BEAT
A ROTTEN EGG
TO THE PUNCH

A Journals of Kate Cavanaugh Mystery

CATHIE JOHN

JOURNEYBOOK PRESS

Journals of Kate Cavanaugh:
BEAT A ROTTEN EGG TO THE PUNCH

JOURNEYBOOK PRESS
is an imprint of
CC Comics / CC Publishing
P.O. Box 542 Loveland, OH   45140-0542
(513) 248-4170
ccpub@worldnet.att.net

Authors photograph by David Koetzle

Logo designed by Steve Del Gardo

ISBN 0-9634183-5-1

First Edition 1998
10 9 8 7 6 5 4 3 2 1

Printed in the United States by:
Morris Publishing
3212 East Highway 30
Kearney, NE 68847
1-800-650-7888

Dedicated to all seekers, survivors, and oddballs.

ACKNOWLEDGMENTS

The authors wish to thank Rick Combs, Chief Deputy Sheriff of the Clermont County, Ohio Sheriff's office, for his expert advice and Fariba Zahedi, owner of The Gourmet Bazaar, Montgomery, Ohio for sharing her knowledge of Iranian cuisine.

AUTHORS' NOTE

Clairmont is an imaginary suburb comprising Indian Hill and parts of Clermont and Warren Counties on the northeast side of Cincinnati, Ohio.

The Circle of Light is a fictional organization and any resemblance to existing groups is purely coincidental.

ALSO BY CATHIE JOHN

JOURNALS OF KATE CAVANAUGH MYSTERIES:

ADD ONE DEAD CRITIC

BEAT
A ROTTEN EGG
TO THE PUNCH

1

IT'S JUST A DREAM, RIGHT? Just a bad dream.

Wake up! Everything's okay.

That was my first reaction. But with the realization that I was, indeed, awake and this was really happening, the terror set in. I felt like a trapped animal, panic-stricken and helpless. I remembered thinking, "So this is the way it all ends." As that thought spread and settled into every cell of my being, it triggered an alarm, waking up the fighter within.

I knew this feeling. I'd had it before. The first time was when the doctor told me I had breast cancer. Now I was crouching in a dark, mouse-infested, vegetable cellar, awaiting the approach of a killer. The parallels intrigued me.

I pushed up against the wooden cellar door with every ounce of strength I had. It felt as though the thumb of a giant hand was pinning the door shut and the other four fingers were encircling the perimeter of the cellar, slowly closing in around me and squeezing the air out of my lungs.

My back muscles burned.

I stopped. My lungs ached for air. The events of the past week swirled around inside my head.

11

Life has a funny way of throwing a lot of truths at you all at once. Boy, did I learn a few things about myself and what people will do for power. I think I was up to *LIFE'S LESSON #2103:* Devils sometimes wear white.

I only hoped it wasn't the last lesson I'd ever learn.

But I'm getting ahead of myself.

I swear, I'm calling the cops the next time I hear people arguing. Why, you ask? Because the last shouting match I walked past wound up being a prelude to murder. And—contrary to local gossip—I've no intention of changing my occupation from caterer to private eye, no matter how many of my long-lost friends wind up as murder suspects.

The chain of events which landed me in the vegetable cellar started nine days earlier. I was just taking Boo-Kat out on an early morning meditative walk.

Saturday, May 17th 6:00 A.M.

"Heel!" I yanked the retractable leash. "Boo-Kat. Heel." Yeah, right. What made me think I could keep him totally under my control? Welsh Terriers are the most obstinate animals on earth. Well, of all people, I should understand how he feels. Mother says I'm obstinate. She tries to keep me on a leash, too.

As a teenager, I was always wandering off the road she had laid out for me. That's when my feelings of claustrophobia began. I always felt as though people were trying to put me in a box. In a place like Clairmont, the blue-blood suburb of Cincinnati, you are expected to look, act, and live by the social code book that is issued you at birth.

But right from the beginning, I was going to go where I wanted, when I wanted. My entire philosophy of life could be summed up in two words: So, there. I've grown up since then. A little bit.

"Damn. Not again." I couldn't get the leash to retract. The

mechanism was probably jammed from the dripping wet cord. Every time Boo-Kat went off the trail he'd splashed through three or four inches of muddy water left over from the previous night's howling, torrential storm. Weather fronts from the North and South clash here along the Ohio, the Great Miami and Little Miami Rivers, spinning tornadoes and ripping roofs off houses, enraging the rivers until they flood downtown, spitting lightning bolts to the ground, and in general scaring the pants off everyone. It's almost enough to send me packing.

The cord was extended to its full twenty-six feet. Boo-Kat charged off the side of the Little Miami Bike Trail and wound his way around a large scotch pine, following the scent of some critter. Self-tied, he finally came to a halt and barked as I followed his trail around the tree, reeling in the line and forcing it back into the plastic case.

"You're a pain in the butt."

He barked.

"C'mon, let's go."

We headed towards downtown Loveland, a small city (really just a small town) on the northeastern side of the Greater Cincinnati Metropolitan area. It was a short walk from my twenty-acre farm in Clairmont.

I wanted to get Boo-Kat used to a leash so I could take him out in public. This was only my second attempt at our new routine, and already I was thinking of giving up. Our training circuit was the Bike Trail, which ran parallel to my farm. In a couple of hours, the trail would be jammed with cyclists, rollerbladers, and other misbehaving dogs, so dawn was the best time for Walkies 101.

It was foggy. The trail was deserted and littered with downed tree branches. The TV news said once the sun burned through, it would be another hot one. I would be splitting my time that afternoon between a steamy kitchen and a stuffy tent.

"Heel." This time Boo-Kat actually decided to obey me. Sort

of. He stopped and sat. I yanked on his leash, and we started up again.

The bike trail cut right through the middle of what the chamber of commerce called Historic Loveland, a two-block stretch of brick storefronts with dusty antiques displayed in most of the windows. Right at the intersection of the trail and West Loveland Avenue was City Hall and the police station. I turned right and headed down towards Tequila Jack's Saloon, one of the landmarks of this little spot on the planet known as "The Sweetheart of Ohio." Stretched across the main drag was a new banner proudly announcing the upcoming *Tour de Loveland* bike race.

My plan was to go down to the end of the block, cross the street, walk back past the old train station, and return to the bike trail. And not at the leisurely pace Boo-Kat had been dictating up to that point. I had a large wedding to cater that day and was already falling behind schedule.

I noticed an emerald green, late model car parked in the otherwise empty street, halfway down the block. As we got nearer I could see it was outside one of the storefronts that was under renovation. Even though a sign wasn't up yet, I could tell the new business had some money behind it. The windows were sparkling, the wood-trim was painted a trendy shade of blue-gray, and there were brand-new, heavy brass fixtures on the door.

For a couple of months, I'd been driving past and watching the transformation take place, curious as to what kind of business was moving in. Now that I was on foot, this was my chance to take a peek.

"Goddamn it! What're you trying to pull?" A man's voice shouted from behind the closed aluminum blinds covering the storefront window.

Maybe it wasn't such a good time. I quickened my pace.

"I want more," answered a second male voice, deeper but with the same loud, angry tone. "Another twenty-five percent."

Boo-Kat, sniffing the ground, suddenly caught a whiff of something interesting. The leash almost snapped out of my hand as he pulled and tugged in a frantic attempt to find its source. He dragged me straight up to the partially opened door disregarding my half-whispered "Heel! Heel!"

The first voice yelled, "You're pressuring *me?* You can be replaced, you know."

"Not with my connections. You need me."

"Forget about it. Big Gabe can't protect you now."

I heard the sounds of a scuffle. I yanked hard on Boo-Kat's leash. A loud bang and clatter on the storefront window right by my head made me jump. One of the men was pushed up against the blinds—I could see his shoulder between two of the aluminum slats.

Boo-Kat let out a typical terrier bark which is loud enough to wake the dead. The hell with "Heel!" Dragging the noisy beast, I took off in a half-trot down the street back towards the bike trail, breaking into a sprint when I heard a door slam.

Someone other than me was running on the sidewalk. Was he after me? Could he see me through the fog? I could run into the police station.

No need. I heard a car door open and shut. The engine sprang to life. Tires squealed, and the car roared into the distance.

I should've gone straight to the police station and reported the scuffle. I might have saved a life. Then again, maybe not.

2

Same day, 3:00 P.M.

SOMEONE WAS WATCHING ME from behind. No, I don't have
eyes in the back of my head, but every tiny hair on the back of
my neck was standing up in alarm. Why this sudden compulsion
to look over my shoulder? I thought. There was no reason to feel
that way. I wasn't pushing through the jam-packed Thieves'
Bazaar in Bombay, India where you always had to watch your
back. I was setting up the buffet table for my friend Cindy's
wedding reception in Clairmont.

But the alarm wouldn't shut off.

I had to find out who was studying me, but I didn't want the
Peeping Tom to know that I'd caught him—or her—whoever.

I picked up a silver bowl of fruit, pretending it just had to be
moved a few feet down the buffet table. As I made my way over
to the new spot and placed the bowl down next to the stuffed
grape leaves, I cocked my head to one side and squeezed my
peripheral vision. I saw him out of the corner of my eye—a pale,
bean pole of a man with white blond hair hanging almost to his
shoulders. He was standing about twenty feet away and staring
at me. I had the sense he was separate and removed from the
other guests in chattering huddles all around him. Something

16

about him made me uneasy, and I jerked my eyes away.

Pretending that the Persian chicken salad had to be placed to the left of the roasted eggplant dip, I busied myself rearranging one whole section of the buffet table. That little make-work project finished, I strolled down towards the far end of the table and stole a quick sideways glance. The pale stick man was gone.

I needed a breather. It was an unusually hot afternoon for May and the air in the tent was stuffy. Before leaving the tent I took one quick look around the crowd. Where the hell was he? I shrugged, pushed the thought of him out of my mind, and stepped out to take a moment to enjoy the blue sky and sunshine.

I inhaled slowly and deeply. The spicy perfume of the nearby rose garden, where Cindy Schmitz and her new husband Ali Hoseyni had exchanged their wedding vows, cleared my mind. I savored the moment knowing my next destination was Ali's hot, crowded kitchen to make sure the entrees were ready to be brought to the tent. After that, I needed to put the finishing touches on the wedding cake.

"Well, there's the little rich girl who caught that killer." The emaciated form of Betty Zender tottered towards me across the grass, the brim of her huge, straw hat flopping up and down with each step. Her voice had long ago been stripped of any smoothness by the four plus decades of pouring scotch down her throat. She waved a half-empty glass. "What is this, Kate? Some kind of Iranian punch? You're the caterer here. Where do I get something decent to drink?"

I instinctively wanted to reach out and catch her before she fell off her turquoise, spike-heeled shoes, but then that's the way Betty walks, drunk or sober.

I had to acknowledge her, but I didn't want to get drafted into being Betty's audience for the usual half-hour monologue of juicy gossip she'd just heard. I could always read it in her *Cincy Life* magazine society column.

"Can't stay to chat, Betty," I said, getting ready to turn on my heels and head for the house. "I've got to go check up on my staff."

Betty's bony arthritic fingers gripped my silk blouse. "Kate, have you been playing Sherlock Holmes lately? Any more dead bodies showing up in churches or on the bike trail?"

"No, but there may be some fires in the kitchen I have to put out. Gotta go."

Betty loosened her grip. "No, no, my dear. I'm sure your excellent staff can do without you for a few minutes." She handed her glass to me and reached into her voluminous shoulder bag, pulling out a gold cigarette case. "So, as I was saying, how's the little rich girl who solved Clairmont's first murder?" She squinted up at me. "I guess you're not so little." Betty grabbed my sleeve and started maneuvering me. "Stand over here, Kate, so I can look at you without that blasted sun burning my eyes. How tall *are* you?"

I was sure my silent groan showed on my face, but Betty's quizzical expression didn't change as she popped a cigarette into a plastic "poison-reducing" holder.

"Betty, you ask me that every time you see me."

She waved her lit cigarette in the air. "Humor me and refresh my poor, addled memory. My sixty-something-year-old brain has been losing cells lately."

"I'm six-foot-three, and I really have to get going."

At the sound of a hacking cough behind us, Betty and I turned and were greeted by Mabel Crank's "Where're ya goin', honey?" The owner of the Cincinnati Twister's minor league hockey team gave a playful tug on my long blond braid. "Helluva wedding you've put on. Like something outta the Arabian Nights."

Mabel's apple doll face scrunched in a smile. Her eyes squinted at Betty through the smoke swirling from her ever-present cigarillo. "Well, if it isn't the Fashion Police. Gonna report all the infractions in your dumb column?" She wagged her stubby finger at the long, curling feather on Betty's hat. "How come nobody writes about your stupid looking get-ups?"

"I swear, woman," Betty said, fingering the sleeve of Mabel's brown polyester pant suit, "your bank account is probably bigger than anyone else's around here, but you haven't shopped for clothing since 1973."

Mabel brushed Betty's hand away. "Haven't you been reading the newspapers, honey? My hockey team's still in the red. Money pours outta that franchise like a leaky bucket, so I've been on a personal budget for years." Her badly painted lips clamped shut. She snorted in disgust and turned to me. "Kate, honey, tell her how tough it is to run a business."

Betty waved her cigarette. "You can't compare your mismanagement of a bunch of toothless French Canadians with Kate's culinary artistry." She smiled at me and then turned her nose up at Mabel while petting my arm. "This is Cincinnati's favorite gourmet caterer, and you're running a business that's—"

I opened my mouth to sympathize with Mabel but realized I was only an excuse for them to launch into their long-running game of antagonizing each other. Mabel and Betty had faced-off, cigarette to cigarillo, and were yammering away, puffing smoke into each other's eyes. I grabbed the opportunity and quietly slipped back into the tent.

Something had to be done about the temperature inside, so I waved over two of my servers. "Hey, guys, help me open up some of these side panels." I started rolling the heavy canvas so I could tie it in place and let the breeze blow through. It felt better immediately. The yards of colored silk draped overhead started to billow sensuously.

Aside from the usual tables and chairs, we had set up a few raised platforms here and there covered in Persian carpets and overstuffed kilim pillows in various shades of terra cotta reds, oranges, and blues. It reminded me of being in a Bedouin tent out on the Arabian desert. I half-expected to see a big, fat sheik sitting cross-legged, propped up against the pillows and sucking on his gurgling hookah pipe.

Instead, I saw Harold Schmitz, Cindy's big fat brother using a piece of flat bread to shovel an enormous gob of feta cheese into his mouth. He moved on to one of the bowls of caviar and proceeded to lay waste to that.

Wedding guests were still straggling into the tent in bunches having spent time lingering in the rose garden. I caught some of their conversations as they milled around in front of the buffet table.

"I especially liked that unusual Persian ritual of symbolically sewing the mother-in-law's mouth shut before the wedding ceremony," said a distinguished-looking middle-aged man with a face I couldn't place. "Don't you think we should incorporate that into American weddings, eh, Kate?" He looked straight at me as though we were old friends, and I couldn't for the life of me remember who he was.

I laughed politely and was trying to think of something to say that wouldn't sound too snide, when my mystery friend's chest started ringing. Without another word, he reached into his jacket pocket, pulled out a cell phone, and walked away.

I preferred the more romantic end of the ceremony when the bride and groom stuck their little fingers in honey and placed them in one another's mouths. I went through the very short list of available men in my life, tried to imagine each one of them putting his sticky little finger in my mouth, and gagged.

The musicians started to play celebratory Iranian music on guitars and recorders, which prompted some of Cindy's new relatives to break into an arm-waving, hand-clapping, whirling dervish kind of dance.

It seemed everybody was beginning to have a good time, so I slipped out the exit at the far end of the tent and headed towards the house.

I waved at a friend of my Mother's and felt relieved that for once she wasn't at one of these Clairmont affairs I was always catering. It was bad enough having Mother fuss about the food at fund-raising galas, but it would have driven me crazy having to deal with her at my friend's wedding. She'd have been nagging me constantly about my "embarrassing singleness" at the age of forty-three.

"Nobody seems to be good enough for you," I heard her say in my head as I crossed the large driveway filled with Mercedes, Jags, and a couple of Rolls Royces. Just imagining what she'd say made me feel claustrophobic. I entered the kitchen door at the back of the house and grabbed my chef's jacket from the back of a chair where I'd left it.

"Hey, Boss." Tony Zampella, my twenty-five year old assistant greeted me, wielding a long, greasy carving knife. "About time you stopped schmoozing with your rich friends and came back to toil with us peasants." He flashed me a grin and winked in that flirty Italian way of his.

"It's a mess in here," I said, slipping into my jacket and starting to stack dirty pots and pans in the sink. Immediately, one of the servers shooed me away with, "I'll do that, Kate."

I could see Tony had finished carving the roast lamb and had arranged it expertly on several silver platters. "How's our Persian Rice coming along?" I asked. "Is it ready?"

Tony shrugged his broad shoulders and scratched his permanent five o'clock shadow. "I don't know, Kate. That stuff makes me nervous. You better look at it."

I had to admit I felt pretty insecure myself. Never in all the years I've been catering had a dish given me so much trouble. But it was an Iranian tradition and Cindy had requested it specifically, even providing me with the recipe.

Special pans had to be provided, too, and Ali's relatives came to my aid. Every spare inch of counter space was taken up by the eight large pans, each with it's own burner, on loan for the occasion.

I lifted the lid of one pan and poked a long wooden spoon through the mounds of fluffy rice, candied orange peel, and pistachios to see if a nice, golden crust was forming on the bottom. Or a charred, blackened mess.

"Well?" asked Tony, putting a hand on his hip. "Is it show time?"

"I can't tell. We'll just have to dump it out and deal with whatever we find."

Tony grabbed one end of the pot, and I the other.

"Do you want to say a prayer first?" Tony smirked.

"Yeah. God help us if this isn't right."

We tilted the pan so I could scoop out the fluffy rice into a warming dish. I could see the crust had formed on the bottom, but still didn't know if it was right, until we turned the pan upside-down and the crust fell out in one beautiful caramel colored sheet. Both of us said, "Wow!"

I broke the crust up into smaller pieces with my spoon, left them sitting on top of the rice and quickly covered it. We had to do this seven more times. I wondered if it was the same feeling experienced by a Hollywood producer, whose movie had been nominated for eight Academy Awards and had to sit holding her breath through the opening of eight envelopes. Food preparation, after all, is a performance.

It was a clean sweep. The eighth one came out as perfectly as the others, and I really wanted a standing ovation, but all I got was a pat on the back from Tony, my assistant director.

I sent Tony and the four servers off on the first of many trips back and forth between kitchen and tent, laden with trays of steaming food to be placed in warming pans. I slipped out of my chef's jacket, tossed it back on the chair, and grabbed a pastry bag full of ivory white buttercream out of the refrigerator.

I don't know what it is about wedding cakes, but they always make my stomach tighten into a little knot, and I was anxious to get this over with. Boy, this whole job was turning into an ordeal. Thankfully, Cindy had chosen a relatively simple, though in my opinion tacky, design. My neck was still sore from the hour spent that morning bent in an awkward position piping colonial scrolls and reverse shell borders.

The wedding cake was waiting for me in an alcove behind the buffet tables, curtained off by large, colorfully patterned hanging rugs. I surveyed my handiwork, which looked like a pastry condominium consisting of three stacked tiers with smaller cakes on either side. There were just a couple of smudges to fix and fresh flowers to arrange between the floors. I still needed to place a pair of winged angels up on the penthouse.

I took a deep breath, planted my feet, and bent over close to the main tier. I aimed my pastry bag at a wonky piece of scroll and squeezed. I've often thought that for my wedding, if the day ever comes, I'd rather have something other than cake. Maybe a nice piece of apple pie. I'd enjoy that more. Mother would have a fit.

"Kathleen," I could hear her say, "you're impossible. You always find a way to embarrass me." And she always found a way to annoy me. Even when she wasn't around, I couldn't seem to block out that *I know what's best for you* voice.

I suppose Mother couldn't help it, Patricia "Tink" Cavanaugh was used to getting her way. And I was her only child, so all her high expectations were dumped on my shoulders. It wasn't as if I was her whole life and she had to live through me—she had plenty of other people to boss around. She managed a large successful business herself. In fact, ever since Dad died, she'd been majority stockholder and board chair of the family Crown Chili Parlor enterprise that now had more than fifty stores in the Cincinnati Tri-State area.

Splat! Damn. The thought of Mother bugging me made me squeeze the pastry bag too hard and an air bubble farted a glob of icing out onto the cake. Calm down. I was sure most women my age had long since graduated from the childhood their mothers tried to keep them in. On second thought, I could remember Mother complaining about Grandma Vasherhann when I was in my teens. Guess the circle never ends.

The Vasherhanns had made a name for themselves manufacturing soap products. They expected their offspring to live a clean life, marry the proper persons, and make a lot of money. I wasn't keeping up the family tradition. My two year escapade traveling overland from England to India and Nepal was the first rebellious act by a member of the Vasherhann clan that anyone could remember. Hopes were raised when I came back home, but then I announced that I was going to culinary school. Despair set in when I moved out to my farm and started my catering business. Dad loved it, but then he came from a long line of rebels. His grandfather had started the Crown Chili Parlor empire as a small greasy spoon in the Over-the-Rhine section of Cincinnati.

"Can I disturb the artist at work?" A deep bass voice burst through my mental meandering, making my fingers leap from the angels I had just placed on the top tier of the cake. I turned and gasped. The booming voice had come out of Stick Man.

I couldn't breathe in or out. I just stood there. Even though he looked at me with a calm, steady expression, I found it difficult to look back. His eyes, with their washed-out icy blue color and piercing black pupils, had an aggressiveness that disturbed me.

I realized I was reacting to his strange, almost-albino appearance and had no reason to feel threatened.

On second look, he was strangely attractive. Obviously, by the way he dressed, Stick Man considered himself very hip. Expensive gray suit. Black shirt with one of those banded collars. No tie.

He took a step towards me and held out one of the two champagne glasses he was carrying. "I seem to have this extra drink that's screaming to be handed over to you."

Hmm. Interesting but weird opening line. "Are you in the

habit of hearing voices?" I asked.

"Once in a while. But I only pay attention when it sounds like it might be a good time."

I held up my pastry bag and gave a weary nod to the cake. "Sorry, but the good time's gotta be delayed. I've got some replastering to do."

He set both glasses down on top of a cardboard storage box and grabbed a folding chair from a stack leaning against the tent pole. Opening it, he sat down next to the box. He picked up his glass by its stem and began rolling it between long, thin fingers. "I'll wait. Mind if I watch?"

"No," I lied, "but is the party so boring that you'd rather be here?"

"I wanted to meet you. You're a famous woman." He seemed to be studying me. "And very pretty."

I never know how to respond to flattery, so to avoid saying something stupid, I dove back into fixing the frosting. Even though I felt pressured by his presence, I took the time necessary to finish the job. But after only a minute, my mind began darting around, searching for some engaging topic of conversation to break the silence. "What's your name?" Hardly brilliant, but at least it was a starting point.

"Brad," he said, his voice resonating like the bass half of the Righteous Brothers. Cool. In my mind I heard the opening to *You've Got That Loving Feeling*.

With an exultant flourish, I piped the final bit of scrollwork. "Done!"

"As I said, you're very pretty. A lot prettier in person than in those grainy newspaper photos and TV clips. You always looked like you were snarling at the camera."

I straightened up and, still with my back to Brad, said, "I didn't like those newspaper photos, either. In fact," I turned and looked down at him, "I didn't want the publicity at all."

"Why's that?" He handed me the champagne glass filled with

25

the screaming-voiced drink. "Did it hurt your business?"

"No, exactly the opposite, I had to turn jobs down. For the past four months, I've been getting calls from all over the tri-state area, people wanting me to cater their parties. But what they really wanted was to flaunt me in front of their friends, like some kind of celebrity bauble." I took a healthy sip of champagne. "You know those dinner parties where someone's murdered and the guests have to figure out who did it? Well, suddenly, people started calling up, asking me to create my own murder theme party. At any other time I'd have thought that would be fun, kind of a Midwestern Agatha Christie atmosphere."

Brad toasted me. "Kate Cavanaugh, Culinary Detective."

"But not so soon after the real thing." I took another swallow of my drink. "The worst thing of all was the media."

"Well, you can't blame them, you did solve the murder mystery. It was big news."

"Yeah, well I gave one interview to a local TV reporter who was a friend. That was picked up by the network news and got national play. Before I knew it, the tabloid TV gangs were camped at the entrance to my farm lying in wait to get a shot of me, the Amazon Chili Heiress Detective or whatever they were calling me."

Warning buzzers went off in my head. What was I doing, talking to this stranger as though we were old pals? How did he get me to start blabbing like that? This Brad guy *was* attractive in a slightly dangerous way. I took a closer look. Although his yellow-white hair almost touched his shoulders, it was clean and well-groomed. On the lapel of his trendy gray suit, which he wore quite well, was some kind of gold pin. Looked like a pair of wings within a circle. Hanging down below the cuff of his sleeve was a silver bracelet, Rajasthani style. "Oh. Have you been to India?"

Brad looked startled. "Uh . . . no. Why?"

I pointed to the thick coil of tarnished silver encircling his pale wrist. "Those kind of bracelets come from a specific region in India."

"Oh, yeah?" The corner of his right eye began twitching uncontrollably. He looked down at the piece of jewelry, fingered the silver clasp, and mumbled his reply without looking back at me. "Um . . . someone gave it to me. A friend. Maybe they'd been there. I don't know."

The warning bells in my head were making such a racket, I could barely hear my own thoughts. Why was Brad so nervous? What had I said? Here I'd spent the last five minutes telling him all this personal stuff about me, but I asked him one simple question and he acted as though I'd pried into some dark secret. I decided Brad was a case and looked to make a quick exit.

Aha! I chose Excuse Number Seven. "Gotta go, Brad. Duty calls. I need to check on the buffet table and make sure the food's set up properly."

Without waiting for his reaction, I gathered up my cake decorating tools and pushed through the curtain into the main section of the party tent. Sensing that Brad would start to follow me, I tried to lose myself in the crowd. Duh. Dumb idea. I was taller than practically everyone else there. No mistaking me for a Munchkin as I wound through the partyers, looking down on a lot of bald heads and smiling at well-wishers who complimented my cooking with their mouths full.

"Kate! Over here!" A loud female voice cut through the noise of chatter and rambunctious Iranian music. No question who owned that pair of lungs. I'd heard that shout thousands of times ringing across the court back when I was on the Clairmont High School girl's basketball team. I looked to my right and saw Cindy. To my dismay, she was talking with Betty Zender and I wished I could reroute my steps. But no, I was committed. Besides, if I turned back, I might've bumped into Brad with his screaming drinks and strange secrets.

Cindy Schmitz didn't look like the typical radiant bride. She was my age, which wasn't ancient, but hardly blushing. A stocky five-foot-ten, she still had the muscular shoulders and the wide-legged stance of a jock. But she was dressed in a white satin caftan-type outfit with long, belled sleeves, gold braided trim, and even a small train gathered on the floor behind her.

I waved a quick "Hi" to Betty and hugged my old teammate. "You look great, Cindy."

"I feel great. This is a wonderful party, Kate."

Betty nodded her head, the feather on her hat flopping up and down. She started to open her mouth to say something, but Cindy still had the floor. "And the food . . . some of Ali's family came all the way from Iran and they are so impressed with your knowledge of Persian cuisine." Cindy leaned towards me in a conspiratorial way. "Quite honestly, they didn't think you could get it right."

My ego wanted to *harumph* at the slight but, instead, I asked, "Is that an Iranian wedding dress?"

Cindy laughed, ending with her customary loud snort. "The last person I talked to asked if I was already wearing my honeymoon peignoir." She struck a runway model pose. "I designed this myself. I wanted to make sure I was comfortable 'cause I certainly wasn't going to wear one of those poufy, beaded dresses like I wore at my first wedding."

Betty jumped in. "I thought you looked beautiful in that dress. That was a lovely wedding, too. I remember how you and your handsome groom—"

Cindy snapped her hand in a traffic cop's *Stop* gesture and said, "That was then. This is now. Don't bring up that disastrous time in my life."

There was a momentary silence. What to say? I almost went down the same road Cindy took twenty-three years ago, and found myself about to marry my high school steady. It seemed as though every one of my friends was marrying her senior prom date. Instead, I hopped a plane to Geneva.

Betty broke the silence with, "There are lots of single men here today, Kate. Any possibilities?"

Oh, great. A day without Mother and Betty steps in to take her place. "No."

Cindy took a turn at pushing my button. "Didn't you meet Brad?"

"Yeah," I monotoned, "what's his story?"

"He's quite an artist. Thought you went for those artsy types."

"Well, yeah. But sometimes they can be pretty weird. What makes this one so nervous?"

Cindy frowned. "Nervous? Whenever I've seen him, he's exactly the opposite—kind of cocky." She smiled. "He likes confident women, so I thought you two might hit it off."

I groaned inside. Another member of the Find Kate A Mate Foundation. On the other hand, I *was* curious about her friend. "How did you meet him, Cindy?"

Betty waved her empty cigarette holder, which she held onto at times when it was inappropriate to smoke—kind of an adult pacifier. "Oh, Kate. You must know. He's the one who designed that wild poster for the Ault Park Flower Show that you see everywhere these days."

Cindy calmly blocked one of Betty's exuberant waves before the pacifier poked her in the eye. "I'm on the Flower Show's Planning Board, so Brad and I spent most Thursday nights together for the past year working on the promotion." She reached out with her forefinger and gave me a little tap-shove. "He's lots of fun."

The band started playing some jumpy Iranian song that made half the guests start whooping as they gathered into a circle in the middle of the tent. Cindy laughed and waved at me to follow her as she was gently coaxed into the middle and tried to imitate the waving dance they were all doing. I shook my head and silently begged off. One of the problems with being a caterer is that I never have time to party. There was still a lot for me to do, like keeping an eye on the buffet table. The guests were gobbling everything in sight and I had to make sure the food flowed from the kitchen. But first I needed to make a restroom stop.

I walked out of the tent and across the lawn, entering the back of the house through the kitchen.

"Hey, Boss," Tony greeted me. "Good timing. I need you to—"

"Hold that thought," I said, rushing past him through the kitchen and down the hallway. The guest bathroom was on my right, but my attention was drawn to the billowing gauzy curtains in the sitting room to my left. The house was supposed to be secured while everyone was out in the tent, so I went over and slid the glass door shut. I looked around, made sure everything was still in order, and went back out into the hallway. It was probably a good idea to report what I'd seen to someone, but I really needed to go to the bathroom first.

The door was shut. Damn. I wondered if I would have to go looking for another bathroom. Maybe there wasn't anyone in there. I tried the doorknob, expecting it to be locked. To my relief, the knob turned all the way, and I pushed the door open.

Brad was fully clothed, but he looked at me in complete and utter horror as though I was his mother and had just caught him with his pants down doing a very nasty thing.

3

"OH, EXCUSE ME," I said, feeling my face burn with embarrassment. It's amazing how in times of surprise or shock your brain can retain an image even though you see it for no more than one or two seconds. A mental snapshot. I distinctly remembered Brad holding a small plastic bag full of white powder in one hand and a tiny silver spoon in the other, both up to his face. He brought them down quickly and turned away. In the reflection in the bathroom mirror I watched him snap the bag shut, roll it up, and stuff both the spoon and the bag into his jacket's breast pocket. So that explained his strange nervousness—probably coke-induced paranoia.

Brad turned back towards me, recomposed and with a *this never happened* smile plastered on his face. "Bathroom's all yours," he said, brushing past me and hurrying across the hall into the sitting room and towards the patio door. He swatted and cursed at the curtains, trying to spread them apart. Finally, he found the handle and yanked the sliding glass door open. The glass rattled loudly as Brad banged his shoulder against it in his rush to escape. The door was left opened and the curtains billowed softly in the breeze. So much for Mr. Cool.

"What's all the racket about?" Tony yelled from the kitchen.

I wasn't going to be side-tracked again, so I quickly stepped into the bathroom and closed the door. I heard Tony run into the hallway and say, "Boss? You here?" Then, a knocking on the door. "Kate? You in there?"

"Leave me alone. I'm busy."

"I heard this loud bang. You stuck?"

"Get outta here."

"Okay, okay, you don't hafta snap at me. But didn't you hear that noise?"

"I'll explain it to you, later!"

WITHIN TWO MINUTES, I was in the kitchen pouring myself a cup of coffee.

"So?" Tony demanded, handing me the cream.

"I caught someone in the bathroom snorting coke."

"And you smacked him upside the head and flushed him down the toilet, right?"

"Not exactly," I said, dropping a couple of sugar cubes into my coffee. "Is that what you'd have done?"

"You bet. I've got no sympathy for rich coke heads." Tony walked over to the oven and pulled open the door.

"But it's okay if you're poor?"

"'Course not," Tony said, peering into the oven to check on the Khoresh. "I feel sorry for the kids in my old neighborhood who got sucked into that life before they could understand what they were getting into. I was one of the lucky ones." He pulled the oven rack halfway out and lifted one corner of the aluminum foil covering the pan. A little puff of steam escaped. "Looks good," he said, and resealed the foil, pushed the pan back in and let the door close with a bang.

I considered myself lucky, too, having Tony as my assistant. He first impressed me with a chocolate chestnut torte he had baked for a *Cincy Life* magazine contest, and in the seven years he'd been with me had learned enough about the catering business to be my right hand. Besides, he looked cute in those baggy chef's pants with the red, green, and yellow chili peppers printed all over them.

"So," Tony said, "you gonna report this scum bag to your friend Cindy?"

"No, of course not. I'm not going to ruin her wedding day." I started rearranging a platter of walnut cookies. "But I'll keep my eye on him. Is this all we have of the cookies. Who's been eating them?"

"We've already taken some trays over to the tent," Tony said with a huff. "I only ate one."

"One whole tray of walnut cookies?"

"No, no. Only one *cookie*. Jeez."

"Okay, well let's get another tray of sugar-coated almonds, and there should be some more elephant ears and almond cookies. I've never seen people eat like this."

I stacked a couple of trays of the rapidly disappearing confections in a plastic carrier rack and threw a last minute instruction over my shoulder. "Watch those servers, Tony—one of them's a cookie monster."

Carrying my precious cargo, I marched off towards the tent. Somewhere between the house and the raucous party with its high-pitched, reedy music I thought I heard the tinkling of bells. The green grass of Clairmont, Ohio disappeared in a whirl of sand and I was loping along over a scrubby hill. Nothing in sight for miles. The horrible stink of the camel I was riding burned my nostrils, and my backside felt pounded and bruised from the bumpy gait of the smelly animal.

I came over the top of the hill. Before me was a single, huge, white tent. The camel screeched and complained as it dropped down on its knobby front knees, almost dumping me over its head onto the sand. I was wrenched back as his rear flopped to the ground, sending up clouds of dust.

The flaps of the tent parted and a dark-skinned man in a flowing white robe and head scarf stared at me, his eyes hard with suspicion. A moment later, those same eyes widened and a gleaming, gold-toothed grin spread across his face. He flung his arms skyward and exclaimed, "Cookies! You have cookies! Come in! Come in!"

I blinked and switched back to the reality channel. "Oh, hi, TC," I greeted Cindy's new brother-in-law, who was not wearing a flowing robe or head scarf—though he did look exotically handsome in his white tux. When he smiled, a hint of gold in the back of his mouth glinted in the sunlight.

"Good goin', Kate. You brought more cookies," TC said, moving aside so I could step into the tent. "You did a great job with the food today. You should set up a booth at Taste of Cincinnati next weekend."

"That event's for local restaurants. I'm just a little caterer." Before TC could come out with the usual corny joke about my height, I quickly added, "Little as in size of business. You know what I mean."

"Well, they're expanding this year and starting to allow smaller businesses to set up at Taste. Like the microbrewers."

A pug-nosed, freckle-faced Thomas Hassenbacher sidled up to us and grabbed a cookie off my tray. "That's the stupidest decision made this year. Those upstarts with their la de da beer. None of it tastes any better than my Hassenbacher Gold. And they're charging a buck a cup more." Thomas popped the cookie into his mouth.

There was never just one Hassenbacher; the four brothers almost always roamed in a pack. I looked around for the other three and, sure enough, there they were a few yards away, surrounding Mabel Crank. On first impression, the four middle-aged men could be mistaken for quadruplets. They looked like they were stamped out of the same mold with their thinning red hair, wide, pink foreheads, freckles, and noses that appear to be continually pushed up against some invisible barrier. On second glance, the eight years that separated Brother Number One from Brother Number Four became apparent.

I said, "What's the problem? Taste is supposed to be the showcase for local food and entertainment. And all those microbrewers that have started up in the past few years are a part of that. There's room for everybody."

Thomas' pink face was darkening into red, reminding me I was breaking one of my cardinal rules: don't get into any controversial discussions while on the job.

TC shook his head in exaggerated sympathy. "Yeah, it's too bad you lost your brew master like that. Must feel awful when someone you depend on gets it in his mind to go set up a shop of his own."

Thomas sputtered. "Th-that's why I said that new Winged Pig Ale doesn't taste any better than my Hassenbacher Gold. *It is Hassenbacher Gold!"*

"Kate, honey." A gravelly voice broke into our conversation. I looked around. Mabel Crank waved me over. "Come here and listen to what these angels are offering me."

Angels? The Hassenbacher Brothers? They were better known for fooling around with other men's wives and spending small fortunes on unsuccessful bids for political office. Business was always being transacted at these Clairmont affairs, but this was a strange little pow-wow. I had to find out what put such a toothy smile on Mabel's face.

Placing his hand on my shoulder, Thomas started to guide me over to the group.

"Wait," I said, "my arms are about to fall off. Let me deliver these cookies to the buffet table first." I did so and instructed one of the servers to stack them in pyramids on their crystal platters.

"Okay, Mabel," I said, joining the group and munching on an

elephant ear, "what's up?"

"Have you ever met an angel, Kate? Well, you're standing in front of four of 'em."

I looked at Thomas, Carl, John, and Henry Hassenbacher and didn't see any halos over their heads. But knowing them I recognized the gleam of profit potential in their eyes.

Thomas, the leader of the pack, spoke up. "Hassenbacher Brewery has always wanted to be associated with sports and Mabel, here, has graciously agreed to consider selling a portion of her Twister Hockey Team to us." He turned to Mabel. "We're very grateful you've given us this opportunity."

"Hell," Mabel flicked her hand in the air, "I'm the one who's grateful. Your money'll save my butt."

"And we've got ideas, too," said Henry, the youngest of the four. "See, what this hockey franchise needs, Mabel, is to get the fans in the stands all pumped. You've got too much down time in between periods. Give 'em some entertainment. Every successful team has a mascot. We could dress up a guy to look like a giant Hassenbacher beer can—"

Carl jabbed Henry with an elbow.

"Ouch. Wait a minute. Hear me out. The Beer Can skates around the ice—"

At that, we all groaned, and a playful shove from Carl caused Henry to almost lose his balance.

"That's right," Henry said, "try to knock me off so you can take my twenty-five percent of our . . ."

My mind's eye replayed that morning's run-in. *I want more! Another twenty-five percent,* the unseen man had shouted just before he was shoved up against the blinds. Twenty-five percent more of what? I wondered.

Mabel patted Henry on the shoulder. "I think you and I are on the same wavelength, Honey. We'll talk later."

I pushed the twenty-five percent question out of my head. No time to think about that. Everyone at these Clairmont events expected me to visit with them, and I had already spent more than my allotted amount of time with Mabel and the Hassenbachers. For the next half-hour I mingled and smiled and stayed out of lengthy conversations. Until I was snared by Betty Zender.

"Are you behind this flocking business, Kate?"

With Betty's raspy voice, I couldn't be sure whether she was cursing or referring to the latest antics of some mysterious and inventive Clairmont hostess.

"I've done some strange things, Betty. But I can't take credit for that. How many flamingos are they up to now?"

"According to your mother—"

"Mother's been flocked?"

"No, dear, but I'm sure she's on the list. As I said, according to Tink the flock is up to twenty-six flamingos."

I had to admit it was a pretty creative way of inviting people to a party, although no-one knew yet who was giving it or where it was going to be. The only thing known for sure was the date and who had been invited. Skip Enburg had reported in his *Cincinnati Enquirer Around Town* column that the first sighting was in March: two plastic flamingos showed up in front of a prominent Clairmont residence with a banner reading, "You've been flocked."

Betty steered me over to one side of the tent where a flap had been opened and pulled out her cigarette case. "Your mother's worried about what the neighbors will say if she gets flocked." She pushed a cigarette into her long plastic holder and lit it. "I guess it's becoming a status symbol, but it's still tacky." Betty turned her head, pursed her lips as far as she could to the side of her face and blew smoke out the tent.

I gazed over Betty's floppy hat and across the party inside. A white–blond head stuck out above the rest of the crowd. Mr. Cool—aka Brad. He appeared to be bobbing and weaving as if attempting to cut a trail through the groups of people congregating in front of the buffet table. But there was no one in his way. He reached for a glass of wine and grabbed empty air. I figured he was probably bobbing and weaving because his interior gyroscope had been knocked out of whack by the drug he'd snorted in the bathroom.

Scrawny fingers wearing several diamond rings two sizes too big shot up right in front of my eyes and wiggled. "You listening to me, Kate?" Betty asked.

"Yes. Sorry. Um . . . you think it's a tacky status symbol."

"Right. Anyway," Betty breathed smoke out her nose, "apparently there's a letter tied around one flamingo's neck explaining the rules of the game. The victim of the flocking is told to add two flamingos and leave them somewhere else. Under cover of darkness, of course."

"Oh, so the flock propagates. But how does the victim know where the herd of birds is supposed to show up next?"

Betty folded one arm under the other's elbow and held her cigarette straight up. I watched the long ash on her cigarette grow even longer as she answered. "At some point within forty-eight hours, the victim gets a call with the address of the next flock drop. However, the flamingos must first be left in place at least twenty-four hours but less than forty-eight. So the neighbors are fit to be tied."

The ash was still growing. I said, "And how long is this supposed to go on?"

"Into August."

CRASH!

A woman screamed.

4

I RAN TOWARDS THE SCREAM, pushing through the crowd as though through a thicket of bushes. Amazing how inert people are in the first few seconds of an emergency situation, but I could tell by the looks on their faces that urgency was needed.

My first thought was of Brad and his champagne-cocaine cocktails. What was I going to do for a drug overdose?

As I got closer, the guests seemed to be even more frozen in place. "Let me through," I yelled, sending a number of drinks splashing onto designer dresses and expensive suits as I forced my way past the solid circle of gawkers standing by an upended buffet table.

I did not find Brad lying dead on the floor. Instead, fat Harold Schmitz, Cindy's older brother, was on his knees surrounded by a mess of spilled appetizers, choking and gasping for air. His eyes bulged, terror-stricken, and his face was quickly turning from red to purple.

Almost slipping on the eggplant dip, I wrapped my arms around Harold's waist from behind. Luckily, my arms were just long enough. I clasped my hands together to form a fist and shoved it into his belly with a quick inward and slightly upward thrust. Harold kept wheezing, and I repeated my thrusts. *C'mon, Harold, spit it out!* I couldn't tell if I was doing any good. His belly felt like a huge squishy foam beach ball.

A fourth thrust.

Pwlahk! A killer-sized gob of Kufteh Tabrizi flew out his mouth.

I let go of Harold's waist. He flopped backwards onto his butt and immediately began breathing normally while color returned to his face. The distinguished-looking middle-aged man who I earlier didn't recognize came to Harold's side. Turns out he was the Schmitz's family doctor and had been to a number of parties I'd catered for them. My brain just doesn't have enough RAM to keep files on everybody I meet.

"Quick thinking, Kate," he said. "I guess you've seen this happen before."

"Believe it or not, that's the first time I've had to do that." I'd been around Harold's food shoveling displays before, but they'd always just been an embarrassment and had never accelerated into a medical emergency.

"Where's Cindy?" I asked, looking around at the circle of guests.

Someone answered, "She's not in the tent. Must be somewhere outside."

"I'll find her."

I stepped outside, looked at the choices: the house, the pool, or the rose garden. The rose garden was closest, so I headed towards that.

For the second time that day, I heard angry voices. I walked under the rose arbor and entered the fragrant garden. Ali was fit to be tied and Cindy wasn't backing down.

"I'm going to kick him out of here right now. I should've done it sooner." Ali's dark eyebrows formed a bushy V and he shook his arms in the air.

"He's just a little drunk," Cindy replied. Her chin jutted out at him in defiance. "He's not hurting anyone. Besides, he's my friend. I invited him. This is my party, too, and you have no right to throw anyone out."

Ali waved in the direction of the pool. I looked. Seated on the end of the diving board out over the water was a thin, pale figure. Mr. Stick Man.

"Your friend Brad has got to go before he creates a scene," Ali shouted.

It wasn't great timing but I had to tell Cindy about the scene her brother had already created in the reception tent. "Cindy?" I called out as I approached the warring newlyweds. "I think you should come to the tent. Harold has just had an accident."

"What happened?" Cindy's expression immediately switched from anger to alarm.

"Well, it wasn't really an accident. Sort of a—oh, he's okay now, but you might want to check on him."

Ali looked at me, then to Cindy, and finally rolled his eyes up to the sky. "Now what?"

Cindy glared at Ali. "What do you mean 'Now what?' It's my brother. I suppose you want to kick him out, too?"

I reached out and touched Cindy's shoulder. "Harold was choking on a meatball, and I had to use the Heimlich Maneuver on him."

Cindy gathered up her wedding caftan and started to rush off. "Where is he now? The tent? I've got to see him."

Ali, still glowering, called out after her. "I'm going to do something about that fool before he falls in and Kate has to perform CPR."

"Don't you touch him," Cindy yelled back over her shoulder as she continued in a half-trot to the tent.

I looked to Ali. He was staring contemptuously at Brad, who was still perched on the end of the diving board, dangling his legs.

"Is there anything I can do?"

Ali took in a deep breath and snorted it out his hairy nostrils. "I don't think so, Kate. I have to deal with this product of American culture all the time. Makes me sick."

My back went up a little bit. "I don't understand."

Ali's eyes softened slightly. "Please don't get me wrong. I love the freedom America has given me. When I first came here over twenty years ago to go to college, I realized I could never go back to living under a repressive regime. But the irresponsible behavior that comes along with that freedom drives me crazy."

Ali flicked a hand at Stick Man. "I have long-haired, disrespectful types like him working for me in my warehouse. They show up late and high, and they don't do their jobs properly. I'm constantly firing these idiots. In fact, years ago, that drunken man over there used to work for me."

"I've been told that Brad is a well-respected artist."

"Ha! His talents may be well-respected, but I don't think he has much respect for himself or others. It's a rotten thing for him to behave like this at a friend's wedding."

"You're right, Ali. It is a rotten thing to do." I could imagine Brad working in the front of Ali's designer furniture showroom or explaining the history of some intricate weaving technique to a customer in Ali's Persian rug emporium next door. But he was hardly the type to be maneuvering a semi up to the loading dock.

Ali pulled a clean, pressed handkerchief out of his pocket and dabbed at the beads of perspiration forming on his forehead. "America is poisoning the rest of the world with its dysfunctional culture. My little brother—my business partner, my best man—got sucked into it as soon as he came over ten years ago. He rejected his heritage. Changed his given name from Habib to TC. Stupid name doesn't even mean anything. He even started palling around with that . . . that Brad scum. Thank God our mother was not alive to see that. Would have broken her heart."

And Ali thought Brad was only drunk. What would Ali think or do if he had seen Brad spilling cocaine all over his bathroom floor?

I also wondered how long his marriage with Cindy would last.

Splash!

Brad fell in the pool.

5

That evening, 7:00 P.M.

I'D HAD ENOUGH. All the windows of my Jeep Cherokee were rolled down. As I sped along Drake Road past mini-estates half-hidden behind walls of stately trees, I hoped the rush of cool evening air would clear away the kitchen smells from my nostrils, hair, and chef's jacket. It was all over me. I was soaked in the sickening aroma of stale cooking oil, lamb grease, and Persian spices. My size eleven feet felt like they'd suddenly swelled to a size twenty-two and throbbed inside my too-tight shoes.

At least I wasn't sitting in wet clothes. Brad survived his impromptu belly flop into the pool without needing me to play lifeguard. Even in his stoned state, he managed to dog paddle to the side and was trying to haul himself out by the time Ali and I got to him.

Ali was really pissed off. Getting his white tux wet yanking Brad out of the water enraged him even more.

"That's it," he shouted, and stormed off to get his brother TC to act as bouncer. But not before other guests became aware of

Brad's poolside entertainment.

Poor Cindy. I wondered if her marriage would survive its rocky start. Ali was so serious and formal, and placed great importance on the proper appearance. I hoped he wasn't going to hold her responsible for the misbehavior of her food-gorging brother and coke-snorting friend.

In front of his guests, Ali was a master of self-control. When he arrived back at poolside with TC, he was all smiles and showed great concern for a dripping, bedraggled Brad who was escorted—well, half-carried—through the crowd of guests and into the house.

That was pretty much the high point of the reception. The presentation and cutting of the wedding cake was a bit anti-climactic. However, the guests appeared to enjoy everything and it looked like it was going to be an all-nighter.

I supervised the first stages of clean-up as food ran out. Tony's day always started later than mine, so he was in charge of final wrap-up. With great relief, I headed home.

Traveling north on Loveland-Madeira Road the traffic was light, so, of course, my big, fat foot lay on the gas pedal like a brick.

I took the bend in the road at sixty mph.

A dark green car in the pull-over up ahead.

Two cars in fact.

Damn. A Clairmont Ranger.

My reflexes shifted the brick to the brake.

No, on second glance it wasn't a police patrol car. My shoulders relaxed as I coasted by and took a look.

A short, round man wearing a white shirt with epaulets and black and gold patches on each sleeve was attaching jumper cables from the green sedan to a red station wagon with rusted bumpers. A young woman with stringy hair watched. I'd seen the man a few times before. Clairmont and the surrounding communities are small enough that you can run into the same

45

people over and over again. Or at least recognize faces in the crowds.

Each time I saw this man, he appeared to be doing some sort of good deed. A few weeks earlier, I'd seen him helping an elderly woman who had just dropped all her parcels in the Kenwood Towne Center parking lot. Another time, I watched him trying to get some little girl's cat out of a tree by holding a chair up to the branch where the frightened animal crouched, spitting at him. Mr.Short Round managed to get the chair close enough for the cat to jump onto the seat, to the sidewalk, and tear off into some bushes.

I wondered if any of the people he helped ever thought of nominating him for Channel 12's Anonymous Angel Award.

TEN MINUTES LATER, I had whizzed through historic Loveland, made a left after the railroad tracks, crossed the invisible border into Clairmont, and was driving up my private laneway.

As usual, I felt I was entering another world as I drove past the towering Douglas fir trees towards my white clapboard farmhouse. Having spent most of my life searching for my place in the world and not finding it, I finally concluded I was an odd ball and decided to create my own oasis.

I call it Trail's End Farm, but there isn't a cow, pig, chicken, or horse in residence. In fact, it's not really a farm at all. I just refer to it as such because fifteen years ago, when I first looked at the property, it consisted of a small, run-down farmhouse surrounded by neglected fields. It had been part of the last working family farm in the area, but when the owner's children, who wanted no part of that life, inherited the place, the acreage was chopped up into lots. They saw the suburbs of Cincinnati approaching and figured they could make a killing and move on to bigger dreams.

To me, that little white house and the twenty acres of rutted fields that went with it were an unfinished canvas on which I could realize my dreams.

My catering business was starting to take off, and I was determined not to go to my family for help. I had enough for a down payment. Over the years, as the money came in, I replanted the fields with trees and added a couple of wings to the house. One was for my commercial kitchen and the other for my personal gym and basketball court. I'm now living my dream on prime real estate just inside the northern border of Clairmont.

I parked my jeep beside the house and started walking around to the front. The sun was just disappearing behind the tops of the trees. Yellow finches living in the bushes that skirted the back edges of the parking area were settling in for the night. I stopped for a moment to listen to their soft twittering and could feel my battered nerves being soothed by one of nature's non-toxic tranquilizers.

At the age of thirty-seven I learned something that changed the way I looked at my surroundings. Suffering through the chemotherapy necessary to treat my breast cancer, I discovered that healing was available to me right here at Trail's End Farm. I'm not one to talk about God, but I think somebody gave us birds and flowers and wind in the trees to calm our spirits when we are troubled. Since then, I have considered it preventive maintenance to notice and appreciate what was around me. Speaking of which, I noticed that Robert Boone, my live-in groundskeeper-handyman, had applied a much-needed fresh coat of paint to the house's white gingerbread trim and black shutters that day.

"Is that you, Miss Kate?" Phoebe Jo, Robert's wife, called out in her Kentucky drawl.

I stepped up onto the flagstone walk and followed it around to the front of the house. "Yeah, it's me."

"Had yourself a long day," Phoebe Jo added. Her head, poking around the edge of one of the front double doors, was wrapped in a yellow bandana, long frizzes of brown hair sticking out the back.

"You don't know the half of it."

I heard a squeal. A furry black and tan bullet shot out from behind my housekeeper's legs and scrambled across the smooth walkway towards me. Boo-Kat skidded to a halt at my feet and began his favorite greeting ritual of nipping the air around my toes—kind of like the way Mother's friends greet each other, kissing the air beside their earrings.

"Well, y'all can tell us about it over supper," Phoebe Jo said, heading for the family kitchen. "I've got some roasted chicken and sweet potatoes in the oven."

"Sounds good," I replied, and stepped into the foyer. I stayed put, giving Boo-Kat's nose a chance to explore the hem of my coffee-colored silk pants and to gorge on all the new smells I had brought with me from the reception.

"Have you been a good boy?" I crouched down and scratched behind his ears. But that wasn't an exuberant enough greeting to make up for my being away all day. Boo-Kat stood on his hind legs and stretched up full-length, trying unsuccessfully to reach my face. I got down on my knees, folding my long frame so he could lick my face, which always turns into more kissing than I care for.

"Enough, enough! You're such an obsessive-compulsive." As I pulled myself up to full height, a white flag hanging down from the upper landing caught my attention. I saw a lacy strap wrapped around one of the balusters.

"So that's how you amused yourself while I was gone."

Boo-Kat looked up at me, tilted his head, and gave his *who, me?* look.

"Be there in a few minutes, Phoebe Jo," I called down the hall to the kitchen. "Just going to wash up."

I took the stairs two at a time, snatched up my stolen bra, and headed for my bedroom. Boo-Kat ran alongside, leaping and snapping at my hand, trying to recapture his quarry.

I tossed the bra back into the laundry basket, shook a warning finger at my bad boy, and peeled off my stinky clothes.

I STABBED A HUGE piece of chicken with my fork, added a hefty chunk of roasted sweet potato, and stuffed it all in my mouth.

Phoebe Jo smiled at me from her seat across the oak kitchen table and shook her head. "Miss Kate, I can't get over the way you eat."

Yeah, I know my table manners after one of my catering jobs aren't the most refined, but, as usual, I was starving. Once I rid my body of the day's cooking smells, I'm overwhelmed by a feeling of emptiness, a hunger both emotional and physical. I feel drained and used up, like I've given everything I've got to my clients and their guests. Food fills that void. But it has to be prepared by someone who cares about me.

It probably all goes back to my childhood. Mother never cooked for us, but Grandpa Cavanaugh would make me his special five-way chili combo whenever he saw me looking a little sad. I guess I inherited his love of food. It's a good thing I also inherited the Cavanaugh genetic codes that govern height and metabolism; otherwise, I'd have an extremely rounded physique.

I savored the simple flavors of the food I'd stuffed into my mouth. I swallowed, then announced to Phoebe Jo, "This is the best thing I've eaten all day."

"I can't believe that," she answered, passing a basket of sourdough rolls to me. I took a couple and passed it on to Robert, who handed it to Julie Ann, the Boones' fourteen-year-old daughter and youngest member of my surrogate family.

"So, how did your Arabian party go?" a wide-eyed Julie Ann asked.

"Iranian," I said, my voice muffled by the wad of sourdough in my mouth.

"Okay," Julie Ann wagged her head side-to-side, swinging her long, brown ponytail, "Iranian. Was there anyone famous there?" She blinked, pushed her eyeglasses back up onto the bridge of her nose, and stared expectantly at me.

"The usual cast of characters from the Clairmont blue book," I replied.

"Well, that being the case," Robert drawled, "ya gotta have at least one good story for us." He stretched a lanky arm across the table and reached for the butter plate.

Robert was right, and I spent the rest of the meal filling them in on the more entertaining episodes of the afternoon. With all the renovating and building that had been done on my house, the family kitchen was the most important room and my favorite place to be. Many hours were spent sitting around the table swapping stories, venting frustrations, and laughing. It was important to keep the business of catering away from the nurturing atmosphere I believed a family kitchen should have. Bad vibes, you know. Besides, to a caterer, the kitchen is the office, and when I leave that cold, stainless steel environment, walk across to the other side of the house and enter the cozy family kitchen, I feel like I've come home. Oak furniture and cabinets, colorful French country floral curtains, and pots of herbs growing on the sill of the bay window all contribute to the comforting and renewing energy I get from the room.

"Wow, Kate," Julie Ann said as I came to the end of my account of the afternoon's activities, "you have so much fun. Some day, I'll be your assistant and get to go to these crazy parties with you."

"Well, if you want the job," I answered, "you better start spending some of your time in front of a stove instead of a computer screen."

Julie Ann jumped up out of her chair and knocked her fork

onto the floor. "I have a surprise for you," she said, crouching down to retrieve it. On her way back up, she banged her head on the edge of the table. "Ouch!"

Phoebe Jo shook her head. "Julie Ann. Just slow down and think before you move." But she beamed with pride as she watched her daughter rush over to the kitchen counter. Julie Ann pulled a towel off an object I hadn't noticed before, turned around, and began processing towards me, arms out, holding her treasure aloft.

"I don't believe my eyes," I said. "Julie Ann, you didn't—"

"Yes, I did," she replied, head held high. "My very first—AAH!" I don't know what she tripped over—probably her own feet. Julie Ann always had trouble maneuvering through the world.

The glass-covered plate tilted dangerously to one side, but the fledgling baker/computer whiz lunged forward and stumbled to the safety of the kitchen table. The pineapple upside-down cake landed rightside-up in front of me.

Never mind that the pineapple slices were slipping over the edges of the cake and the texture was a little gritty, it was Julie Ann's first cake. I loved it.

* * * * * * *

I knew it was a dream, but I couldn't stop it.

The forest was dark, and I was alone. The only sounds I was aware of were the beating of my heart and the pounding of my feet on the hard ground. I ran towards the small wooden structure I could just make out through the trees at the end of the path. The door. Must reach the door.

Too slow. My leg muscles strained as though I was trying to push through thick mud.

I heard what sounded like the beating of a single pair of tiny wings behind me. Why was I scared?

51

I tried to turn my head to see what it was, but my neck felt like it was locked in a heavy brace. I could only look forward.

The door. Safety. Running through mud.

Whatever was chasing me had grown from a single pair of wings to a flock.

Must get to the door. I tried to reached out. My arms . . . too heavy.

6

Sunday, May 18th 6:00 A.M.

"OH, STOP!"

Boo-Kat immediately plopped down on his little rear end in the middle of the bike trail.

"No, Boo, not you. I was talking to myself."

We were out on our new ritual, the Sunrise Walk, and I was trying to curb the upsetting memories of the previous night's dream, not my dog.

It was supposed to be a meditative walk, but until I figured out what the dream meant, there would be no peace and I was doomed to keep running that memory loop over and over again. My obsessive-compulsive behavior matched my dog's. I could chew on the same old bone for days, too.

Boo-Kat looked up at me in confusion.

"Good, boy," I said, and we continued walking down the trail towards Loveland.

In the past my crazy dreams quite often turned out to be predictors of something important. It's not that I could read the future, but every once in a while someone, or something, would send me messages that would get all scrambled up in my brain's dream factory. I'm embarrassed to reveal that, 'cause it sounds kind of flaky. But I've learned to read my mental E-mail and take it seriously.

When we reached West Loveland Avenue, I decided to add some variety to our exercise and turned left this time, reversing our route. I crossed the railroad tracks and over to the opposite side of the street. Things were going well with Boo-Kat. His nose was to the ground, but there must have been an interesting scent trail right in our path, because he didn't pull me off on any little side trips. Our steady pace all the way down the sidewalk allowed me to continue replaying my dream without interruption.

We passed the old train station. I noticed the figure of a young man in a white windbreaker running away from the row of storefronts a couple of blocks down and on the other side of the street. He obviously wasn't on a morning jog. There was something frantic about his pace as he disappeared around a corner. I scanned back along the length of storefronts to see if someone was chasing him. There was no one else around, but I noticed an open door. My heart started to pound and I could feel a fluttering in my stomach.

The day before, I had heard someone run from that same doorway. Automatically, thoughts of my dream were pushed aside by the recollection of the previous morning's strange occurrence.

What had they been yelling about? I remembered an angry voice saying, *"I want more. Another twenty-five percent."*

Then the other guy said something about not wanting to be pressured and shouted *"Big Gabe can't protect you now."*

That's all I could remember.

I was just across the street from the opened doorway. As far as I could tell, there was no one else around. Maybe I'd just witnessed a burglary, but of what? The place hadn't opened for business yet, so I didn't know what there was to steal.

I decided to be a good citizen, but I also couldn't resist snooping. Too many unanswered questions in my head drives me crazy. I had time to take a quick look before reporting it to the police—after all, they were only a couple of blocks away.

I walked across the empty street, but as I reached the curb the cautious side of my brain began arguing with the impulsive side.

Don't go in there. What do you think you're going to accomplish by sticking your nose in someone else's business?

I'm just going to take a peek. There's no harm in that.

Oh yeah? I've heard that one before.

Maybe someone needs help.

That's what the police are for. Just go down a couple of blocks and report it.

I'm here. Might as well look.

The open door loomed in front of me. Even though the sun had risen over the tree tops, the interior of the storefront was still dark because of the closed aluminum blinds. The darkness was sucking me in. I couldn't stop myself.

Oh. Boo-Kat. Forgot about him. Can't take him in there.

I quickly tied his leash around the door handle.

What are you going to do if you find something you don't want to see?

My palms began to sweat. "Hello? Anybody there?"

Silence.

I stepped into what looked like a small reception area. I felt immediately woozy from the suffocating smells of fresh paint, adhesives, and plastic. The white walls were still bare. A desk looking like it belonged on the set of a Jetsons' cartoon was right in front of me. It had been set up with telephone equipment and a computer. Two beige love seats, still wrapped in plastic, and a marble, triangular-shaped coffee table, with sharp edges that looked like they could knife your knee caps, filled one corner. It appeared that some trendy business was almost ready to open.

What kind, I couldn't tell.

There was a wide doorway beside the receptionist's desk leading to who knew where. I repeated my "Hello's." Boo-Kat, indignant at being excluded from the tour, whimpered and squealed from his make-shift hitching post.

I stepped through the second doorway and scanned the room. I didn't know what I was looking for. That guy looked like he was being chased. But who or what was he running from? All I could see before me was a room full of drafting tables and computer equipment. The room was still in semi-darkness, except in one far corner where a single artist's lamp was turned on. In its spotlight on the floor was my answer.

"Oh, shit."

A body was stretched out, face down and very still.

Yellow-white hair.

Mr. Stick Man.

7

STOMACH HEAVING, I instinctively covered my mouth with my hand. I wanted to turn away, but was transfixed by the sight of blood that had seeped out the hole in the back of Brad's head. I stared in disbelief. The man had been making passes at me less than twenty-four hours earlier.

From my vantage point at Brad's feet, I noticed he still wore the expensive gray suit he'd gone swimming in the day before. It was dry but looked like he'd slept in it. His right hand was outstretched and partly hidden by a wastepaper basket under the drafting table. The impulsive side of my brain made me take a step forward to see if he was clutching anything. I heard a little clinking noise down by my feet. I saw that I had kicked a small object against the hard plastic mat under the table. It came to a halt at the edge of the bloody puddle around Brad's head. I felt compelled to check it out, but that meant having to get closer to Brad's body than I wanted to when he was alive.

Realizing I'd stumbled onto a murder scene and could be a potential contaminator of evidence, I was paranoid about brushing up against anything. Pulling in my elbows and moving slowly, I held my breath and crouched down. It was the pin I'd noticed on Brad's jacket at the wedding reception.

My face was only inches away from the sticky, oozing wound at the base of his skull. Another wave of dry heaves made me choke. I'd had enough of this snooping. It was way past time to report it to the police. I straightened up, left the room, and untied my anxious dog, who bounced with joy when he saw me. Leaving the door open as it had been before, we headed for the police station.

"THAT'S HER!"

It wasn't the type of greeting I expected at the police station. Jabbing his finger at me was a young guy with curly dark hair and long sideburns. He was wearing a white windbreaker. The runner.

I looked from the pointing finger to the beer-bellied policeman behind the complaint desk. He hitched up his belt and nodded towards me. "She's the one you saw?"

The runner shrugged his shoulders with a quick jerk. "Yeah."

"You sure?" The policeman thoughtfully scratched his military-style mustache.

"How many tall broads like her live around here?" The young man pointed at me with his thumb.

"Good morning, Ms. Cavanaugh."

I'd never met the officer who addressed me, but I wasn't surprised he knew who I was. After my solving what *The Cincinnati Enquirer* called "The Murder of the Critic from Hell", every policeman in the tri-state area knew what I looked like.

"What's going on?" I asked.

"This man has just reported a possible homicide and has placed you at the scene."

The insides of my stomach jumped, leaving me with a queasy feeling. I took a breath to steady myself, and replied to the policeman, "That's what *I'm* here to report."

I walked straight up to the complaint desk, stopped in front of my accuser, and stared down into his impudent face. "I saw you running away from the building. That's what made me go in there in the first place."

"You're crazy, lady."

The policeman waved his hands at both of us. "Wait a minute, wait a minute. Let's get this story straight." He directed his attention to the guy. "When did you get there and what were you doing?"

"Well, first of all, it's no story. I got a perfectly logical explanation. Just listen."

"Okay, okay. I'm listening."

"Well, see, it's like this. I work for the guy, Brad Holtmann. I was coming in to finish setting up. We were supposed to be ready for business tomorrow. I see the door wide open, so I know right away something's wrong. Brad never comes in that early, especially on a Sunday morning. Even if he did, he wouldn't leave the door open. So I'm walking up and see there's a dog tied to the door handle, making all these pathetic noises. Not exactly your vicious watchdog type. I think to myself, 'Something's screwy', and I go in real quiet like."

"You just walked past the dog and it didn't bark?"

"When he first sees me, his tail starts waggin' a mile a minute. So I just reach out my hand, he licks it. I walk right in and I see this lady looking down at my boss who's stretched out on the floor."

I couldn't believe my ears. "He's lying," I blurted out, "I saw you run away before I even got to that side of the street."

The officer gestured with his hand for me to stop. "Ms. Cavanaugh, please let him finish his story. Then we'll get to your version."

Version? How did I get into this? I'm a suspect? He can't be serious.

"So," the policeman prompted, his pen ready to record more

lies, "you went in and saw what?"

"I told ya," the young man's unshaven face scrunched up in frustration, "that lady was hanging over my boss's body. I didn't stick around and take notes. I came straight here."

"Is there a body, Ms. Cavanaugh?"

"Yes," I replied.

The policeman turned to a second officer who had been sitting in the background and said, "You better go down and secure the place." Then he nodded towards me. "Okay, Ms. Cavanaugh, your turn."

I was really pissed with the situation and myself. I should've listened to that irritating little voice inside of me that kept saying *don't go in there.* But no, I had to be a snoopy Good Samaritan. After last December's escapade, trying to keep the Clairmont Rangers from pinning that community's first murder on the wrong person, I promised myself no more getting involved with the police.

I wanted to get this over with as soon as possible, so I quickly and succinctly related the events of both that morning's walk and the previous day's when I heard the argument in the same building. I offered what I could remember—one guy demanding he wanted twenty-five percent more of something and the other shouting, "Big Gabe can't protect you now."

The officer took notes and, when I had finished, remarked, "Do you have any idea what any of this could mean?"

"Not a clue."

"Where's your dog now?"

"He's tied up to the bicycle rack outside."

The officer craned his neck, looked past me and out the picture window next to the front entrance. "Oh, yeah. I see him. He really is a quiet pup." He looked back at me. "Did you happen to know the alleged victim Brad Holtmann?"

What did he have to go and ask that for? I didn't want to get pulled into it even further, but I couldn't lie. I told him about meeting Brad at Cindy's wedding reception and briefly mentioned his inebriated behavior. Then, hoping to divert attention away from me and onto other possibilities, I said, "I barged in on him in the bathroom, by mistake of course, with a nose full of white powder."

The cop looked at me with a quizzical expression. "Who had the nose full of white powder? You? Or him?"

I was getting in deeper. "*He* did, of course."

"You talking cocaine?"

"I don't know. But judging from the look on his face it was something illegal."

"And the last time you saw him alive, he fell in the pool and Mr. Hoseyni and his brother were carrying him off to the house?"

"Right."

"Did you inform Mr. Hoseyni about the incident in the bathroom?"

"No."

"You didn't think the host should be aware of what was going on under his own roof."

I bit my tongue. If I told this policeman about Ali's temper, that he was already angry with Brad, then Ali would automatically be a suspect. I couldn't do that to Cindy, so I just said, "I didn't want to ruin the day for him and his bride, who happens to be an old friend of mine."

"We should talk to Mr. and Mrs. Hoseyni. Are they still in town?"

I checked the clock on the wall. "They're on their honeymoon. Probably on their way to the airport right now to catch a flight to Paris."

The policeman punched a button on his telephone and spoke into the intercom. "Call the Cincinnati/Northern Kentucky International Airport and have them page Mr. and Mrs. Ali Hoseyni." He spelled the last name. "They're booked on a flight

61

to Paris. We need to talk to them."

The policeman turned back to me. "Where can we get hold of Mr. Hoseyni's brother? Does he live in the area?"

"Yes." I told him what street TC lived on.

He recorded the information on a form, and the station was silent except for the sound of his pen scratching across the paper. And the irritating *rat tat tat* of my accuser's fingers drumming on the counter.

"Uh, Mr. Alberto . . . " The policeman looked up and cocked a bushy eyebrow at the young man. "Frank, isn't it?"

The drumming stopped. "Name's Frankie."

"Okay. Well . . . Mr. Alberto, were you aware of Mr. Holtmann's drug use?"

"Nope."

"Did he have any enemies?"

"How would I know? He was my boss, not my drinking buddy."

"Do you know anything about yesterday's altercation?"

"Altercation?"

"Fight. The one Ms. Cavanaugh alleges took place where you work?"

Mr. Alberto shrugged and held his hands out in a helpless gesture.

"Who's this 'Big Gabe'?"

"I haven't the foggiest idea. I was nowhere near the place yesterday."

"Well, do you know who'd be angry with Mr. Holtmann?"

"I don't know. He was a cool guy. Lots of laughs. Why ask *me* all this stuff?" Mr. Alberto turned abruptly and aimed a finger at me. "She's the one who was partying with him yesterday, and *she's* who I found standing over his body."

8

SO MUCH FOR MY meditative walk. I climbed the steps to the back door of my house and into the kitchen, feeling more stressed than when I had started out that morning. The smell of fried pork sausage welcomed me home to my sanctuary.

"Miss Kate!" Phoebe Jo, dressed for church in her special occasion flower print dress with a lace collar, jumped up from her seat at the breakfast table, rushed towards me, and threw her arms around my waist. "Oh, thank the Lord you're safe!" she said into my arm pit. Throwing her head back so she could look me eye to eye she asked, "Where've you been?"

"I think I was in an old episode of *The Twilight Zone*."

I went to the door and held it open for Boo-Kat who had stopped for a pee in the yard. He bounced in, sniffed the air and ran over to the counter. Stretching up to his full height, he placed his front paws against the edge, and danced along its length searching for a stray sausage.

"Don't joke with me," Phoebe Jo said, hands on hips. "I've been beside myself worrying about you."

"Yeah," Robert joined in, "Phoebe Jo had visions of you falling into the Little Miami River."

I sat down across from him and Julie Ann at the table. They too were dressed in what I knew to be their best outfits, and I remembered that this was the Sunday they were providing the music for their church's morning service. Julie Ann was chewing on her last bite of waffle and staring at me with a look of someone who was anticipating a good story. I unlaced my walking shoes and began telling the tale.

"So," Julie Ann interrupted, "was it that hunky Matt Skinner who took you and Mr. Alberto to ID the body?"

Much to my dismay, I had already allowed Clairmont Ranger Matt Skinner to snake his way into my thoughts. It was difficult not to recall my first attraction to him and make the comparison between his sexy good looks and the pot-bellied physique of the Loveland police officer. Yeah, Matt was hunky. But he was also a cop. And I have this problem with cops.

Ranger Skinner, who had been assigned to Clairmont's first murder, had pushed all sorts of buttons in me. Some of them pleasurable, others downright aggravating. It probably wasn't fair, but I could trace the beginnings of my attitude back twenty years ago to my dealings with foreign police while on my travels. In one particular situation, I was falsely accused and mistreated by some London bobbies.

"No, Julie Ann." I sliced a chunk of sausage, swirled it around in a puddle of maple syrup and stuck a piece of waffle on top. "The Loveland police are investigating this murder. And they're really ticked off that it happened just down the block from them." I stuffed the first forkful of my long-awaited breakfast into my mouth.

Robert sipped his coffee thoughtfully and peered at me over the edge of the cup. "I suppose catering isn't a very exciting occupation, but this is the second time in less than six months that you've been tangled up with police and dead bodies. You gonna make a habit of this?"

"I wasn't looking for trouble—just trying to be a Good

Samaritan. But next time, I'm minding my own business. The cops have pegged me as one of the suspects."

Phoebe Jo dropped a plate she was putting into the dishwasher.

"They're wrong," Julie Ann shouted, her expression serious and determined. "We'll just have to solve it, Kate. I'll help you like I did the last time."

"Thanks, Julie Ann, but I really doubt it'll come to that. I'm sure that once the police dig into Brad Holtmann's background and activities they'll find more solid leads." That's what I said to keep my little "family" calm. Inside, I ran through the list of experiences I'd had where the police I encountered jumped to the easiest conclusions and tried to make the evidence fit. My thought patterns were threatening to plunge me into a bad mood. I switched gears. "So, you're playing today?"

"Yep," Robert said, tightening the silver and turquoise clasp on his bolo tie. "Want a little live music with your breakfast?" He looked at his wife. "We should warm up. It's almost time to go."

Phoebe Jo dumped the dustpan full of broken plate into the trash, sighed, and pulled off her apron. "I suppose singing is the best thing to do when you're troubled. But, all of a sudden, my heart's just not in it. It pains me to see all these tribulations heaped on you, Miss Kate."

I sliced a piece of sausage. "Phoebe Jo, you're the one who's always saying 'Tribulation worketh patience.' Someone up there is just working on me." I slipped the chunk of meat under the table to Boo-Kat. "C'mon, I'd love to hear you guys sing."

Robert reached into a small, black case and handed her a mandolin. "Here, honey. It'll make us all feel better."

Julie Ann rolled her eyes as Robert picked up his guitar, strummed a couple of times, and retuned it. He looked at Phoebe Jo, bobbed his head once, and, on cue, they broke into a soft, slow chorus of *Go Tell It On The Mountain.*

I could never understand why they hadn't made it big as a country singing duo. Their voices were strong and clear and harmonized perfectly. They had even cut a few albums. But I guessed there were a lot of good country singers out there and I had heard the stories about how tough it was on the road, especially when Julie Ann came along. They, too, had found sanctuary here at Trail's End Farm, and that made me happy. I slipped a couple of pieces of waffle to Boo-Kat, who made a project out of giving my fingers a tongue-cleaning.

After a verse or two, Robert picked up the tempo slightly, and a smile broke out on Phoebe Jo's face. Still seated, I held Boo-Kat up by his front paws and rocked him side to side to the beat of the music. Even Julie Ann joined in and began singing.

"...over the hills and everywhere;
go, tell it on the mountain,
that Jesus Christ is born."

Robert sped the music up to a rousing tempo. I got to my feet, still holding my dog by his front paws, and began to dance him around the kitchen.

Faster and louder, we whirled and sang. Boo-Kat couldn't keep up, so I bent down and he jumped into my arms. I danced across the kitchen floor with my happy, panting bundle of fur. Around and around and around we went.

"Why is everybody singing Christmas songs in the middle of May?" Mother stood at the front entrance to the kitchen, dressed in her expensive and show-offy Sunday best. She did look nice in her powder-blue silk suit and pearl necklace with matching earrings. But I suspected she never slept well. Her silver hair was always arranged in perfect waves and had such a stiff appearance I couldn't imagine she was able to relax with that hair-sprayed, metallic helmet between her brain box and the pillow.

I said, "Good morning, Mother. I didn't hear you come in." Boo-Kat squealed at the sight of his grandmother and wriggled in a desperate attempt to free himself from my arms. He always wants to greet her, probably because he senses how much it annoys her. I carried my squirming pet to the back door and dumped him outside, not wanting to deal with pulled stockings, muddy paw prints on blue silk, and a lecture on child-rearing.

"Nobody's answering my question," Mother said, walking into the kitchen. "Why is everybody singing Christmas songs in the middle of May?"

The Boones started putting their instruments back into their cases. "Just needed a little pick-me-up," Robert answered. "And that song always does the trick for us."

Phoebe Jo locked her mandolin case and started towards the coffee maker. "Can I get you a cup, Mrs. Cavanaugh?"

"No, no. Thank you," replied Mother, coming up beside me. "I'm just here to pick up my daughter." She took a half step back in order to look up into my face. "I thought we were going to church, Kathleen."

Church? "We were?"

"Yes," she said with a brusque nod of her head, then inspected me from top to bottom and frowned. "What *are* you doing in that tatty sweat suit?"

Seems Mother was stuck in a time warp. "Church was last week."

"Well, they have it every Sunday, you know. I thought we were starting off on a new foot."

"Last week was Mother's Day." Give a parent an inch and she'll take a yard.

"Well, whatever, it would be good for you to go, Kathleen. They have a lovely singles group there."

"Oh, Mother, give it a rest." Why was she doing this to me? "I'm forty-three. Too old for that sort of stuff."

"No, you're not, dear. I happen to know that some of the boys you went to high school with are quite active in that group."

Yeah, the ones I ran away from. As long as she lived, Mother would continually try to match me up with some man from a family with the right pedigree. At some point she was going to have to give up on the notion of grandchildren. *And soon.*

"Well, Kathleen, I worry about your not having any religion. That's not the way your father and I brought you up."

Oh, great. We were going to get into one of those discussions.

"You're missing out," Mother said, patting her helmet. "You really should go to church."

"I am having church. Right here. That was our worship service you just walked in on."

Mother's mouth clamped shut so tight there were little puckers at the corners of her rose-painted lips. Behind her, I could see Phoebe Jo smiling and shaking her head. Robert stifled a laugh as he cleared away the breakfast dishes.

"This is not church," Mother whispered through clenched teeth as she smacked my arm.

"Well," I said, "it's too late for me to get ready. I would need to shower and change . . . it's already been a busy morning."

"Yeah." Julie Ann's high-pitched voice startled everyone. "Kate found a dead body."

Mother's jaw dropped. Her head jerked to look at Julie Ann, and then back at me, eyes wide with horror. "What? Here on the farm?"

"No. I was taking a morning walk with Boo-Kat, and it seems we stumbled onto a murder scene in Loveland."

"Oh, please, Kathleen. Don't get involved." Mother clutched at my arm. "I couldn't handle a repeat of last Christmas."

There she was, always thinking of others. "I'm sorry, I have to be involved. I'm one of the suspects."

Mother stared at me speechless for almost a full half-minute, her hand slowly reaching up to touch her lips with the tips of her manicured nails.

"Don't worry," Julie Ann jumped in, "Kate'll solve it. She'll figure out who did it."

"Oh, Kathleen . . . "

I raised my hand. "Don't worry, Mother, I'm not going to play private eye. As soon as the cops get into the murder victim's background they'll find some more plausible suspects. I won't get pulled into it." That is, if they did their job right. I wondered how much weight they were going to give the story Frankie Alberto told them. He really went overboard in trying to pin the murder of his poor, cocaine-sniffing boss Brad Holtmann on me. The man was obviously trying to cover up something and I didn't believe he had actually spied on me inside that studio. I'd have felt his presence.

"Well," snapped Mother, her eyes regaining the haughtiness they had momentarily lost. Her chin shot up and I knew she was back into her matriarchal mode. "The best thing for you to do, Kathleen, is to go to church and pray to God that He keeps our family name out of the papers. That's what I'm going to do. I don't know what this world is coming to. The younger generation is abandoning all traditional values."

Mother paused. Her eyes widened with renewed indignation as a second thought occurred to her. "And they have no sense of what's in good taste. On my way here this morning, I drove past the Beckers' place. You know that new monstrosity on the corner that looks more like a bank than a house. The front lawn was littered with dozens of those atrocious pink plastic flamingos. I'm sure we have laws against that sort of thing here in Clairmont."

After a curt "Good day" to the Boones, Mother swept out of the kitchen with such a royal flourish, I found myself humming *God Save the Queen.*

A moment's silence followed her departure. I've noticed whenever Mother leaves a room, the people left behind need a few minutes to recover. Even the room's energy seems to need a chance to settle back into its normal vibration frequency after being shaken up by one of her appearances.

Phoebe Jo broke the silence. "Well . . . Miss Kate, here, has had her church, and Mrs. Cavanaugh has gone to hers . . . so," she said, turning to Robert and Julie Ann, "we better get this show on the road or we'll be late for ours."

Robert gathered up the guitar and mandolin cases. "We'll say a prayer for you, Kate. Like we always do."

"Thanks, guys," I replied. Then, remembering this was their special music day, "Knock their socks off. See you later."

THE SUN WARMED my back as I bent over and pulled last year's rotting daylily leaves out of the beds. This was one of my favorite times of the year. It felt good to be looking forward, digging in the earth, and cleaning out the old dead wood.

The gardens at the back of my house were more than a source of fresh vegetables and herbs; they were a symbol of healing and renewal. For years, I had constructed garden plans in my head, but never seemed to find the motivation to actually start digging. Until right after my surgery. Having a breast removed not only makes you feel less than whole, it also stiffens up that side of your body to the point where you can't even brush your own hair. You're supposed to do all these tedious exercises to stretch out the muscles, and for the thousandth time you think, *Why me? Why do I have to deal with this?* I was getting negative and downright depressed. I had to find some way to turn this exercise into something positive, so I picked up a shovel and started to dig. I know the doctor warned me not to do any heavy lifting, but it felt so good I kept right on going.

In six years' time, I'd managed to dig up six separate flower beds for my collection of old roses, daylilies, poppies, and herbs and to rototill a fifty-foot-square bed for vegetables. I don't even use all that ground I turned over, but once I started, I couldn't stop. Another example of my compulsive nature.

I'd go so far as saying the garden helped save my life. I never questioned why I was taking the trouble to plant seeds whose flowers I wouldn't even see for two years. Hope and a gut feeling I was going to survive must have created positive energy. And you need all you can get when you're facing an unpredictable disease. That in itself probably caused the T-cells in my body to aggressively go after all the nasty cancer cells and gobble them up.

That's what I believed on the good days. On the bad days, I was just as certain I was going to die within the week.

So, there I was dressed in my shorts, Cincinnati Reds T-shirt and cap—it was, after all, baseball season. I had a lot on my mind. Edging the flower beds sounded like a good physical release for my frustrations. I jabbed the shovel into the trench around one of the beds, placed my work boot on the top edge of the blade and put all my weight on it. The hard clay we have to contend with here in Clairmont resists all effort, unless you throw yourself into it whole hog and with great determination. My thoughts turned to Mother.

Boy, she pisses me off the way she treats me like a child. Was it because I still acted like one or was it impossible for her to let go of her need to control? I suppose, in her eyes, I wasn't going to be an adult until I was married. I would like to find someone, fall in love with him, and live happily ever after. But who was I kidding? I couldn't quite figure out what my problem was—if I had a problem. Was it fear of commitment, looking for my father, or just that I'm too goddamn picky? It was a mystery to me.

But a mystery with a more compelling need to be solved was: what the hell was that Frankie Alberto trying to do accusing me of murdering Brad Holtmann?

I didn't believe that slimy little guy snuck up on me while I was in Brad's studio looking at his lifeless body. I'm sure I would have felt the same crawly sensation up and down my spine as I did when I caught Brad spying on me at the wedding.

Maybe Frankie Boy had it in for his boss. Even though he

denied it, maybe Frankie did come in early Saturday morning and have an argument with Brad—that is if it was Brad I heard yelling at someone behind the aluminum blind.

How do I get myself involved in situations like this?

I finished stamping my shovel around the first flower bed, and moved across the lawn to work on another. The clay on this side of the house was always solid as a rock, and the shovel clanged against the ground and sprang back in my hands. I repositioned it, stepped up onto the rim of the shovel with both feet and gave it a good, hard bounce as though I were trying to jump-start a pogo stick.

I made a little dent in the ground and was about to try again, when I heard the rhythmic beeping of a car horn in the distance. No one traveled down to the end of the road unless they were intending to come to Trail's End Farm. I could hear the beeping getting closer. Dragging the shovel, I walked around to the front of the house to where the split rail fence ended, and looked down the lane, waiting for whoever it was to come around the bend.

The beeping grew louder and more excited, losing its syncopated beat. Whoever was announcing their arrival did so with frenzied blasts of the horn.

As soon as the vehicle turned up the laneway, I knew, even at the distance of a couple of hundred yards, it wasn't someone from the Cincinnati area. You couldn't miss knowing about this van. It would've been touted in all the local media as a moving landmark. A huge, yellow sun face covered the front end. As it got closer, the side of the van I could see was painted with a detailed scene that included elephants, palm trees, and a dancing, blue-skinned Krishna playing a flute. There must have been crystals hanging from the rearview mirror, because little sparkles and shards of light danced beside the driver's head.

I couldn't believe my eyes. A giant cosmic hand had just come down and flipped back a few chapters in my life's journeybook.

9

I KNEW WHO IT WAS even before the van came to a stop, but didn't know if I was ready for her.

Twenty years ago, I traveled over eight thousand miles in a van painted like that, and a flood of outrageous memories and crazy, mixed-up feelings pinned me to the spot. The whole scene had a dream-like quality to it.

Through the windshield, I could see a mass of silver, frizzy hair encircling her round face, eyes hidden behind a pair of aviator-style sunglasses. One side of her nose was still pierced with a small gold ring. Jasmine Woods stuck a rubber chicken out the window, waved it wildly, and pulled it back in to the give the horn another series of quick beeps!

Dark memories were pushed aside and I laughed until tears formed in the corners of my eyes. The van came to a halt beside me.

"I can't believe you still have that dumb old chicken," I said, as Jaz threw open the door with the multi-colored mandala painted on it and tumbled out.

"Katie," she shouted.

"Jaz!" I bent over and caught her as she flung herself at me, wrapping her arms around my waist.

"Katie, Katie, Katie," she screeched, her energetic embrace bouncing both of us in a little dance, accompanied by the tinkling of tiny silver bells on her bracelets. "It's so good to see you."

"It's great to see you, too." I gave her soft body another hearty squeeze and buried my face in her thick tangle of hair, breathing in the warm scent of patchouli oil and sandalwood.

Jaz held me out at arm's length and looked me up and down, accenting each comment with a vigorous shake of my shoulder. "You haven't aged a bit. It's like you stepped out of a time warp. I don't see a line on your face, an extra pound on that bony body, and your braid is as golden as ever."

"You haven't seen me under fluorescent lighting."

"Well, get a load of this old lady." She gave her hair a quick flick. "Betcha never thought I'd live long enough to turn this color, huh?"

"I'm surprised any of us survived. But you look great, Jaz." Though she must have been fifty years old by now, and had turned silver-haired and acquired a few lines around her eyes, she was still dressed in that hippie-in-India style. She wore a gauzy, ankle-length skirt with a complex pattern of orange and purple floral designs and geometric borders. Strings wrapped in gold wire with little beads on the ends hung from her waist. A gauzy, purple shawl, with gold threads woven through it, covered her shoulders and the orange silk, sleeveless top she had on underneath.

I put my hands on my hips. "How'd you ever find me?" The answer came to me as soon as I asked the question. "Klaus?"

Jaz nodded. "That crazy German we met in Goa has a web site on the Internet. He's made a hobby out of keeping track of everyone and letting others know where we all scattered to after that winter in India."

So I'm on the Web. I had this feeling of not being in control. Now anybody from my past could find me. I wasn't sure if that was good or bad. "So where's Colin? You two still together?"

Jaz averted her eyes and brushed a strand of hair from her face. "Oh, him. That was a long time ago, Katie. We split up." She looked back at me. "No surprise, uh? Our battles always seemed to be fought in public, but I have Mike now, so I'm okay."

I nodded towards the painted van. "That's not the same one we drove overland from London to Bombay, but I recognize your artwork." Studying the pictures closer, I said, "Your technique has improved."

"Come and take a look at this side." Jaz grabbed my hand and pulled me towards the rear of the van. She pointed out the two painted angels, one on each corner, their wings spread across the back and sides of the van as though hugging it. "Remember that time we were stuck in that little village outside of Teheran? After the accident? You and I sat in that van for days waiting to get towed and we talked about the angels. Didn't we have some good times, Katie?"

The memory created a hollow feeling in my stomach. It wasn't pleasant. I let Jaz chatter on.

"The angels are pushing the van and bringing me to wonderful places like your farm. Now come around here and see what I've done on this side."

I did. "Oh!" It felt like someone had punched me in the chest and left me a coded message. Painted on the passenger side from front to rear was a huge representation of the gold wing pin I'd seen on Brad Holtmann's lapel. Only this one included rays of light shooting out from its center, and a large dove along with dozens of tiny angels hovering about.

"Katie? Are you okay?"

I couldn't answer right away. My mind was racing around trying to understand what was happening. This was the third time in the last two days that I'd seen those gold wings, and that wasn't counting my dream. From where I stood, I could still see those painted angels pushing Jaz's van. If there was a message in this for me, I wished the angels would just speak up and explain it. But instead, it felt like they were silently pushing me down the road towards another strange adventure.

I collected those thoughts and stuffed them in my Review Later File. "Yeah, just felt a little funny there for a minute." I patted my chest. "Everything's okay now. Uh, your artwork is very impressive."

"Thank you. It's a lot more meaningful than those flowers and stars I painted on that old hippie van."

I didn't understand the difference between the old van and this shiny, new version. It still looked like a hippie van to me. But it was definitely a work of art. "It's beautiful. Um, what is the significance of this?" I asked, pointing to the huge wing pin symbol.

Jaz's eyes widened with excitement. "Katie, it's The Circle of Light. I'm surprised you haven't heard about it." The excitement that had been visible first in her eyes obviously began coursing through her entire body, because she started bouncing around on the balls of her feet like she couldn't stand still. "They're a community of magical people with the most enlightened ideas about life and the world and how we all fit together." She waved her arms as though conducting some cosmic orchestra. "We're really going to change things. We're making an evolutionary leap into a whole new consciousness. Aren't you still interested in that?"

"Yeah. I'm still interested. But I guess I'm trying to make evolutionary leaps in my own way." Suddenly, I felt like a solid clump of earthbound matter that had planted itself in some old rut and was missing out on all these supposedly magical things.

"That's good, Katie. I'm glad living here in the Midwest hasn't closed your mind to the mystical realities of the universe." Jaz reached for my arm. "Come to our Open House tomorrow."

"Open House? Where? What are you talking about?"

"It's The Circle of Light's annual leadership retreat."

"Here?"

"Yeah. At the Golden Valley Spiritual Center. They have it in a different part of the country every year at this time, and this year The High One chose Cincinnati."

I knew the Golden Valley Spiritual Center well. Ever since that eccentric millionaire donated land on the southern edge of Clairmont, there'd been a lot of controversy. The wealthy neighbors valued their privacy, and saw the constant stream of out-of-towners with unconservative beliefs as a threat. They even got lumped into the same category as the Gypsies who showed up every spring and left a trail of burglarized estates in their wake.

"So," I said, "how long are you going to be in town?"

Her shawl momentarily slipped from one shoulder and I caught a glimpse of a large bluish-green bruise, before she yanked it back up.

"Just a week," Jaz replied quickly, "but it'll be very full. The new High One will be chosen by mid-week and the rest of the retreat will have seminars with visiting speakers, meditation, and Dynamic Energy Healing sessions."

I bit. "What are 'Dynamic Energy Healing sessions?'"

"Oh, Katie, you would just love that. Especially since you're such a physical person. They play these tablas, you know, Indian drums." Jaz's fingers tapped imaginary tablas. "As the rhythm gets faster and more complicated, you feel it come into your body and you start jumping up and down. You're like one with the beat. It's all one energy and it wakes up all your electromagnetic circuits."

"And what does that do?" I said, withholding judgment.

"Well, if you do it with all your heart and soul, you can literally detach yourself from old, wounding perceptions and attachments. And that frees you up to receive healing."

I pictured old, frayed electrical cords popping and sparking as

I hopped around and ripped them out of the childhood baggage I was dragging behind me—Mother, right on my heels, trying to plug them back in.

"Oh," Jaz continued, "and another thing you might enjoy at the Open House, Katie, is the totally organic vegetarian feast they're going to serve. Do you grow organic vegetables on your farm? You should, you know. Wait'll you see the fields and fields of pure, nontoxic veggies at the spiritual center."

"Yeah, I know what they have there. Every now and then, I buy some herb plants from them." I waved my hand in the air. "Anyway, I'm sold on it. I'll come to your Open House. So, are you part of the leadership of this, uh . . . group?"

"No. I'm just one of the helpers who are here to set things up and keep the events running smoothly."

I pointed to the Circle of Light symbol on the van. "Do you have gold pins like that?"

"Sure." Jaz nodded. "We've got a whole catalog of stuff. You can get pins, earrings, T-shirts, books, drums, whatever you need."

"So, anyone can buy one of your pins and it doesn't necessarily mean they're a believer?"

"Yeah, but I don't know why they would want to. Why do you ask?"

"Well, I met someone the other day who was wearing a pin like that."

"Oh? Who?" Jaz looked like she was going to start bouncing again. I wondered whether she was trying to heal an old wound or if this kind of enlightenment required constant maintenance.

"A guy named Brad Holtmann—a graphic artist in the area."

Jaz stood still and frowned for a few seconds. "Nope, don't know him. But that doesn't mean anything. There are thousands of people in The Circle."

"Well, this one's no longer in any circle. I found him dead this morning, shot through the back of the head."

"Oh, that's awful," Jaz said. She looked down at the ground and shook her head quickly. "He couldn't have been a member."

"How would you know?"

"First of all," she said, looking up at me, "he wouldn't put himself in a violent situation. True believers are enlightened people and are repelled by anything other than peace and harmony. Besides, anyone who's really in The Circle of Light is protected from earthly violence. The energy from their aura connects with God's energy and forms an invisible shield around them. There is documented evidence of believers escaping harm when that should have been impossible."

Yeah, we thought we were enlightened people on the beaches of Goa, too. But I remember the Arabian Sea coughing up more than one murdered body.

10

Monday, May 19th

I PADDED THROUGH the dark kitchen in my bare feet and nightshirt, opened the refrigerator door, and pulled out a glass baking dish. I turned on the light over one of the counters. The grandfather clock in the foyer chimed once, indicating it was half past midnight.

I spooned a huge portion of Phoebe Jo's apple-rhubarb cobbler into a cereal bowl and topped it off with four scoops of butterscotch pecan ice cream. Big girls eat big. Especially after being harassed all evening long by phone calls from *The Cincinnati Enquirer, The Post,* and every TV and radio station in the tri-state area. Everyone wanted an exclusive quote from the Amazon Chili Heiress Detective. I finally let my answering machine handle the calls with the recorded message "No comment."

Even so, I was prepared to see my picture and name screaming from the morning's front page. I guessed Mother's prayers wouldn't be answered to her liking, and she'd probably find a way to blame it on me. As though I had God's ear.

The one call I did take was from Cindy, whose honeymoon

plans had been aborted. First, she expressed concern about my finding Brad and wondered how I was dealing with it, then launched into the real reason for her late night call.

Cindy said, "It's a good thing they paged us at the airport, because Ali and I were in the middle of creating a scene."

Apparently, their flight had been delayed and they were killing time when they heard the news report about Brad's body being found. That got Ali going on another tirade about American culture which made Cindy angry and defensive. She said, "It's a wonder we heard the page, we were arguing so loudly. The police want us to hang around town, which is probably for the best. Ali and I have a lot to work through."

I told her to call me anytime, that when I heard her voice on the answering machine I'd pick up.

The pine flooring creaked under my feet as I made my way along the dark corridor and into the foyer. Shafts of silvery moonlight shining through the leaded glass window over the front entrance illuminated the mustached faces of The Chili Kings. The four paintings honoring the men responsible for the Cavanaugh Crown Chili empire, from great-great-grandpa to Dad, hung on the wall going up the oak staircase.

I tiptoed past them to the top of the stairs and stopped at the landing that crossed over the foyer and connected the two wings of the house. No sound came from the Boones' living quarters down the hall. They'd had a long day, visiting relatives in Kentucky after church and had gone straight to bed when they finally got home. All I could hear was the faint ticking of the grandfather clock downstairs.

I turned and headed in the opposite direction down the corridor, past three guest bedrooms, and into my master suite.

Boo-Kat was snoring in his little bed at the foot of my four-poster. Hoping he wouldn't wake up and start begging, I carefully set the cereal bowl down on the bedside table and went to my walk-in closet.

In a far corner, on a shelf behind some old clothes, was a cardboard box. I pulled the heavy carton off the shelf, placed it on the floor and opened it up. You would think I'd give such an important part of my life history a more impressive time capsule than this beaten up, saggy old piece of cardboard. The flaps were half torn off from the constant opening and closing over the years. The musty smell of old paper made me sneeze as I rummaged around, looking for the tattered journals that documented my travels. I couldn't remember which notebook had the memoirs of Iran in it, so I grabbed all five, turned off the closet light, and climbed into bed.

Once Jaz had left to go back to the spiritual center earlier that evening, I started thinking about her version of the dramatic events that almost kept us from getting out of Iran. She was one of those personality types that could tell you a story about going to the grocery store and make it sound like one of the most hair-raising experiences a person could ever have.

We had spent the afternoon and evening reminiscing and catching up with one another, and I had concluded that she had not changed one bit. I had the same feeling about all my friends—that they just stayed the same, while I went through all these earth-shaking changes. But I guess that doesn't show on the outside, and I look the same to them as I did twenty years ago.

I stuffed a spoonful of cobbler and ice cream into my mouth, grabbed the orange notebook, and opened it up. A thin, folded sheet of newsprint fell out. I laughed. "The Goan Pig!" Klaus's newsletter. Here was another example of someone who apparently hadn't changed much. Always the one trying to keep track of everybody, he apparently was still at it with his web page reports on the whereabouts and activities of our beach tribe.

Carefully picking up the fragile newsletter, I held the orangey-pink paper up to my nose and breathed in Goa.

In my mind I saw clusters of small cow-dung cottages

surrounded by palm trees, their trunks bent by the winds so that they grew parallel to the beach and then shot up like crowned towers. A woman in a vivid green and gold sari gathered water at the well and headed off into the grove, balancing the heavy clay urn on top of her head. A cow plodded along behind her, its marigold necklace swinging with each step. Stoned hippies on the beach. Wrong book.

I slipped the newsletter back in between the pages and flipped through the rest of the notebook. Here and there I stopped to read a recipe I had jotted down. They sounded good and were making me even hungrier. Making a mental note to myself to try out some of the dishes, I set the notebook aside and shoveled in another spoonful of cobbler and ice cream. Recipes, recipes, recipes. Always focused on food. Guess I haven't changed either.

I picked up the green notebook and started skimming through its pages.

We were such an odd group to be traveling together. Three American women—a six-foot-three inch tall blond, a redhead standing just barely over five feet in her cowboy boots, and a brunette who looked like she was about to give birth to septuplets. But the Arabs were most impressed with the guy—a Brit. They thought we were his harem.

Cherry Jublanski and I had already traveled many miles together when we hooked up with a very pregnant Jaz and her husband Colin. We found them by answering an ad, posted in the London American Express office, looking for two more people to share expenses on an overland drive to India.

Colin and Jaz were already experienced Asian Trekkers, making a business out of traveling to India every two years, buying up loads of silver and ivory jewelry, and Indian clothing. On the way back to London, they would make a detour to the Greek Islands, sell the bulk of their treasures at enormous markups to the summer tourists, then head back to London and sell whatever was remaining to the local retailers.

Jaz became a tribal legend when she had her baby boy Raji on the beach during a Christmas Eve celebration. She took it as some giant cosmic joke that Raji was now, at twenty-five, a fabulously successful Wall Street analyst. Seems every generation has to rebel.

As I continued leafing through the notebook, a title jumped out at me with three exclamation points punctuating it: *A Cold Morning in the Cotton Fields!!!*

Yeah, this was it. I hadn't read these particular entries for many years and I was curious to see how my version compared with Jaz's.

November 20th, Middle of Nowhere, Iran

We'd been driving all day along endless stretches of empty, boring countryside. Finding a place to spend the night had been impossible. None of the small, rural villages were prepared for tourists. But we thought, that's okay. We have our camper van. So we pulled over to the side of the road and crashed for the night.

The next thing I remembered was Jaz shouting, "Why is it so bloody cold in here?" Then, she yelled at Colin to get up.

I opened my eyes and could tell by the light coming through the curtains that it was sunrise.

"Something's wrong," she said, and climbed through to the front of the van and screamed, "What the bloody hell is going on?"

When Jaz opened the van door, I could hear the tinkling sound of pieces of broken glass falling to the ground. The rest of us got up and opened the side door and climbed out. Jaz was standing by the front passenger door with the broken window and pointing to something on the seat. It was a rock the size of a small football. All four of us stood there, dumbfounded. Colin asked if anyone had heard anything in the night. We shook our heads, still too stunned to speak. Our extensive collection of music tapes had been dumped out on the floor of the van, but it didn't appear any of them was missing.

All of a sudden, we realized the packs and bags that held our possessions were gone. But the robbers would've had to crawl all around us to get them. It was hard to believe we had slept through the whole thing.

"We've been ripped-off," Cherry finally said.

Behind me, I could hear the sound of horse's hooves, and I looked up, squinting against the rising sun, to the top edge of a cliff. Five Iranian men on horseback looked down on us with great interest. When they saw me looking back at them, they came snaking down a narrow, rocky trail to join us. Everyone started talking at once, but the Iranians couldn't understand us and they chattered excitably in undecipherable Farsi.

One of them kept shouting and pointing across the highway towards a small village in the distance. Then they disappeared back up into the hills as quickly as they had appeared. All four of us walked across the road, plunged into the field of waist-high cotton, and headed towards the village. The plants were bursting open and our legs were soon covered with the white fluff.

Cherry turned back to look at me. "This is stupid," she said. "We're going to walk through all this and then what? They won't understand a word we're saying."

Suddenly, Jaz shouted, "Over here." She bent down and came back up waving her rubber chicken. "Guess they realized this wouldn't taste too good."

Not caring about the trampled cotton plants, we ran across to where she stood and found the beginnings of what turned out to be a trail of our belongings. We spent the first hour of that cold, sunny morning gathering up our stuff.

In the end, all that was gone was our money and a couple of passports. But we almost lost more than that. Back at the van, as we were cleaning out the broken glass and putting things back together, we found Colin's six-inch-long hunting knife, which we kept on the dashboard, removed from its leather sheath and lying on the bed beside Jaz's pillow, the cutting edge facing where her head had been.

We could never understand why nobody heard anything. Jaz was certain she would've been the first one killed if we'd woken up.

Angels must have had their hands covering our eyes and ears.

This afternoon, Jaz had remembered the story pretty much as it had happened. I remembered those long conversations about angels back then, although we weren't believers in any specific spiritual doctrine. All kinds of people in all kinds of cultures believe in guardian angels. Why did the Circle of Light think they had cornered the market in angelic protection?

I finished my ice cream, put the notebooks down on the floor beside my bed, and turned off the light.

* * * * * * * * *

I COULD HEAR A BEAUTIFUL SOUND. It was far away. Like hundreds of tiny bells. I wanted to get closer to it, but my body felt so heavy, I didn't think I could move. Golden lights started dancing above my head and seemed to pull me out of some deep pit.

The golden lights came into focus. There were hundreds of angels hovering over me. Some didn't have bodies and were just wings of gold spinning in the air. Others were large and white with beautiful faces and gossamer wings. But as my eyes focused in even more, I saw the wings were actually made of stiff netting just like the angels on top of Cindy's wedding cake. The spinning wings were brass mobiles and, like the wedding cake angels, were attached to thin wires.

I was lying in the back of a van. A strangely familiar van. I turned my head and saw the blade of a knife lying right beside me. Blood was still dripping from it and staining the pillow my head was on. I jumped up and found myself entangled in the wires that suspended the fake angels from the roof of the van.

Tearing myself free, I slid open the side door and stepped out onto West Loveland Avenue, right outside of Brad Holtmann's studio. Frankie Alberto was standing by the open doorway, jabbing his finger at me in slow motion, and shouting, *You! You! You!*

11

"HEY, BOSS. WHAT'CHA GOT COOKIN'?" Tony sauntered into the commercial kitchen and grabbed a clean apron off the wire shelving next to the back door. "That is, if you're cooking. You playing Sherlock Holmes or Julia Child today?"

I was sharpening knives—kind of an inappropriate job, since I was trying in vain to shake off my dream. "Here, take over for me. You always do a better job anyway."

He flashed his crooked, smirky smile at me, bumped me off to one side with his hip, and picked up a knife. "So, what's this I hear on the radio? You gonna tell me about your secret life, snooping around the mean streets of Loveland and tripping over murdered bodies?"

"It's going to be an easy day," I said, ignoring his question and walking to the cork board. Just as I'd expected, that morning's *Cincinnati Enquirer* had printed one of their bad, grainy photos of me under a headline that read *Chili Heiress Discovers Murder In Loveland.*

I unpinned the day's printout. "There's a new art gallery opening in Madeira this afternoon. They just want the usual appetizers. We can whip that up in no time, and you can run down there in the van and deliver it. I may have to go to the vet this afternoon with Boo-Kat."

"Before or after you help the cops nab the killer?"

"Before," I said, hand on hip. "First things first."

"What's the matter with the little squirt?"

"Well, Boo-Kat was limping around this morning, holding his front left paw up. We had to cancel our walk because of that." I continued down the list. "Mrs. Treadway is having another one of her cocktail parties. Same old crowd, so we have to come up with some new nibbles. Can't give them the same thing they had last month."

"Oh, they don't care," Tony said, pushing the edge of a chef's knife across the stone. "Her guests probably don't notice what they're stuffing in their mouths."

"Oh, yes they do. That's why people call us, Tony. Everyone knows we'll give them something unusual."

"Unusual. . . Hmm. . . What about. . ." Tony made a big show of inspecting the edge of a blade. "How about some frozen pizza rolls? Betcha they never tasted those."

Wise guy. "Start chopping the onion and garlic for Peruvian Dipping Sauce. I'll prepare the crudités."

The phone rang. It was the business line, so I couldn't ignore it. "If it's one of those damn reporters," I told Tony, "I'm gonna rip the phone off the wall and toss it into the pond." I took a breath and answered on the fifth ring with my polite "'Round the World Catering, Kate speaking."

A tough male voice on the other end of the line asked bluntly, "Tony there? I wanna speak to him."

I pointed the receiver at my assistant. "One of your pals."

Tony wiped his hands with a towel and grabbed the phone. "Yeah? Who's this?"

I headed into the walk-in to check our supply of vegetables, and when I came back out a few minutes later an exasperated Tony was still on the phone.

"Oh, man. Give me a break. You had all that time and now your back's up against the wall, so you call good old Tony." He listened for a few seconds to his caller. "You shoulda thought about that before." A few more seconds of silence. Tony sighed. "Look, let me check with the Boss. I'll call you back. But no deals. You gotta pay full price." He listened. "Yeah, well, just remember you owe me for this." Tony banged down the receiver.

"What was that all about?"

"That was my cousin Carlo. He's going to be the Best Man at a wedding, so he's throwing a stag party for the groom this Thursday night. My stupid cousin doesn't know you have to call the caterer at least a couple of weeks ahead of time, so naturally, all the caterers he called over the weekend said they were booked."

"I hope you told him we were booked, too."

"Well. . . not exactly."

We both headed over to the job calendar on the cork board. Every day was booked. But they were relatively small jobs. Tony looked up at me and pointed to the Thursday square. "It's not that heavy, and I'd do all the work. Besides, Carlo is family and if I don't help him, my mother'll be on my back."

I knew exactly what that was like, so I rolled the logistics over in my mind. "How big of a party?"

"He says thirty, but knowing Italians, I'd plan for fifty."

"Fifty to a stag party?"

Tony shrugged and went back to chopping garlic. "Yeah, well, what can I say? The groom's a popular guy in the neighborhood and everybody knows everybody and would be insulted if they weren't invited. Like the time Frankie Morano's mother forgot to invite the Campezza's to his sister's christening. That started a feud that lasted three years."

I had never thought about it, but Cincinnati's Italian community is kind of small. Tony's mention of the name Frankie immediately brought Frankie Alberto to the front of my mind. I interrupted Tony before he got too far into the narration of the operatic goings-on over on his side of town, and told him about Frankie Alberto's accusation.

Tony's hand froze in mid-chop. "That's the guy who said he found the body, too. The cops didn't say anything about him fingering you—not in the reports I heard."

"Well, that's what he did. And to complicate things, the victim is that cocaine-snorting wedding guest I surprised in Ali's bathroom."

"Shit, Boss." Tony set his knife down on the cutting board. "How do you get into these things? You think maybe Ali found out and . . ."

I dismissed the idea with my hand. "Anyway, back to Alberto. Do you know him?" On impulse, I threw in, "Or heard of anybody named Big Gabe?"

"Big Gabe? Sounds like mafioso."

I filled him in on Saturday morning's fight.

"No . . ." Tony appeared to chew it over. "Never heard of either one, but that doesn't mean somebody else don't know them." He looked at me and it was obvious my plight had stirred up his macho protective instinct. "I'll make some phone calls."

12

6:00 PM

WHY WAS I GOING to The Circle of Light's Open House? It had been an impulsive decision, but afterwards, the question rolled around in my head. I came up with a variety of reasons, from as simple as grabbing an opportunity to taste some good vegetarian cooking, to wanting to see what an old friend was up to. But what really compelled me to get into my Jeep Cherokee and drive to the southern border of Clairmont was the unquenchable need to see what was around the corner, the same need that pulled me half-way across the globe when I was twenty years old.

I had tried unsuccessfully to fight it off yesterday morning when I walked into Brad Holtmann's studio. Now I found myself at another corner. Who were The Circle of Light and what was Brad's connection to them?

A utilitarian, green and white painted sign informed me I was entering the Golden Valley Spiritual Center. I turned onto the narrow, gravel road that cut straight through acres of newly planted fields. In the distance, a two-story, rambling, clapboard house—my destination—stood surrounded by old pines and a white rail fence.

Every time I came to this place to stock up on herb plants and organic produce, I hoped to see something unusual. Like maybe the house levitating. Or at least, I thought, it should be radiating some golden glow. But it looked so farm-like and ordinary. It seemed more likely that Granny Clampett would come out onto the wrap-around porch and greet me with a piece of elderberry pie.

It was a good thing I already knew how to get there. On the seven mile drive from home, I'd been directed by the occasional piece of cardboard, tacked to a telephone pole, with "RETREAT" and an arrow scrawled on it. Not exactly the most comprehensive directions ever given. But then again, I was discounting the fact that the participants of this retreat were people who lived on a different plane than the rest of us. They must have followed the vibrations, because the parking lot behind the house and down by the barns was jammed with all kinds of vehicles tagged with license plates from all corners of the country.

I managed to wedge the jeep into what looked like a parking space and walked up to one of the barn-like buildings with a sign above its door identifying it as the conference center. Even though I'd been on the grounds many times, I'd never had a reason to enter this building.

Stepping inside, I was surprised to find myself in a newly renovated welcoming room. The floors were polished pine with Indian carpets here and there. A desk with displays of pamphlets and a guest book sat at one end of the room. I could smell incense and heard some kind of chant and gong music softly playing from hidden speakers.

On my way over to the desk, I stopped to admire the woven wall hangings, textile art pieces with feather and bead tails, and vibrantly colored paintings of mandalas that covered the walls. It came as no surprise, since the Open House had already been in progress for two hours, that no one was stationed at the desk to greet me. I glanced at the guest book but didn't bother signing it. Stuffing a pamphlet about organic gardening into my purse, I turned back and pushed through the double doors.

Nobody noticed me as I entered the main conference hall. How unusual and liberating. Normally, wherever I go, people always stare at me because of my size. But this time, I felt like an invisible giant surveying the packed room. People were running back and forth, looking very busy. At least half of them were wearing white or saffron-orange and yellow tunics and pants. Some were in white robes. I noticed The Circle of Light symbol being worn as various forms of jewelry—either pins, earrings, or pendants. I looked down at my denim skirt and striped cotton shirt, and wished I had worn something a little less conservative. I should have rummaged deeper into that old cardboard time capsule and dug out one of my Indian skirts and embroidered vests with the tiny mirrors sewn into the design.

Across the room, a gang of little kids chased each other, playing some kind of tag game, amongst the tables of the dining area. Their screeches echoed off the wall of floor-to-ceiling windows at that end of the hall.

To my left, long wooden tables were set with bowls and trays of food. A line of guests moved along its length, piling their plates high with rice and stews and little pastry turnovers. The room had very bad acoustics, and the enthusiastic chatter of what looked like a couple of hundred people, and the screaming kids, created such a din that my ears started to buzz.

Opposite the buffet, another line of wooden tables was filled with displays of books, tapes, jewelry, soaps, and little bottles. A myriad of merchandise that nobody seemed to be looking at. I was hungry—at this moment physically, not spiritually—and decided to investigate the trinkets later. I headed for the food.

I picked up a tray, set a plate on it and joined the line. Immediately, a friendly couple greeted me. It was probably a safe guess that the man and woman were Circle of Light followers. They were wearing white cotton outfits and smiled up at me with a joyous expression that said *We are all one and you are accepted unconditionally and there can be true peace and harmony in the universe.* I smiled back and asked, "What's good to eat here?"

The woman said, "It's all good. But talk to him." She indicated with a nod of her head the small man, with an all-knowing smile, standing behind the buffet table. "He's the chef."

"It's all vegetarian," the small man said. "Ayurvedic cooking. Do you know what that is? It's the Indian form of medicine which brings the rhythmic patterns of our individual temperaments into harmony with nature's vibrations so that we are a part of the universal energy. The elements in these dishes will bring your frequencies into proper balance. Very good for you."

"Yes," I said, swallowing a laugh, "I know all about that, but it's been many years since I've eaten that way." I held my plate out and a young woman with a calm, half-here, half-in-another-universe expression put a scoop of brown basmati rice on it.

"Help yourself to the dal," she said, pointing to three warming pans. The chef came over and rattled off a description of each one. "Chick peas and potatoes, split moong beans and fenugreek, and red lentils with leeks and beets."

I took a ladle of each of the vegetarian stews.

As the line moved along, I picked up a little bowl of raita, a spiced yogurt condiment, and helped myself to a banana and a couple of samosas, small pastries filled with potatoes, peas, and spices. Just as I was reaching for a cup of chai, milky tea with the wonderful smell of cardamom steaming out of it, I heard a voice behind me.

"Katie, I've been watching for you for hours, I thought you weren't coming, oh, I'm so glad to see you."

Jaz was about to fling her arms around me and I quickly set

down my tray of food and I gave her a big hug. She was wearing orange cotton pants that fit tight around her ankles and calves, ballooned out around her knees, and disappeared under a long-sleeved cotton tunic in a bright marigold yellow. Her mass of silver curls were pinned back and I could see gold wings dangling from her earlobes.

"You've already missed a couple of demonstrations and some live music and dancing," Jaz said, stroking my braid and straightening the collar on my shirt. "But the things I really wanted you to hear about haven't happened. We're going to have a presentation on some of the rage and healing workshops we do. And the musicians are going to come back and we'll do some chants, and I'm going to play the flute. What are you eating? Is that enough? Do you want more? Come and sit at my table, I want you to meet some people."

I followed Jaz to the dining area, but had to stop short several times as little kids darted in front of me in their continuing game of tag-and-scream.

"Here she is. Someone get another chair." Jaz motioned for me to sit in her spot, then grabbed a vacant chair from the next table for herself.

Landing safely at my destination, I smiled and nodded at Jaz's tablemates, another woman and two men. They were all dressed in versions of what appeared to be The Circle of Light uniform, Indian-style outfits in white or bright colored cotton.

Jaz pointed first to the thirty-something, dark haired man sitting by her side. "Katie, this is Mike," she said, looking up into his face with a sweet smile.

"Mike Dyer," he said, extending a hand, "I've heard a lot about you over the past few years." His handshake was quick, businesslike. So this was the Boyfriend. His dark, thick hair curled around a finely-featured face. He wore a safron-orange tunic and pants. Through the low, open collar of the tunic, I could see his chest was covered with a thick mat of black, curly hair. Mike grinned at me, showing the most beautiful lips and teeth I'd ever seen on a man. But his eyes had an intensity that said he wasn't someone who was easily amused. He had the same sharp, penetrating gaze that I remember Jaz's husband, Colin, having.

Jaz waved a hand at the other two. "This is Patricia Ebbes, and Adam George. And you guys," she placed an arm around me and laid her head on my shoulder, "this is the famous Katie Cavanaugh. She's been my friend for ages and I probably know her better than anyone else. If you have to spend weeks cooped up in a van, you couldn't ask for a better traveling companion. Together we went to hell and back on that road." She gave me a quick shake. "And it was fun!"

I noticed, during Jaz's exuberant introduction, Adam George's eyebrows arching as he gave me a not very subtle once-over. The man looked like he belonged on the cover of some steamy paperback romance novel—long, brown hair tied back in a thick ponytail, heavy-lidded dark eyes, three-day stubble, a small gold ring in one ear. He slowly got to his feet and reached across the table.

"Adam George," he said, as though he wanted me to record it in my address book. I grasped his hand and noticed a huge silver and moonstone ring on his pinkie finger, a heavy silver Rajasthani bracelet encircling his wrist, and a gold Circle of Light wing pin on the collar of his orange shirt. In stark contrast to Mike, who was plainer and unadorned, Adam was a flashy dresser.

"Pleased to meet you," I lied as we shook hands, his giving mine a subtle caress. I immediately wanted to go wash. That feeling, and the sight of his Rajasthani bracelet, made me think of Brad Holtmann. I wondered if the two knew each other, but now wasn't the time to ask.

I turned and smiled at Patricia Ebbes, who was seated between Mike and Adam. She needed a kiddie chair. The table edge cut across the top third of her thick torso, forcing her to hold her pudgy arms up at an uncomfortable angle as she ate. For some unknown reason she gave me a frosty look which, combined with her blond buzz cut, round head, and white outfit, brought to mind a disgruntled Pillsbury Dough Girl. Hmm, guess not everyone in The Circle was the smiley type. I focused my attention on the food in front of me.

Patricia scraped up the last bits of rice and dal, noisily stacked her plates and cutlery back on her tray, and pushed out of her chair with such a violent motion, it teetered and almost fell over. She stomped away without saying goodbye.

"What's her problem?" I whispered to Jaz.

"Oh, don't mind her. Pattycake's a bit nervous. She's on next with her Rage and Healing presentation. Oh!" Jaz jumped up from her seat. "I've got to warm up. I'm next." She put her hands on my shoulders. "But you'll be okay here with Mike and Adam. Well, maybe not Adam. Mike, stay here and take care of Katie."

"Where're you going?" I asked.

"Just outside," Jaz answered over her shoulder as she quickly made her way around the dining tables. "Gotta warm up my flute." She hurried out of the hall.

I heard Jaz's chair scrape against the floor, and got a sudden whiff of musky perfume. I turned to see Adam settling in beside me. Fast mover. He leaned in a little closer and peered at me with exaggerated concern. "I can tell by your aura that you are uncomfortable."

You got that right. I hopped my chair a good six inches away. "Probably because I'm starving. My aura will positively glow once I get this food into me." I took a big bite out of a samosa.

Adam read my body language and stayed put. "Maybe you'd like to get out of here? After you eat, of course, we could take a walk."

Oh, brother. "No, thank you. I'm here to see these

presentations and find out a little bit about The Circle of Light. Besides, Jaz'll be on soon. Can't leave now."

"Well, I can tell you all about The Circle. It's my job."

I looked across at Mike, my supposed protector. He seemed to be entranced by the activity in the center of the hall. Patricia Ebbes had started her talk and was having difficulty with the microphone. It screeched back at her every time she held it close to her mouth.

Mike must have sensed I wanted to talk to him, because he turned just then and looked at me. I grabbed the opportunity to ask, "Do you know a guy named Brad Holtmann?"

Mike's head jerked a little with what appeared to be surprise. He recovered, frowned slightly and shook his head. "No. Why?"

I turned to Adam. "Do you know anyone by that name? I think he was a member of your Circle of Light."

Adam arched an eyebrow. "Not off the top of my head." He made an exaggerated show of flipping through his mental Rolodex, but I suspected he only kept female names in there. "Nope."

"I thought you might," I said, pointing to Adam's wrist, "because you both wear the same kind of bracelet. They're not common around here. Besides, this Brad Holtmann also wore one of your pins."

Adam leaned back and stared blankly at me. "So, what about him? Why're you asking."

"Didn't Jaz tell you?"

Adam looked at Mike, and they shrugged their shoulders.

"What?" Mike asked.

"He was murdered yesterday. It's front page news."

One corner of Mike's beautiful lips lifted in a sneer. "The whole idea of going on a retreat is to be cut off from the world so that you can be renewed. We're not watching TV, reading newspapers, or even listening to the radio."

Why was he talking down to me like I was some ignorant kid?

99

"I understand that. I just thought you'd be aware of it because he might have been a local member taking part in this retreat."

Adam gave Mike a quick look of disapproval, and smiled at me. "Well, first off, there are thousands of believers across the country, who come together on their own to form circles here and there. One of the purposes of this retreat is for the leaders of those circles to elect a new High One, so, unless Mr. Holtmann was part of the leadership or one of the volunteer helpers, he wouldn't be registered."

"There's no circle in Cincinnati," Mike added, in a flat voice. "But let's say he was registered and didn't show up. I would still have seen his name on the list, since I helped coordinate this retreat."

Adam sat straight in his chair and closed his eyes. I thought he was going to levitate, but instead he intoned, "Besides, no physical harm can come to a true believer."

A horrendous scream of pain filled the conference hall.

13

PATRICIA EBBES' FACE was contorted in an ugly snarl, her eyes squeezed tight and her head thrown back. She lunged forward and brought the heavy stick in her hand down hard on what looked like a large tambourine. Her squatty, pastry dough body moved across the center of the floor in a jerky dance that made me think of a drunken frog hopping from lily pad to lily pad, trying to get across a pond.

I watched, awestruck by the ferocity of her presentation. I wondered what caused all her rage and when the healing part was going to kick in. The bellowing frog dance stopped as abruptly as it had started, leaving the onlookers unsure how to react. A tentative smattering of applause accompanied Patricia back to her seat across from me. I was trying to come up with some intelligent way to acknowledge her efforts, but the glazed look in her eyes told me I didn't need to bother. Mike and Adam kept their faces averted from mine, so I took my cue from their perfunctory applause and clapped politely.

Three men filed into the hall and sat cross-legged on the floor with their Indian drums and stringed instruments. They started playing a hypnotic rhythm. Just as I was beginning to wonder when Jaz would join them, I heard the sound of a flute playing something soft and dreamy from behind me. I turned and saw her standing further back on one side of the hall. From the other side, a woman began singing. A high, clear chant wove a counterpoint melody with the instruments and I found myself beginning to relax as I watched Jaz and the woman chanter, in her long, white robe, move in to the center of the room and join the other musicians.

The music was strange, other-worldly, but they were all expert musicians, and I found myself being transported to a calm and enjoyable place.

Jaz's eyes were shut and she swayed with the mesmerizing flow of the music, appearing to have traveled to another sphere. I knew that at this moment she was truly happy.

Gradually, the piece built to an exuberant and joyful finale. When it was over, the applause was spontaneous and loud.

Jaz snapped out of her revery and came running to the table. "What did you think about that, Katie? Adam, get out of my chair."

Adam grumbled something and went back to sit on his side of the table next to Patricia.

I said, "That was fantastic, Jaz. I really enjoyed it. When's your CD coming out?"

"Well, surprise, surprise. We got three recordings. You can buy them over there at the resource table." Jaz pointed to where I had seen the trinkets displayed.

I leaned close to her and whispered as quietly as I could, "I'm not sure about Ms. Ebbes, though. She lost me."

Jaz started to laugh, but then her expression suddenly turned serious. Her attention was pulled past me and fixed on the center of the room.

I followed her stare and watched a tall, attractive man in a white tunic and pants stride up to the microphone. He adjusted the mike stand, pulling it up a good six or eight inches, and smiled out at the audience in such a way that each person must have felt personally greeted. I did.

"Who's that?" I whispered in Jaz's ear.

"Shh." She replied.

I took it from Jaz's gentle chide that the speaker was important.

"Friends," he started in a warm, sensual voice, "for those of you who don't know me, I'm Charles Sutcliff, spiritual leader of the Southern California Circle, headquartered in Malibu. We are the largest and longest running circle of believers in the country."

I noticed Patricia Ebbes' glazed expression had switched to one of rapt attention. At first, I had a wild idea that they might be lovers, but on second thought, and after witnessing Patricia's bitter energy, her fawning attention to the man told me the worship was probably distant and one-sided.

"And as leader of the largest and most influential circle, I am taking this opportunity to call us all to a higher spirituality."

I heard a low growl come from Adam. It reminded me of a dog's warning when he doesn't like what you're doing and wants you to back off. I looked at Mike, but he was expressionless.

Charles Sutcliff continued. "In a moment, I will call up our High One, Lowell Lindsay. However, before I do, let me say this about him. Over the past two years, we have reaped the benefits of Lowell's higher consciousness and been inspired by his poetic wisdom. In my extensive travels to the other circles around the country, I have witnessed the tremendous growth and expansion under his unique brand of leadership. This, of course, is desirable. But let us not forget our beginnings, our core beliefs. As it is written: 'The believer who roots his life in truth will enjoy an abundant harvest. But the one who squanders his life gazing only at the beautiful leaves, will end up a rootless failure.'

"With that in mind, let's resolve to put a hundred and ten percent of ourselves into the work ahead. I know this is going to be a life-changing week that will bring great spiritual renewal to

The Circle. And now I introduce The High One, Lowell Lindsay.

Applause filled the room as an elderly, white-haired man dressed in a simple white robe got up out of a chair at a nearby table and shuffled towards the microphone. He walked with his head hanging down, and I wondered if the large Circle of Light pendant, suspended from a thick gold chain and covering half his chest, was the cause of his sad posture.

The clapping died down. The room grew silent.

Stopping at the mike stand, which was still in position for the much taller Charles Sutcliff, The High One began fiddling with the pendant's chain, sliding the golden wings back and forth, trying to reposition it. I could just make out a mumbled, "This thing isn't on straight."

My line of vision included Patricia, Mike, and Adam. There was a quick exchange between the two men that consisted of exasperated smirks. Patricia had reverted back to her glowering self.

Charles returned to the microphone to lower the stand, just in time for all of us to plainly hear The High One make a loud *snufugh* with his nose. I half expected him to use one of his belled sleeves to wipe it. Instead, he raised his head and, staring at the ceiling, said, "We are all walking The Path together in search of the Hidden Gem. Untie those chains of misconceptions and break away from those tongues that betray and poison. For the Gem is but a reflection of your god nature. And in your mute transcendent journey you will come to the Bliss of No Thought. You ask for someone to point to the One Way, but on The Circle there is no point."

The High One unexpectedly shuffled off to stand beside Charles Sutcliff. All was quiet, except for the almost discernible hum of two hundred brains trying to process all that poetic wisdom. A lone clapper broke the silence. And everyone else joined in. I leaned towards Jaz, and in a low voice said, "Does all that mean something?"

Jaz rolled her eyes. "We used to think so. It's a good thing his term is up and the leaders will probably elect a new High One. Two years of this gobbledygook is enough."

"What about this Charles Sutcliff? He sounds like he's campaigning."

"Yeah. He wants it pretty bad."

When I looked back, Charles was at the mike. He announced, "That's the end of our program. Please visit our resource tables. The grounds around us are very beautiful this time of the evening, and we would encourage you to go out and enjoy them. Just a reminder—please stay on the designated walks. We don't want anyone trampling through the fields and disturbing the newly planted gardens."

As chairs scraped and chattering reverberated around the hall, we stood up. I had a desperate need to stretch out my body, but I ignored it. Didn't want to scare anyone with my huge wingspan.

I noticed Charles and The High One approaching our table.

Jaz whispered loudly in my ear, "Be right back. Gotta go to the bathroom." She disappeared into the crowd.

Surprisingly, Charles came straight up to me and held out his hand. He was tall, but still had to crane his neck slightly in order for his blue eyes to lock on mine. I found myself smiling back at a face that was confident and handsome in an outdoorsy way. His skin was leathery and lined and the hair over his ears was graying. I guessed him to be in his fifties.

We shook hands and, even though he didn't let go right away, his lingering clasp had the opposite effect of Adam's slimy caress. I was charmed, whether or not I wanted to be.

Charles said, "You must be a friend of some fortunate person at this table."

I allowed him to continue holding my hand. "I'm with Jaz Woods. We go back a long way."

Charles nodded. "Oh, yes. Jasmine."

"I'm Kate Cavanaugh."

Charles looked at me with half-closed eyes as though recalling some past conversation he'd had. "Ah. One of those three amazing women who left a trail of trampled hearts all over India and the Middle East. Jasmine has told me some of the stories."

"Charles." A smiling Patricia Ebbes sidled up to our little gathering and stroked his arm. I watched her turn on her worshipful look as he glanced in her direction. In a little girl voice that didn't match the rage-filled personality she'd exhibited earlier, she said, "Your speech was so inspiring. You can count on getting a hundred and *twenty* percent from me."

Charles patted the arm which she had linked around his. "I'm sure we can, Patricia. Your dedication is appreciated."

"I . . . I have some ideas I'd like to discuss with you."

"Write them down and bring them to the Elders meeting later on this week." Charles turned to me. "So pleased to make your acquaintance. If you have any questions about The Circle, please feel free to call me."

Out of the corner of my eye, I watched Patricia slink off and give me a look that threatened to burn holes right through me.

As abruptly as Charles had dismissed Patricia, he turned from me and addressed Mike and Adam. "I meant what I said up there at the microphone. This needs to be discussed at the Elders meeting. I know you gentlemen have your own agendas to put forth, but I'm sure you see as plainly as I do how The Circle has spun away from its spiritual moorings and is drifting rapidly towards a superficial and worldly view."

The High One, Lowell Lindsay, had been standing by our table all this time in silence. He continued to stare at my tray as though contemplating the crumbs and the banana I'd left uneaten.

Charles continued his uninvited analysis of the organization. "The growth and expansion over the past few years has brought in a lot of energetic and talented people, but they're putting all that energy into promotion and merchandising instead of meditation and study." He waved a hand at the display tables. "You know that's nothing but crass commercialism."

"We still need to pay the bills, Charles," Mike responded.

"Save it for the meeting," Adam said.

Lowell snuffled. He reached down to my tray, picked up the uneaten fruit, and handed it to me. "Bananas are holy."

I thanked him and, addressing all four men, said, "If you'll excuse me, I'll go see about making a contribution to your cash flow." I headed for the trinket display.

A lot of other people had the same idea and I joined the long line shuffling along the length of the merchandise table. Apparently not everyone agreed with Charles' assessment, and wads of money were being handed across to smiling Circle salespeople.

First, I studied a display of pins, earrings, and pendants, though none of these were as big as The High One's. It certainly was easy to get hold of a Circle of Light pin, but I wouldn't wear it unless it symbolized my acceptance of and belief in The Circle's teachings. I tried to picture Brad Holtmann with this group of people. I supposed he could have fit in—there were all sorts of strange types here.

As the people in front of me moved forward, I shuffled along, picked up a copy of one of The Circle of Light's booklets, flipped through and started reading the section on the presence of angels. It described the various classes and duties of angelic beings, from messengers to healers to protectors. I hung onto the booklet. There was a collection of expensive video tapes, which I ignored, picking up instead one of the music CDs after checking on the back to see that Jaz was one of the musicians. The last third of the display table had been set up with all sorts of oils, soaps, and candles that claimed to have healing properties. I picked up one small glass bottle marked "Shining". The back label claimed that, when the oil was massaged into the skin, it would protect the body against germs and restore a healthy glow

107

to the skin and all internal organs.

I sniffed the contents of the bottle and my nose wrinkled at the bitter scent. I put it down and picked up another one that said, "Fiery". The label on this one stated: "Application of this oil provides inspiration, courage, and determination—most important for self-realization and growth." It had an earthy, sexy smell to it. I added that to my booklet and CD.

"Chandrika Ayurvedic soap!" I picked up the green and maroon cardboard box. "I remember this stuff."

A fresh-faced man beamed and nodded at me as I held the soap box up to my nose and breathed in. Suddenly, I was standing beside a palm tree, my face held up to the hot sun. I poured cool water out of a clay pot over my head.

"Who is she?" An angry voice burst my day dream bubble just as I was beginning to enjoy it. "Don't give me any more of your lies."

I recognized the furious voice and turned to see a red-faced Jaz confronting Mike Dyer. They were standing in the doorway of a small alcove, just twenty feet away from me. With a feeling of embarrassment, I quickly paid for my items and, not wanting to be caught eavesdropping, started walking in the opposite direction. I was beginning to wonder where I should go and what to do next, when I heard, "Katie. Wait up."

Jaz clutched at my arm. Her eyes were puffy and still wet with tears.

14

"LET'S GO FOR A WALK," Jaz said, pulling me towards the exit.

I stuffed my purchases in my purse and followed her through the foyer and out the door. The last rays of sunlight shone through the tall pine trees, making long black shadow lines across the lawn. In the distance, lone figures strolled around the grounds and disappeared down marked trails through the woods. The warm evening air had a soft, peace-filled quality, in complete contrast to my friend's obviously distraught frame of mind.

I pushed aside my discomfort at having accidentally witnessed the lovers' quarrel and asked, "What went on back there, Jaz? I overheard the last part."

Jaz linked her arm in mine and steered me off to the right, around the corner of the conference hall and down a dirt road that didn't appear to be attracting any nature lovers. She wiped her eyes and made a little sniffing sound. "I'm okay, Katie. Really I am." She turned her face up towards me so I could see for myself, in her bright, pasted-on smile, that she was fully recovered.

"I'm not convinced."

"Oh, Katie, you know about me and the jerky men I always choose. You'd think I'd be enough for them, but they always seem to wander off and find someone else to play with. Maybe I'm too much for them and they need to get away." Jaz flicked a chunk of unruly hair over her shoulder and sighed. "I don't know. It's the same old story. No big deal. So what did you think of the presentations? And the food? Betcha liked the food."

I did, but wasn't given the chance to say so.

Jaz rattled on without even taking a breath. "We've got the greatest chef. He studied for years, living in a Brahmin household in Poona. Remember Poona?"

"Ah, yes. One of the Great Mysteries of the East."

We both said at the same time, "How Do You Get To Poona?"

Jaz laughed. "I can't remember why we chose to take the back roads up to Bombay, but we sure saw another side of India, didn't we, stopping at all those little villages and asking for directions."

"Yeah," I said, "every time we stopped, we'd attract the entire male population of that town. We were the most exciting thing to happen all year. But we never did get a straight answer from any of them, did we?"

"No. They'd all be shouting and waving their skinny arms in the air. Everyone claimed they knew how to get there, but they'd all be pointing off in different directions. Then, they'd get into a big argument with each other and we'd drive off, even more confused."

I laughed and, at the same time, remembered Jaz's talent for orchestrating and manipulating conversations away from anything she found uncomfortable. Bury it. Don't deal with it. "How long have you been with Mike?" I took over the conductor's baton.

"Oh, a while." Jaz waved my question off. "Maybe too long.

110

What about you, Katie? Any men in your life?" She grabbed the baton back and I knew this tug-of-war could go on all night.

"Nope. Trying to keep my life simple."

"Well, I see the guys are still coming on to you. Adam was falling all over himself, trying to impress you. And Charles probably charmed the pants off you, too."

"Yeah, what about this Charles. He gave me the impression he knew a lot about us."

Jaz's face flushed slightly. "Yeah, I had a thing with him, too, once upon a time. Told him some of our adventures."

"And knowing you, the stories became a helluva lot more colorful than they were in reality."

"Believe me, those didn't need any more color. Back then, we were all experimenting and searching—it was an exciting and spiritual time. Looks like you've abandoned all that, Katie."

What? My neck almost snapped as I jerked my head to look at her.

"And that worries me." She kept her gaze on the dirt road ahead of us. "I sense that your life is out of balance. You know, too much living on the physical plane. You used to be so into the medicinal herbs and natural remedies and meditation, and you'd tell us all about the vibrations of different foods. There was a different feeling about you back then."

Every muscle in my body stiffened and I felt my teeth clench. "How do you know what I'm all about, Jaz? We've spent less than twenty-four hours together in the last twenty years. I suppose you're making these judgments based on my aura?" (And probably getting ready to preach at me.)

Jaz looked startled, as though I'd pointed my finger and hit her with a bolt of cosmic energy. "I don't mean to sound judgmental. I'm just concerned. You can't live in such an imbalanced state for very long before your body starts breaking down and becomes diseased."

This coming from a woman who just finished screaming at her

lover? "I don't see perfect balance in your life, Jaz, and in my understanding, if you keep avoiding dealing with negative issues, that can make you pretty sick, too." I had been intending at some point to tell Jaz about my experiences with cancer, but changed my mind. I'd had enough of the know-it-alls who blamed me for causing my own illness. "I don't think it's possible to be perfectly balanced. Besides, I don't believe we have total control over what happens to us." We came to the end of the road and the end of my preaching.

"Oh, Katie," Jaz said in a sing-song voice. She wrapped her arms around me. "There's no reason to argue. I love you and that's all that matters. Oh, look." She pointed to an old barn. "Let's go exploring."

Jaz, Jaz, Jaz. None of us ever changes.

The rotting old barn that Jaz was using as a diversion from our prickly conversation stood just off the road in front of a thickly wooded area. The sun had completely disappeared behind the trees and at that moment I didn't fancy the notion of nighttime exploration. Besides, after finding Brad's body, I'd resolved not to enter any buildings I hadn't been invited into. Especially dark ones. "We really should be getting back, Jaz. It's getting dark out here."

She ignored me and was already yanking on one of the large double doors. "We got a few minutes, Katie."

The door gave a loud creak and I pictured it falling in pieces on top of her head. Instead, it swung open, and she disappeared inside. Standing outside by myself felt stupid. With a grudging sigh I plodded in after her. There was still enough light to make out the interior, and I could see old tools hanging from nails on the walls. A collection of rusty horseshoes and license plates were tacked along the length of one beam. It reminded me of my grandfather's garage. I took in a deep breath. It smelled the same, too—musty wood, earth, and rusting metal. Straw covered the floor and a mud-encrusted wheelbarrow filled with bricks sat in

112

one corner.

"Wow." Jaz had found something. "Katie, do you know what these are?"

I joined her alongside a wooden workbench near the entrance. She was pulling glass jars out of large open boxes and holding them up to the pale light coming through the dirty window over the workbench.

"Sure. Pickling jars," I said. "Sometimes the old ones are worth a lot of money, but I suspect, since they've been left out here, these are worthless."

Jaz put the mason jars back into the boxes. It was time for us to wrap up this nosy foray and go home, but before leaving, I made one last visual sweep of the barn's interior. A black painted wood sleigh sat in the far corner. It was the kind you see on nostalgic Christmas cards loaded with top-hatted, fur-muffled couples laughing all the way.

Now that was interesting.

I walked across the center of the barn and, just as I was alongside the sleigh, I heard a sudden rustling followed by the beating of large wings.

Jaz screamed.

Up in the rafters a black shape darted frantically back and forth over my head. It swooped down towards me. I stepped to the side, heard a squeaking *crunch*, and felt my heel sink into the straw. I jumped back onto firmer ground.

Jaz screamed from the safety of the doorway, "Get outta there."

As I quickly retraced my steps, the barn monster made one finally circle over my head, then swooshed through the door and escaped into the twilight.

"What happened back there, Katie?"

"I don't know. Surprised me. My foot must've gone through some wood flooring. I thought it was all dirt, but you couldn't tell with that straw covering everything."

We started back down the road towards the conference center. "What was it?" Jaz asked. "A bat?"

"No. Too big. Probably an owl. It's disturbing, though."

"What is?"

"The sound of those wings. It was just like a nightmare I had recently, and I've learned to pay attention to my dreams. No matter how strange they are, there's usually a warning or message for me."

I heard an odd rattling and chinking sound behind us. Turning, I saw a hulking figure dressed in white walking a few yards back. A husky male voice spoke out. "This is a time of great angelic activity." The man came closer. "The Messenger Angels are trying hard to communicate with us. But those damn fools aren't listening."

15

"HI, BRUNO," Jaz said, coming to a halt. "Where did you come from?"

I smiled politely as the gigantic bear of a man caught up to us.

"Too many people on these trails. Went wandering in the woods."

We resumed walking, and I heard *ka-chink, ka-chink*. Looking over Jaz's head, I saw this Bruno guy had an unusual habit. In his right hand, wound around his middle fingers, was a short leather thong strung with large amber beads—seven or eight of them. Twirl and catch. Twirl and catch. He manipulated the worry beads with the same rhythmic absentmindedness of an old-time beat cop twirling his nightstick.

"Bruno, this is Kate Cavanaugh. She's an old friend of mine. I invited her to the Open House—she lives around here. We were just looking at that old barn. Oh, and Katie," Jaz continued, fluttering her hand in his direction, "this is Bruno Marcello. Bruno's an Elder. He's been with The Circle from the beginning, which makes you one of the pillars, doesn't it, Bruno?"

The Bear Man said in a very serious voice, "Back in the early years we were a lot more on track. And now here we are at a crucial time and nobody's prepared."

I asked, "For what?"

Bruno abruptly stopped walking and the beads stopped swinging. An owl hooted in the distance. Bruno looked down at me. "The End."

"The end of what?" I asked, stupidly.

"This." He flung his arms upward. "This beautiful, frustrating, glorious mess we call life on Earth."

"So how do we prepare ourselves?"

Bruno kept looking up at the first stars in the night sky. "We stop. Can't hear the messages if we're running around busy with our own ego-driven pursuits. Sounds like you're already aware of a higher intelligence. You keep listening to those messages in your dreams. I get them all the time."

The end of the world was not what I had in mind when I told Jaz my dreams had messages.

"And we should be watching for the signs. Why do you think we're getting all these earthquakes, floods, and tornadoes? There will be more signs, but no one is paying any attention. Before you know it, we'll find ourselves part of the slaughter."

"Slaughter?" I asked, feeling a little twinge of anxiety in my stomach.

"There's a battle brewing. Has been for centuries. Soon it will become an all-out war, and those of us who are prepared will escape annihilation. But the violent struggle between the forces of light and dark will destroy the Earth."

I tried to read Jaz's reaction to all this, but her face was a blank.

Bruno continued, looking intently at me. "Those messenger angels that speak to you through your dreams? They're not pretty things with their delicate wings and golden halos. They're giants with ferocious energies and when they finally clash with the angels of darkness, who are just as powerful, there will be such an explosion that the very atoms creating this planet will be

116

pulled apart."

Maybe an angel whispered in my ear. Just then, a little voice in my head said, *time to go home.*

I SAT CROSS-LEGGED ON MY BED, the thin, orangey pages of the *Goan Pig* spread out in front of me. "Published bi-Moonly," it said under the crudely drawn picture of a pig standing under a palm tree. It was eight pages densely packed with lines of type so small, I had to hold it almost at arm's length so my forty-three year old eyes could read it. There were editorials, jokes, classified ads, bad poetry, and very amateur artwork. But it surprised me that Klaus managed to put together a professional-looking publication—though professional at that time in India was pretty funky.

I carefully turned one of the frail pages and found an announcement of the birth of Jaz's son Raji "on December 24 at 11:26 PM. (Sun: Capricorn, Moon: Pisces)."

As I skimmed through the articles and read the by-lines, faces of people I'd forgotten came back to mind. One particularly smug sounding treatise was written by a French guy on a mission to recruit every female on the beach into the cult he belonged to, using his sexy good looks to attract his victims and bedding them with the expectation of closing the deal. Another article made me laugh right out loud. A startled Boo-Kat looked up at me as if wanting me to share the joke. An article on Karma, written in an earnest and passionate voice, sounded very similar to that afternoon's words of wisdom from Lowell Lindsay. Both seemed enlightened but had a meandering logic that escaped me.

Boy, we really thought we were something, all playing at being spiritual seekers of Truth. But now in these writings, I could see our beach community was involved in the same kind of empire-building and power struggles that I suspected were going on in The Circle of Light. Both communities were made up of the same personality types. In Adam, I saw the Recruiter. Charles, the Man Who Wanted to be King, thought he had a clearer vision than all his naive subjects. And then, of course, there was always a Bruno who thought The End was coming.

I was relieved when Jaz said to me as we parted that evening, "I'm not into this Doomsday stuff. Some of the members get carried away." Jaz was a Follower and had always lived by a kind of wishy-washy philosophy that grew out of the opinions of those around her rather than from her own questioning. A go-with-the-flow type.

Everyone had a part to play and got their sense of identity from the role they chose. They'd invested all their energy into making that part important.

Not being a member of the inner circles of the Goan community, I didn't understand the subtleties and complications of the relationships between the players. I could only assume there were tensions brewing under the peace, love, and harmony facade we were all buying into. When that facade was shattered at times by the appearance of some beaten or stabbed body floating up onto the pristine sand, I was horrified and confused. Now, thinking back, the realization hit me. Though the victims were white Europeans, they were never visible members of our beach tribe. Nobody admitted knowing them. But there must have been a connection. Whatever it was, it was hushed up. In India it was possible for loose ends to be left dangling. Someone could disappear and there'd be no questions.

Brad wore a pin, which meant at some point he must have been involved with The Circle of Light. He even made a joke at Cindy's wedding about hearing voices. Maybe he meant it. But if he was getting messages from the same angels Bruno was, it sure didn't save him from a violent end—despite what Jaz said about true believers being protected by some energy force.

Frankie Alberto, who didn't seem to be a part of any community but was connected to Brad, had some hidden reason for throwing suspicion on me. Even Ali had his agenda that came into conflict with Brad's behavior. I shook my head. That's really stretching it.

And, of course, there were all those people coming together for a week of spiritual renewal. That was certainly a facade. The power struggles and tensions among some of the Elders were barely hidden. So, in a way, it was like Goa. Brad's body washes up and people claim they don't know who he is. Why would he wear a pin if he had no connection?

But this isn't India. Loose ends can't be left dangling.

16

Tuesday, May 20th

"COME ON, BOO-KAT. Up you go. Don't look at me like that. Doctor Baer said there was nothing wrong with you."

My dog and I were standing beside the open passenger door of my Jeep. Boo-Kat looked up at the seat, then rolled his brown eyes at me with a helpless expression.

I threw my hands up in the air. "You've had an x-ray. There's nothing wrong with your foot. You're just a big, fat faker."

His bottlebrush tail curled down between his legs.

"Oh . . . all right." I gathered him in my arms and deposited him on the passenger seat. "If you were a human being, you'd never get away with this behavior." I slammed the door and walked around to the driver's side, as frustrated with myself as I was with my surrogate child. My tires screeched as I pulled out of the parking lot of Dr. Baer's Veterinary Clinic for spoiled suburban pets.

On the drive home, the vet's lecturing words to me were still stinging. Glancing over at my passenger, I said, "It's not your fault. You've just got a stupid mother." He took that as an invitation to try to climb onto my lap and lick my nose.

"Sit!" I stiff-armed him back into his seat. "Watch it, buddy. I'll pull out that old seat belt you hate."

The radio was playing one of my favorite Diamond Rio songs. I turned it up. The song did nothing to ease my guilt. "Boo, you're gonna have to go on a diet, the doc wants you to lose five pounds. And that means no more sausages. Or marshmallows. Or pancakes." I looked at the road. "Talk about irresponsible. It's not your fault, I'm the one in control . . . and I'm screwing up."

I don't think Boo-Kat was listening. At a stop sign, I turned to look at him. His nose was pressed against the window and he was growling a doggie curse at a couple of horses standing on their side of the split rail fence beside the road.

I made an impromptu decision to turn the corner and drive through Mother's part of the neighborhood in hopes of sighting the famous flamingos. The morning's *Enquirer* Tempo section had Skip Enburg's update on what was happening with that migration. His column's heading was *Flamingos are A-List*.

That was really going to irk Mother.

I toured slowly through the old money section of Clairmont, past the sprawling Cavanaugh estate that Crown Chili built, with its huge stone mansion, long, winding driveway, and fountains I remember stocking with tadpoles when I was a kid. No birds. I traveled on down the street. A few acres later, I caught a glimpse of pink through the bushes as I rounded the bend.

"Ha!" I couldn't believe it. I stepped on the brake and backed part-way up the driveway of the Schinkelberg estate, Mother's next door neighbor.

"The flamingos have landed," I announced to Boo-Kat, "but definitely in the wrong yard." Mother was going to be livid at the sight of several dozen scrawny-legged plastic birds wearing every kind of trashy accessory from rhinestone necklaces to sunglasses to hats. Some were gathered together in groups of threes and fours. A few of them were hanging around a plastic kiddie's wading pool. There was even a cardboard bus with flamingos peering out of its cut-out windows. Someone had bent the rules and had added an ugly stuffed dog in a pink T-shirt.

"Okay," I said to Boo-Kat, "now we can go home." I pulled back out of the driveway, and sped off to resume my original route.

The radio announcer was starting to give the news, and I was going to switch stations when I heard those two words that always capture my immediate attention. Breast cancer.

The opening line of the news report referred to study results apparently proving that drinking alcohol increased your risk of breast cancer. I groaned, but continued listening for the details.

Just recently, I had been rejoicing over the discovery that a glass of wine a day was good for your heart. I didn't want my nightly glass of wine with my dinner taken away from me. The announcer referred to the earlier reports on the heart benefits, but ended the segment with a caution to women who were already at risk for breast cancer. I sighed and made a mental note to run that by the oncologist at my next check-up.

Switching off the radio, I said to Boo-Kat, "I shouldn't be eating sausage, either." Maybe I was being as irresponsible with myself as I was with my dog. Looking back, I used to be careful about my diet, teaching Phoebe Jo how to cook lowfat. But just like anything else, over time, I became less disciplined and reverted back to the things that made me feel good.

And what about my catering business? Here I was, cooking up all this rich, wonderful food without any thought to my clients' health.

"Wait a minute. Since when do I have to be responsible for *everybody?*" Boo-Kat stared back at me with what I like to think was deep understanding.

Then there was my family's wealth and status, all created by feeding people artery-clogging chili with almost a quarter pound of cheese on top. Now we were talking major guilt. When my grandfather started the Crown Chili franchise, they didn't know about these things. But now that we know better, maybe Mother should be making changes. Then, the business would take a dive because customers would complain that we were skimping on cheese and the chili didn't taste like it used to.

I pulled into my parking lot and opened the door for Boo-Kat, who jumped out with no sign of a limp.

"It's not my fault people like fat. I like fat, too. And I want a glass of wine with my fat. What's the matter with that? So I kill myself. And I might as well kill everybody else around me while I'm at it. They say that, deep inside, anyone is capable of murder. Well, I'm getting in touch with my inner self. It's coming out. I'm a murderer. What do you think of that, Boo?"

I stomped into the commercial kitchen. "Call the Clairmont Rangers, Phoebe Jo. Tell 'em to come and arrest me. I confess. I'm a mass murderer."

"What in heaven's name are you talking about?" Phoebe Jo asked over her shoulder. She shook the colander of grapes she was washing at the sink.

Tony leaped to the phone and grabbed the receiver. "What's 911's number?" He winked across the room at somebody.

I turned to look. "Jaz. Hi. How long you been here?"

My friend was sitting on a stool at one of the stainless steel counters. "Oh, I got here about a half-hour ago. Your lovely staff have been very hospitable. Gave me a cup of coffee," she lifted a mug, "best I've had in weeks."

Tony said, "We saw her drive up the laneway and head for the front door. I knew right away she was your traveling buddy, but then I see this pin she's wearing and I said, 'Hey, you a flight attendant now?'"

We all laughed.

Tony continued, "So I brought her in, gave her a cup of coffee and she told us about The Circle of Light angels."

Jaz cut in, "And he was starting to tell me about the picture of his guardian angel that his mother still has hanging in his old bedroom, when you came stomping in."

Tony smirked. " Yeah. What's got you so riled up? Did Doctor Baer growl at you?"

I explained what led up to my emotional outburst.

When I was finished, Phoebe Jo said, "Of course you're not responsible for giving yourself cancer and for everyone's state of health. There's nothing wrong with having a special meal now and then to mark some important occasion. People look to you, Miss Kate, to help them celebrate."

Tony added, "'Course that doesn't mean you and Boo-Kat can celebrate every day. A diet'll do you good. We want you around, Boss, and don't want anything to happen to you."

A wide-eyed Jaz sat on her stool, both hands wrapped tightly around her mug. I suddenly realized this was the first time Jaz was hearing about my battle with breast cancer.

Phoebe Jo said, "Miss Kate, we'll go back to what we did when you were first diagnosed. I'll pull out those recipes you modified into low-fat versions. We got a little lax over the years, but it's not a disaster. We'll get back on track."

Robert had sauntered in during the course of our discussion. "Does this mean I'm gonna have ta start eating my pork rinds behind the shed?"

I answered, "Sounds like a good idea." I shook my finger. "But don't give any to the dog."

Tony hoisted a bag of flour and poured it into a bin. "What did ya do with the little pisser? Give him away?"

"You know he can't come in here. He's out patrolling, looking for some rabbits to chase."

Jaz looked very uncomfortable. I guessed maybe this was too much family business for her, and she was feeling left out. So, I decided to fill her in on a little of my medical history but didn't get too far before she waved her hand and said, "No, no, Katie. That's okay. You don't need to tell me. I don't want to know."

That was a slap in the face. I'd met people before who didn't want me to even mention the word cancer, and I suppose maybe there were times I talked too much about it. But for an old friend to react that way . . . I wasn't expecting that. For the second time, I found myself biting the inside of my lip to keep my anger at Jaz hidden.

"Okay." I shrugged. "What's happening over at the spiritual center? You've got some time off? Aren't you supposed to stay there, cut off from the world, for the whole week?"

Jaz was visibly relieved at the change in subject and just waved my question away. "Today is the election of the new High One. All the elders and leaders will be locked up all day in meetings and meditation sessions. Mike's one of the elders. I'm just one of the volunteers, so there's nothing for me to do." She took a sip of her coffee. "I thought I'd come and hang out with you. Maybe we could do something together? Tony told me you didn't have any big jobs this afternoon. We could cook up an Indian dinner. That'd be a good way to start getting back to healthy eating."

I wanted to *grrr* at her. Instead I said, "That sounds like a good idea. I already have lots of ingredients on hand, but we could make a quick trip to the Indian grocery. Let's go right now." To Phoebe Jo and Tony, I said, "We'll be back in about an hour."

As Jaz and I headed for the door, Tony called out, "Hope to see more of you, Jaz. Kate's friends from her past are a lot more fun than the ones she has around here. Cherry and I got on real well, didn't we, Boss?"

"Cherry?" Jaz asked, her face distorted by a very unfriendly look. "She was here? When?"

"C'mon, I'll tell you on the way." I hustled her out the kitchen door and into the Jeep.

As I was still doing up my seat belt, Jaz demanded, "What was that bitch doing here? Trying to steal your lover?"

"I'm sure that wasn't the reason for her visit—she was out of luck if it was. You're still angry at her?"

"You'd be angry, too. I had a husband and a baby, and I was trying to build a life for myself. Colin and I were a little stressed out when the baby arrived and that little tramp saw her opportunity to hurt me and seduced my husband away from me."

"You think she was trying to hurt you intentionally? Colin was hardly the passive type. You told me yourself, his eye was wandering the moment we arrived in Goa."

"Cherry was jealous. She's always been competitive with other women. I never understood how you got along with her as well as you did."

I shrugged. "Maybe she didn't like my taste in men." I pulled onto I-275. We were silent for a few minutes. "What eventually happened to you and Colin?" I asked carefully.

"Oh, he made sure I got back to England safely. Guess I have to be thankful for that, but then immediately, I was hit with a divorce petition. He just disappeared. I don't know where he went. My son doesn't know him."

"Have you been single all this time?"

Jaz looked out the side window.

"Didn't you tell me, yesterday, that at some point you had a thing with Charles Sutcliff?"

Jaz stayed quiet.

"Don't you think it's funny that none of us has found a mate? Cherry's still roaming around on her motorbike by herself, and I'd like to find somebody, but . . ."

"Yeah . . . well, I have Mike now."

I guess Jaz got something out of her rocky relationships, but I didn't understand them.

Another period of heavy silence divided us as we sped along the freeway towards Sharonville.

Jaz spoke abruptly, with a little crack in her voice. "That

relationship's not going too well, either. No surprise, right?"

I decided to keep my mouth shut. This was big for her—she was actually trying to face her troubles. I felt sympathy pushing away my earlier anger.

"And now the same thing's happening all over again. I'm sure Mike's having an affair with someone, and I think she's here at the retreat."

We pulled into the parking lot of a rundown strip mall. I brought the Jeep to a halt in front of the storefront with the lurid movie poster advertising *The Iron Man of Bombay*. I started to get out but realized Jaz wasn't finished yet. I thought she was going to start crying. Instead, she said, "I gave him a special gift and I'm sure he just turned around and gave it to her. That's what we were fighting about when you heard us."

"What was it?"

She sighed noisily. "Oh, Katie. I don't want to dump all this on you. Just forget about it." Jaz looked up and out the windshield. "Where've you brought me? What is this place?"

17

THAT EVENING'S MEAL was a great success for some of us, and an exotic, but almost inedible, adventure for Robert and Julie Ann. I was whipping up a mango lassi for Julie Ann in an effort to win back her trust. Robert was still pushing the rice and dal around on his plate. Phoebe Jo, spooning out another portion of raita, said, "I just love this chicken. There are so many spices on it. I've no idea what any of them are, but it kind of tickles on your tongue. Robert, try some more. Then you have a spoon full of this raita stuff and it cools your mouth right down. I think it's kind of fun."

I smiled over at Jaz, who was pouring out cups of chai. The afternoon with Jaz had smoothed out our ragged reintroduction to each other. We had poked around the Indian grocer's, buying spices for our dinner and, once home, had spent most of the afternoon in the family kitchen. That is, after I had finished arranging hors d'oeuvres and cute, fancy sandwich trays for a couple of small parties.

Early on, Jaz and I abandoned our idea of cooking a vegetarian meal, knowing it was asking too much of the Boones. After all, this was to be their dinner, too. But I laughed to myself when I

128

saw Jaz, who professed to being a strict vegetarian, helping herself to two juicy chicken thighs and then licking her fingers with pure enjoyment.

Robert innocently asked if I had taken Jaz to a Crown Chili parlor yet, and Jaz with mock indignation replied, "No she hasn't. I hadn't even thought of that. What a great idea. I've got to see one, Katie."

Hmm. I could see it all now: The Circle of Light elders condemning me for leading this poor girl down the road to Cholesterol Hell. They'll never come back to Cincinnati, Land of Bratwurst, Five-Way Chili, and Flying Pigs.

The Boones are such kindly, gentle folk, and I never know when they're just being polite, or if it really is sincere and friendly interest in people, but they seemed fascinated by Jaz and her lifestyle and asked all sorts of questions about The Circle of Light. As we ate at the oak table in the family kitchen, Jaz entertained us with her talk of auras and cosmic energy, ideas that wouldn't even occur to the Boones.

When we got to questions about the retreat and the Open House, I joined in with some of my own observations. I asked Jaz, "Where does Patricia Ebbes get all that anger from?"

"Well, she believes we all have that anger in us, Katie. And you've got to release it."

Robert asked, "What do you do? Go out and howl at the moon?"

I laughed. "You're not that far off." I turned to Jaz. "Do you do what she does to get rid of your anger?"

"Well, she does kinda go overboard. I think she does it because it pumps her up. She wouldn't have any sense of herself without the anger. It's like her identity, you know. She's the elder who's become known as the expert on rage."

I asked, "Where does the healing part come in?"

"I guess she gets healed, but there's always something happening to her that fires her up again. It's a vicious cycle. She turns people off and then gets angry 'cause nobody likes her."

"Yeah, I noticed an awkward moment with Charles Sutcliff."

"Oh, yeah! She's got the hots for him. And he keeps pushing her away. She's a scorned woman, over and over again. That really feeds the fire."

This was slightly tabloid-ish dinner conversation, and Julie Ann was lapping it all up with her usual enthusiasm. "So, what do you mean 'she goes overboard?' What does this woman do?"

Jaz and I looked at each other. I said, "You show her, Jaz."

"No, you show her."

I looked across the table to Julie Ann. "She just does this crazy dance and screams and yells a lot while beating on a drum."

"Show me."

"No, Julie Ann."

Jaz got up and pulled on my arm. "C'mon, I'll do it with you."

We started doing our drunken frog leapings and an inferior imitation of Patricia's wails and screeches. All three Boones broke out into laughter. Boo-Kat, already traumatized by not getting any nibbles from the dinner table, was stunned. I don't think he knew what to make of us.

"Wait," I said, "we need drums." I ran to the cabinets and pulled out a couple of large pots and grabbed two wooden spoons. "Here." I handed a set to Jaz. We began pounding away and resumed our leaping and wailing.

It freaked the dog. He took off, probably heading upstairs to safety under my bed.

I was spinning around, when I caught sight of a silver-helmeted figure in the kitchen doorway, slapping a rolled up newspaper against the side of her leg. I halted. Jaz was facing the other way and let out a couple of lusty hollers before she realized I had stopped.

"Oh," Jaz said.

I laughed. "Hello, Mother. You always come at just the right

130

time."

"You're all mad," Mother answered in a measured tone.

I laughed again with sheer pleasure at the look of bewilderment on her face that said *I can't believe that girl came out of me.*

"What are you doing, and who is this dance partner of yours?" Mother lifted her chin at Jaz. "I'm assuming that circus vehicle outside belongs to her."

"Mother, this," I wrapped an arm around Jaz's shoulder, "is Jasmine Woods. She's the one who kept me sane in that van we drove to India."

Mother had the ability to look up at me and down her nose at the same time. "Kathleen, nothing you did during that phase in your life was sane. But I'm forgetting my manners," she said, extending her hand towards Jaz. "Glad to see you're still alive."

For once, Jaz was speechless.

I said, "Mother, you really should call first." That way she could avoid these embarrassing situations.

"Kathleen, if I called first, you would probably tell me you were busy and I couldn't come over. This is the only way I get to see you."

She was probably right, and I felt a little twinge of guilt.

"Besides, I do have a reason for coming here. I have a job for you."

I wanted to tell her I was busy, but she'd just accused me of always saying that, so I kept my mouth clamped shut. Skip Enburg smiled impishly from the section of newspaper Mother was holding. A red marker had left an angry-looking circle around the *Flamingos are A-List* headline of his column. I wondered when Mother was going to start ranting about the plastic lawn ornament road show that had set up shop next door to her.

She laid the newspaper face-up on the kitchen table and said, "It'll be fun and casual—your kind of thing. I want to have a Memorial Day barbecue."

"You mean with burgers, hot dogs, and potato salad?"

"Well . . . I had grilled shrimp and maybe some beef tenderloin in mind. But whatever the menu, I want the party to be festive. I want it to be patriotic, you know flags all around and good old fashioned fun."

"Oh, how about a sheet cake decorated with blueberries and sliced strawberries to look like the Stars and Stripes?"

"Kathleen, are you joking with me? I know when you're pulling my leg. Don't do that to me. I want this to be an intimate gathering with family and my closest friends."

"Well, that could mean about a hundred people, right?"

Mother's confident Cavanaugh smile began to droop.

"Are you alright, Mom?" Something had obviously upset her—her mask wasn't staying in place. Mother slowly sat down at the kitchen table, and I was surprised to see a look of defeat in her face. She smiled weakly and nodded at the Boones, then directed her weary eyes at me. "I know you don't want me here, and I suppose that's my fault. Nobody wants me. Even my own friends and neighbors are ignoring me."

Phoebe Jo got up from the table. "Let me get you a cup of tea, Mrs. Cavanaugh."

I said, "Yes. That's a nice idea. Thank you, Phoebe Jo."

Mother slowly reached up and massaged her temple, rubbing out a third of her penciled-in eyebrow. "People I've know for years and years have shut me out."

"Mother? What are you talking about?"

She took a deep breath and let it out with a little whine. "I looked out my front door this morning and even that snobby Mrs. Schinkelberg had pink flamingos all over her front lawn. I couldn't believe my eyes," her voice squeaked. Mother grabbed the newspaper, her fingers tight around Skip Enburg's photographed neck and cried out, "I want to be flocked!"

WHILE DRINKING my morning coffee and planning out Mother's All-American Barbecue menu, I received a phone call that heaped one more major item onto my rapidly filling plate.

"Katie? It's Jaz. I need you. Something awful's happened. Can you come to the spiritual center? I just found Charles Sutcliff. Dead."

18

I LOOKED AT THE RECEIVER for a second, then put it back to my ear. "What do you mean 'dead'? He collapsed?"

"Murdered." Jaz's voice was shaky.

"How do you know he's been murdered? Where'd you find him?"

"On the Diamond Path . . . you know, one of those trails around the conference hall. I went out there to walk and think through some stuff and there he was lying in some brush by the trail. It's a real wooded area, further away from the conference center than the other trails go. He was staring up at the sky. He was dressed in his ceremonial robes."

"Ceremonial robes?"

"Charles was elected High One last night."

I guess someone had a problem with that. "Did you call the police?"

"Um . . . no. Not exactly. I just found him, Katie. I haven't told anyone around here."

I looked again at the receiver. "Jaz—"

"I know, I know, but I want you to come here first. All of a sudden, I don't trust anybody around here. Any one of them could have killed him. How do I know who I'm talking to? That person could be the killer and turn around and slash my throat."

I said, "Okay. Calm down. You're getting kind of carried away. You just found the body. It's not like you know something that'll get you killed. Or do you?"

"No!" Jaz squealed from her end. "But I need you. I can't handle this by myself. Maybe I should come over there?"

"Jaz—Just call the cops, and stay put."

"Please, Katie, hurry."

I calmly said, "Okay, I'm coming. But as soon as I hang up, you call the police. It'll take me about twenty minutes. I'm leaving right now. 'Bye."

Here we go again—the second time in three days I'd be looking at a murdered body. This time I was going to make sure I had some fuel in me before dealing with the police. I was already dressed in shorts and a clean Reds T-shirt, but I hadn't finished my breakfast. I filled up a commuter mug with coffee, sliced open a bagel and slathered it with chunky peanut butter and cherry jam. It was probably going to be a long morning.

I was about to scribble out a message to the Boones when Phoebe Jo showed up in her flowery robe, rubbing her eyes and yawning. I told her, "Something's come up at the spiritual center. I'm going to see Jaz. Tell Tony to . . . aw, never mind. I'll call him later. He knows to check the job calendar." I let the back door slam behind me as I rushed out to my Jeep.

I TOOK WARD'S CORNER ROAD down to the end and then wound my way around the hills, over the river and through the woods. I wished there really was a Granny Clampett waiting for me with a piece of elderberry pie in this house I was going to.

Instead, there was a good chance I was headed for Norman Bates' Psycho house where granny never got out of her rocking chair.

I turned onto the road that led up to the spiritual center. The house wasn't levitating or glowing, and it sure didn't seem like there were any angels hanging protectively over the grounds. But it looked peaceful. Not even a cop car in sight. Jaz, dressed in a Circle of Light outfit—white baggy pants and white tunic—came running up towards me, waving her arms as I parked by the conference center where I had done so two days before.

I yelled out the window, "The cops shouldn't be taking this long. Did you call them?"

"Yes, yes, of course I did," Jaz said, coming up to the side of the Jeep. She was breathing hard. "Uh, well, it might have been just a few minutes ago."

A bruise on Jaz's cheekbone and around her eye caught my attention. "What happened to you?" I asked, getting out of the car.

Jaz put her hand up to her cheek. "Oh. What d'ya mean? This? Um . . . nothing. Just an accident. It doesn't matter. I'll tell you later."

I was shocked at her appearance. "Jaz, you and I need to talk. You realize the police are going to ask about that bruise."

Jaz was silent.

"Does that have anything to do with why you didn't call the cops right away?"

"No, no," Jaz shook her head and waved her hand impatiently, "I . . . I wanted you to get here first. I didn't want to deal with any of this by myself."

"Still nobody else knows about Charles?"

"No. Katie, my insides are jumping like Mexican beans. I—I—I don't know what to do. I'm so nervous. People are starting to get up and go out for walks. I should've just let someone else find him. The cops'll think I did it."

I hugged her. "Calm down. You're huffing and puffing like you've been running a marathon. Do some of your spiritual breathing exercises."

"I'm too hyper to do it right. It's just making me dizzy. Oh, Katie, Charles is still lying there with this horrible look in his eyes, like he saw the devil himself."

"Jaz, everything's going to be okay." I squeezed her tighter. I desperately wanted to know how she got that bruise and was starting to think maybe we should block off that trail, when I heard the crunch of tires coming up the gravel driveway. I turned to see two green Clairmont Ranger patrol cars come to a halt.

Stepping out of the driver's side of the first one was a familiar figure. I was surprised by the little leap my heart made. The policeman reached back into the car, pulled out his Smokey Bear hat, and positioned it smartly on his head. Looking over at us, he caught my eye. I saw surprise and a quick smile before his official *Just the facts, Ma'am* look settled on his face.

Officer Matt Skinner had arrived.

"Ms. Cavanaugh?" Skinner bobbed the brim of his hat at me. "Didn't realize this was one of your haunts." He looked over at Jaz. "Who placed the call?"

Already he was pushing the wrong button in me. This was hardly one of my "haunts" and he didn't even give me a chance to tell him so.

Jaz raised her hand. "I called."

"So you must be Jasmine Woods." Skinner squinted down at Jaz. "Ms. Woods, how did you get that bruise?"

"It was an accident. It has absolutely nothing to do with why I called. Please, can we hurry?" Jaz started bouncing. "I want to show you what I found."

Neither one of the Rangers objected when I trotted along behind Jaz. Probably it was because I stayed silent as Jaz answered Skinner's questions.

Sometimes I shock myself. I'm embarrassed to admit that

even in the most serious moments my thoughts can be terribly inappropriate. Walking behind Skinner was a rare and pleasant experience. It wasn't so much his broad shoulders and tight buns that made it so enjoyable. It was the fact that he was actually taller than me. I hardly ever get a chance to look up at people.

Skinner asked Jaz, "When did you discover the body?"

"I think it was about five-thirty, six o'clock this morning," she answered. "Let's see. I got up about five. Then I dressed in the dark, but I realized I put my clothes on inside-out, so I had to get dressed again. I didn't look at the clock after that, and I don't know how long it took me, but as soon as I got myself straight, I went for my walk."

"Are you a member of this Circle of Light? Are you staying here?"

I was surprised that Skinner was so on top of things. But then I realized that the influential citizens of Clairmont expected their Rangers to keep an eye on "questionable" groups of people who were coming into their community.

Jaz answered, "Yes, I'm a member. This is the annual retreat for our leaders, but I'm just one of the volunteers who help set things up and keep them running. Last night, the elders chose our new High One. It's Charles Sutcliff. Or it was Charles. He's the dead body I found at the end of this trail. This is really a disaster. He was going to do such great things."

The sun was up, but the trail was in a heavily wooded part of the grounds and the lighting was weak. I tried to picture Jaz stumbling around in the night. What was she doing here? I wouldn't have chosen such a wooded and dark path if all I wanted to do was go out for some predawn reflection.

Matt Skinner seemed to be reading my mind. "It would have been nearly impossible to see where you were going on this trail a couple of hours ago. What were you doing?"

Jaz pulled a flashlight out of her pocket. "I'm used to going out for early morning walks in the country."

"So, you weren't looking for anyone or anything in particular?"

"No. Lots of people go out and do their meditations at this time of day."

"But you didn't see anyone else on this trail?"

Jaz shook her head. "No."

Officer Skinner looked over his shoulder at me. The brim of his hat was set so low on his forehead I couldn't really see his eyes. It made him appear menacing. "And how are you involved in all this, Ms. Cavanaugh?"

"Jaz is my friend. She's not from around here and called me for support."

"Oh yes. I've witnessed the high degree of loyalty you show your friends."

I know he was only making a statement, but I couldn't help reacting to everything he said as if it were a criticism.

"There he is," Jaz said in a loud whisper, pointing off to one side. She stopped in her tracks, turned back to me and said, "I can't look at him, Katie."

I put my arm around her and she buried her face in my shoulder.

A foot or two away from the trail was a white form. It was Charles Sutcliff dressed in what appeared to be the same white ceremonial outfit Lowell Lindsay had worn at the Open House.

The only difference was that the golden wing pendant was sticking out of Charles' chest.

Skinner immediately checked to see if Charles was breathing. He told the other Ranger, "Go back to the beginning of the trail to secure the area and call in the Coroner." Skinner began taking photos of the late High One with a small camera he'd pulled out of his pocket.

I wondered if someone like Officer Skinner ever got used to seeing dead bodies. Skinner's face showed no emotion. This was the second time in four days I'd seen a dead body. I felt the same nausea and disbelief. I kept expecting Charles' eyes to blink. He'd been so vital and ambitious and full of ideas the last time I saw him. But then, those ideas might have got him killed.

Skinner said, pointing to Charles, "Can one of you tell me what that is sticking out of his chest?"

Jaz started to explain, but my first thought was: *Looks like a screaming political statement to me*. And I bet the screamer was going to keep his or her mouth shut.

19

DURING THE NEXT HALF HOUR, the Coroner arrived. After ordering photographs of the entire murder scene, he started examining Charles' body. Jaz and I were whisked back to the main conference hall, where Skinner interviewed us separately.

Jaz was first and followed Skinner into one of the small offices off the main room. I paced up and down in front of the windows, watching the quickly forming crowd of as yet unenlightened onlookers. At least unenlightened to the fact their newly elected High One had not been protected by the angels.

It didn't seem too long before Jaz emerged, looking shaken and nervous. "That policeman wants to see you, Katie."

Skinner was right behind her and he'd taken his hat off and was running his fingers through his thick, dark hair. He didn't appear quite so menacing as before, and actually smiled at me as I approached.

"Have a seat." Skinner motioned me to a chair and sat on a corner of the desk directly in front of me. He gazed into my face, and I thought of dipping strawberries into his chocolate pool eyes. "Quite a surprise to run into you here, Ms. Cavanaugh, though I see you've been pretty active lately in police matters."

He flipped over a page in his notepad. "I heard from the Loveland Police Department—and from every news source around town—that you were over there helping them."

I set the strawberries aside and reminded myself this was serious stuff. "It wasn't my intention to get involved in anything. I had my fill of that last Christmas."

Skinner nodded and gave me a smile that created friendly-looking crinkles at the corners of his eyes. "Yes, I'm sure you did. Haven't seen you since then. Let me take this opportunity to say how much I admired the way you handled yourself. Facing down and capturing that killer was a brave thing."

A bolt of surprise shot through me. I thought he'd been irritated with me for getting myself into that situation.

Skinner tapped the notepad with his pen and cleared his throat. "Okay. Now, maybe you can help me. I need to ask these questions. First, what's your involvement with The Circle of Light?"

"None whatsoever, other than knowing Jaz."

"And you're here at this moment because Ms. Woods called you?"

I nodded.

"You don't know anyone else here?"

"Well . . . I did meet some people at the Open House this past Monday."

"And what's your opinion of what's going on here?"

That didn't sound like a routine question, but I was glad to get the opportunity to set him straight about my so-called "haunts." I reluctantly admitted to myself that it did matter what he thought of me. "I've been around a lot of people on different spiritual paths. This is not a path I would chose, but," I shrugged, "to each his own." I think I saw relief in his eyes.

"Being an outsider at that gathering, did you witness any animosity towards the victim?"

I thought a moment. "Yes. Some of the elders seemed to be at odds with his plans for the organization. But no more so than you'd see before any kind of election. These people are supposed to be anti-violence."

"You say you're friends with Ms. Woods. Are you aware of any relationship between her and the victim . . . uh," Skinner looked at his notes, "Mr. Sutcliff?"

"Jaz and I haven't seen each other in twenty years, so I don't know first hand."

"Well . . . how about second hand?"

"Does that count?"

"If it turns out to be true."

I didn't want to point him in a direction that would cause undo trouble for my friend. But I didn't know what Jaz had already told him. I squirmed a little in my chair. His eyes studied me. He seemed to know I was delaying and weighing my answer.

"Ms. Cavanaugh?" Skinner leaned forward and I caught a whiff of his spicy aftershave. "Kate? Please don't keep anything from me. We have to find the person who killed this man."

I realized my hesitation was making it appear I knew more than I did. I straightened up in my chair. "Jasmine told me she once had a 'thing' with Charles. But I think that was years ago and that's all I know. No. Wait. There is something else, but it may not mean anything. Brad Holtmann, the man I found murdered in Loveland, was wearing one of The Circle of Light pins. But when I asked some of the elders if he was a member, they said they'd never heard of him."

I watched Skinner take this information down on his pad. His hand moved in broad, self-assured strokes, dotting his i's and crossing his t's with energetic flair. I also liked the way he said "Kate". But chances were nothing hot and passionate would ever develop between us if our only meetings were over cold, dead bodies. Too bad.

* * * * * * *

143

JAZ AND MIKE'S ROOM was a small, starkly furnished cubicle in a long line of identical rooms that made up the dormitory building next to the main conference hall. Jaz had obviously brought in some of her own possessions to brighten up her surroundings. We sat on a red and purple bed cover rimmed with a tasseled border of elephants walking trunk to tail. The bed was piled high with silk and velvet pillows, and the air was thick with the scent of sandalwood incense.

I said, "Jaz, do you mind if I open the window?"

"Oh, sure, Katie, no problem." Jaz jumped up, went over to the small window, and cranked it open a few inches.

The frenetic sounds of police talk on car radios, chattering onlookers, and shouts of Rangers and emergency personnel trying to do their job came through the window.

"I can't believe all this is happening," Jaz said, plopping down on the floor. "I wish I wasn't the one who found him. I don't know if I can deal with this, Katie." Jaz reached into a duffel bag next to her and pulled out a small plastic bag. "Want a Zen Bun with your coffee?

"What's that?"

"They're cinnamon raisin buns made with totally organic ingredients. I brought them from California. Even half-stale, they're so good I don't like to go a day without having one."

As I munched on my bun and sipped my coffee, I was wishing I had Matt Skinner's authority to launch into the list of questions I wanted to ask Jaz. I had to find a friendlier way to get some information out of her.

"Where's Mike?" I asked with forced nonchalance. I figured he should have searched her out and offered support by this time. Either he didn't know that Jaz had found Charles or he didn't care.

Jaz's smile momentarily faltered, then switched back on. "I haven't seen Mike since I left him sleeping here this morning. Probably an elders' meeting was called as soon as word got around that Charles was dead. Or maybe the police are questioning him." She slapped her hand over her mouth. "This is awful. Do you think they're going to talk to everybody?"

"Yeah, I'm sure they will." I accepted Jaz's answer and moved on to riskier ground. "You and Mike resolve your argument from Monday? How's everything's between you two?"

Jaz was absentmindedly picking apart her Zen Bun, rolling the bits of dough into little balls and dropping them into her coffee cup. "Oh, Katie. I can't keep secrets from you. Things are not going well at all. He was with her again. I'm sure of it."

"Who is 'her'?"

"I don't know. But it's been going on for at least a year. At home in California, he'd disappear for a couple of days and just say it was Circle business and he had to travel somewhere. Since coming here, he's been out every night. Doesn't even bother with any excuses."

"But he was here in bed this morning when you went out? Why'd you go out for a walk in the dark? Even with a flashlight, that's gotta sound strange to the police."

"I know, I know." Jaz's Zen Bun had been totally mutilated. "I'm a strange person and sometimes I do go for walks that early. But honestly, I was so upset with Mike I didn't want to be here when he woke up. At least, not until I figured out how I should handle things. So I walked up and down every trail, killing time. I knew I couldn't come back until around seven o'clock when he'd be at the elder's morning meditation."

I tiptoed into the next question. "Uh, Jaz. As a friend who's been with you through other hard times, I have to ask you this Are you afraid of Mike?"

"No! Of course not," Jaz said too quickly.

"I want you to come and stay with me on the farm."

"Yeah, I know what you're thinking, Katie. But . . ." She got up and walked over to the closet. "One of the hazards of trying to sneak out in the dark." She opened the door and looked back over her shoulder at me. "I slammed right into the bloody thing." She pointed to her cheekbone. "This is what you're asking about, right? The bruise on my face?"

That was an unacceptable answer. I couldn't believe she expected me to be fooled by such an overused lie. "So, how do you explain the bruise I saw on your shoulder Sunday when you arrived at Trail's End?"

Jaz remained quiet.

"Did Officer Skinner ask you again about that bruise on your cheek?"

"Yeah."

"And you told him your door story?"

Jaz nodded. "Of course. It's the truth. My problem with Mike's fooling around seems insignificant now in comparison to what is happening in The Circle."

Okay. Conductor Jaz just switched the train of thought onto another track. Grudgingly, I went along for the ride. "With that pendant sticking out of Charles' chest, it kind of looks like someone was very unhappy with the election results. Do you have any suspicions, Jaz? Must've been awful for you to stumble on him like that when you were already upset."

Jaz moved to the bed and sat beside me, with one leg tucked underneath her. She grabbed a pillow and started winding the gold tassels around her finger, at the same time, swinging her free leg which made her hunched body bounce up and down. There was a quiet moment.

Jaz broke the quiet with, "I've got to tell somebody about this." She was staring at the tassels and didn't seem to be talking to me.

I waited. I think I was even holding my breath. Jaz appeared to be arranging her thoughts. Finally, she said, "Charles and I used to be married."

That was a bombshell. I felt like *I'd* just walked into the

146

bloody door. "Married? That's what you meant when you said you'd had a 'thing' with Charles?"

"Uh-huh." Jaz was really busy twirling those tassels and swinging her leg.

"When?"

"Well, let me tell you the whole story." Jaz stopped her jittering and folded both her legs underneath her. She hugged the pillow tight against her chest. "After Colin divorced me, I left London with Raji, who was still just a toddler. I had a few bucks left in my pocket, enough to get us back home to California. I was really down and heard about this group in Malibu. I knew some of the people had been to India, so I looked into it.

"It was like a commune. We all lived together in this old ranch house up in the hills. It was just like family. That's where I met Charles. He made sure Raji and I had everything we needed, and I fell in love with him. We sort of got married. It was never legal—we just kinda had our own ceremony. It was beautiful, Katie. We were on top of a hill, looking out over the ocean and the sun was setting, all orange and pink.

"Anyway, we moved to Vermont to start a new life. That was the place to go. There were a lot of interesting and artistic people settling there. We started a New Age bookstore and it grew real fast to a small chain of three stores in the state. I was working real hard."

Jaz leaned towards me, emphasizing her words with her entire body. "It was the only time in my life I ever worked that hard and made a lot of money. It was fantastic. We were living in a style you wouldn't believe, Katie."

Jaz flung the pillow up in the air in disgust. "Then suddenly Charles, out of the blue, says he's had this vision. That God spoke to him and told him to get rid of the business. That it was an idol. Charles said spirituality was meant to be free and that merchandising it was wrong. So he up and sells the whole damn thing without consulting me, and I was the one putting all my blood, sweat, and tears into it. I could've killed him."

I could tell by the way Jaz tossed off that last line that she didn't realize how incriminating it sounded. I asked, "Did you tell the police any of this?"

"No."

I wanted to hear the rest of her story, so I let that go. "Well, you must have made a lot of money on the sale. What did you do? Give it away?"

Jaz huffed. "Not exactly. Just as Charles had his 'revelation,' this guy appeared with a proposal, and Charles thought the whole thing had been divinely orchestrated. I wasn't so sure that God wanted Charles to invest our money in this guy's condominium apartments. But I had no say in our financial matters." She looked down and shook her head. "That's my own fault. I let that happen. I've never had much of a business mind."

Jaz sighed and straightened up. "Anyway, then the old mill they were renovating into these apartments burns down one night and this 'partner' disappears with the insurance money. We were broke, but Charles kept saying, 'It's part of the journey.' So, we went back to the commune in Malibu, met Bruno Marcello—you know, the big doom 'n gloom guy we bumped into down by the barn Monday night?"

I nodded.

"Well, Charles and Bruno turned that commune into the first Circle of Light."

I said, "How could you stay with Charles after all that?"

"Simple. I was broke, I had a son to raise, and I had nowhere else to go. The Circle was the only family I had. But then Charles started acting cold towards me and became very detached. The Circle of Light was the only thing he was interested in. He didn't even have any sexual need for me anymore and started living like a monk. Then Mike joined our circle and gave me the attention I needed."

I still didn't understand something. "Jaz, can you explain

148

why, if Charles and Bruno started The Circle of Light, they needed to elect a new High One? Wouldn't one of them already be in that position?"

"Well, they used to be. But so things wouldn't get corrupted by one person being in power too long, they limited the term of office to two years. After what's happened under Lowell's leadership, Charles felt it was time to take back the reins."

That filled in one blank. I returned to another one. "The police didn't ask if you were connected with Charles in any way?"

Jaz reclaimed her security pillow and was tassel twirling again. "I lied. Dumb mistake. Now I'm worried the police'll find out."

"Go tell them."

"But I have no alibi."

"But you'll look more suspicious if they find this out on their own. It's better to be truthful and clear it up right now."

"Oh, Katie, if I tell the cops I was involved with Charles, that'll open the door for them to start snooping around our past together and then there's a chance they'll find out about our financial troubles. Wouldn't they see that as a motive?"

"That was years ago. They'd really be stretching things to dig that far in the past." I thought for a moment. "You weren't still angry with Charles? Were you?"

Jaz gave a shrug of her shoulders that didn't tell me one way or the other. She looked down and slowly shook her head. "I don't know what to do."

"Is that why you delayed calling the police? You were wondering what to tell them?"

Jaz raised her eyes to me and spoke in a soft voice. "Katie, I'm afraid. The cops don't need to know about me and Charles. Do they?"

Before I could say "Yes", the door opened and Mike walked in. He looked surprised when he noticed my presence.

"Jasmine?" Mike said. "I've been looking all over for you. They tell me you found Charles. Are you okay?" He put an arm around her and kissed her lightly on the unbruised cheek. Jaz flinched almost imperceptibly.

"Yeah, I'm okay. But only because Katie's here."

Mike turned to acknowledge me, his beautiful lips framing a smile. He directed his attention back to Jaz. "I've just been with the police, answering their questions. And now I have to meet with the elders, so I just wanted to make sure you were all right before I got tied up with them."

Mike looked at me. "We need to get a new High One in place right away, so we can make some decisions. As you can imagine, Kate, things are in turmoil. We will be seeking direction through meditation before we come up with a plan of action."

Also known as Damage Control, I thought. The Circle of Light was not looking too spiritual at the moment, which brought to mind a sticky theological question the elders would have to answer. Why, as Jaz had explained to me, didn't the aura of the most spiritual man in The Circle connect with God's energy and keep him from such a violent end? And why should anyone believe they were under Godly protection?

Right now, I believed those of us outside The Circle were safer, and, to paraphrase the "also-very-spiritual" Lowell Lindsay, "The Circle has no point."

20

IT WAS DIFFICULT LEAVING JAZ, but I had to get back to my kitchen—after all, I had a business to run. Jaz accompanied me to the parking lot, and on the way I repeated my invitation to stay at the farm. She refused, putting on a good show of being in control. But I saw a little hint of panic in her eyes. Although her explanation that the police wanted all Circle members to stay on the grounds sounded reasonable, I remembered her saying earlier she didn't trust anyone. She wasn't really making sense, but I couldn't drag her away against her will.

My parting words were, "Don't wander down any trails alone. I'll be back at six to take you to dinner."

I watched Jaz join a couple of other volunteers and go into the main conference hall. She looked pale and vulnerable as she gave me one last wave.

My watch said it was almost eleven, and I realized I hadn't touched base with Tony. I strode across the parking lot towards my Jeep and figured I'd give him a quick call on my car phone to let him know I was leaving and would be home soon.

"Who said you could leave, Ms. Cavanaugh?"

I whirled around and saw Clairmont Ranger Matt Skinner

slouching against the side of his patrol car, one leg crossed over the other and arms folded across his broad chest. He laughed right out loud at the look of indignation I instinctively shot him.

"Don't hit me," Skinner said, "I was just joking." He pushed away from the car and walked towards me.

Quick, girl, I thought to myself, say something smart. Keep this conversation going.

In certain situations, like this one, my mind freezes up. I stood there like a dumb twit, staring at him as he opened my car door for me. It looked like my only course of action was to climb into the driver's seat, but there was a pathetic little voice inside my head that said *I don't want to go just yet*.

Skinner looked directly into my eyes, grinned, and said, "I hope we run into each other again, soon."

I was surprised at hearing myself answer, "Yes, I would like that." I felt like I'd just leaped off a cliff and wondered where that answer would land me. What was I doing? I hate cops.

I was still free-falling, when some activity behind Skinner sparked my curiosity. A Clairmont Ranger was carrying what looked like a three foot long tree branch stuffed in a plastic bag.

I said, "Is that the murder weapon? I thought Charles was stabbed with his angel wings."

"That's not something I can discuss with you."

"Well, I don't think the Rangers came out here to trim trees."

Skinner chuckled. "Are you pushing me for information?"

I smiled and cocked an eyebrow.

He looked back over his shoulder and watched the Ranger deposit the branch in the back of a police van. "I'll say this much, your powers of observation are impressive."

I took that as Skinner's way of saying yes and not breaking police department rules.

There was an awkward moment when I think each of us was waiting for the other to either officially end the conversation or come up with a new way to prolong it. It seemed we were both about to say something, when Lowell Lindsay shuffled up, a child-like smile on his face. I noticed he was still wearing the same white robe he'd worn on Monday. His posture was just as stooped even without the weight of The High One pendant which was, at that moment, sticking out of Charles' chest.

Lowell said, "Good morning." He bowed slightly, and I half expected him to hand me another holy banana. Lowell turned and bowed to Skinner and said, "I will be meditating with great intensity. I do not know how long it will take, but I trust the messenger angels will provide a solution to this terrible situation."

Lowell gave me a serious look. "The air is full of talk from loose, undisciplined tongues. Keep your ears covered. The Truth can be heard within you."

"There you are," Adam George said as he came loping up towards us. He was shadowed by Patricia Ebbes, whose little feet were working twice as hard in order to keep up.

"Everybody's wondering where you wandered off to," Patricia said, glowering at Lowell.

Adam gently, but firmly, grasped the older man by the arm. "We've got to get this meeting off the ground. There's lots to discuss." Adam turned to Skinner. "Is it alright if he comes with us? Or do you need to ask him any more questions?"

Skinner waved him off. "We weren't doing anything official here."

Skinner and I watched the three "enlightened ones" go into the main conference hall. Skinner sighed. "We've asked the usual questions, but we're not getting straight answers around here. It's like questioning a bunch of Zen Masters. All you get are riddles."

That last statement startled me. "Have you talked to many Zen Masters before?"

"Not as a policeman. Which reminds me," he said, glancing at his watch, "I have to check with the Coroner. Drive safe." He touched his fingers to the brim of his hat, giving me a little salute, spun on his heels and strode off across the parking lot towards the police van.

Well, that was a pleasant diversion, but I needed to get back on track again, too. Folding up my gangly legs, I slid onto the car seat and grabbed the phone. 'Round the World Catering was busy and I hoped Tony wasn't getting swamped with job requests. I pulled out of the parking lot, feeling a little anxious about being away from my kitchen for so long. The morning was almost completely used up and there was still plenty of work to be done at home. I pushed the gas pedal to the floor, leaving the Golden Valley Spiritual Center behind. But my mind couldn't leave behind what I'd seen or heard.

Anyone could wield that tree branch, whether it was a tall, strong person like Adam George, a rage-filled Patricia Ebbes, or even gentle Jaz, with her old wounds.

With a combination of enough anger and adrenalin coursing through her body, Jaz could have done it. It bothered me that she didn't give me a direct answer when I asked if she was still angry with Charles. I knew Jaz was capable of lying, so the fact that she couldn't even pretend one way or the other was significant. That told me she was still grappling with strong, conflicting emotions.

Maybe Jaz had been participating in too many of Patricia's Dynamic Energy Healing sessions. If I remembered Jaz's explanation correctly—"it wakes up all your electromagnetic circuits" and "you can literally detach yourself from old, wounding perceptions and attachments"—then maybe her wounds were too intense, too much for her to deal with. Maybe her circuitry became so overloaded that something popped inside and, instead of avoiding confrontations as she usually did, she actually had a deadly one.

I didn't know what to think.

21

WHAT WOULD I DO WITHOUT TONY? I didn't want to think about it. I hoped he was happy working with me. He probably enjoyed being left with the responsibility of taking over while I was running around playing the Amazon Chili Heiress Detective.

When I got home, Tony wasn't there. But I did find, cooling on the counters, trays of that afternoon's orders. The hazelnut, walnut, and coconut macaroons were completed, and empty éclair and tart shells were waiting for my finishing touch.

I filled the last tart shell with a brandied chestnut purée and squeezed out the last gob of it onto a piece of broken pastry. My stomach was rumbling and I didn't want to stop for lunch. Besides, it was a shame to waste such divinely delicious stuff. Just as I was pushing it into my mouth, I heard the kitchen door swing open.

"Miss Kate, what've you got in your mouth? You look like a chipmunk."

"Oh, hi, Phoebe Jo," I tried to say through the wad of buttery pastry in my mouth.

"Tony went off to Trader Bob's to pick up supplies for his cousin's bachelor party. I think he's quite anxious about it 'cause he said it was his responsibility and he didn't want to take up too much of your time with it. So he's using his lunch hour to go there, and he told me to tell you he'd get back as quick as he could."

"He didn't have to do that," I said, stuffing another piece of tart shell in my mouth.

Phoebe Jo tilted her head to one side and frowned slightly. She pointed her finger timidly at me. "Do you realize what you're doing?"

"What?" I said, looking down at the trays of desserts and at the floor around me. "Am I dropping something?"

"You were all upset yesterday and we had a big talk about going back to lowfat eating around here. You said that Rule Number One was: don't lick the bowls."

I swallowed. "Oh, yeah."

Phoebe Jo walked over to the counter and sat on the stool across from me. "They look real pretty," she said, surveying my—and Tony's—handiwork. "What delicious, lowfat, low-calorie dish would you like for dinner tonight? We've got to work out some menus for the next week and I don't know how strict you want to be."

I sighed and looked at the bowls of pastry cream and melted chocolate waiting to adorn the éclair shells. "I'm gonna have to find a new profession."

Phoebe Jo gave me a little slap on the wrist. "Now you don't mean that. Don't be dramatic."

"Well, I'm taking Jaz out to dinner tonight."

"Oh yes. What happened with her? You ran off in such a hurry this morning."

I told her, as undramatically as I could, what had occurred at the spiritual center.

Phoebe Jo just sat quietly for a moment, appearing to ponder what it all meant. "Do you think it's one of those crazy cults you read so much about in the paper these days? They're always thinking God will show up on television announcing that He's coming, or they'll be whisked away on the tail of a comet." She shook her head. "Jasmine seems like such a nice person. Why does she believe in all that crazy stuff? You don't, Miss Kate."

I picked up a pastry bag and started filling the éclairs. "Well, some of their beliefs are a little wacky. But some of them are legitimate. I think. You and I both know that sometimes my dreams predict things. I don't know if it was angels sending me messages or what, but the way I first knew I had cancer was through a dream."

Phoebe Jo picked up a pair of tongs, grasped a filled éclair and dipped it in its chocolate bath. "Hmm. Yes, I remember that," she said. "Even the mammograms didn't show anything wrong."

"Well, I'm certainly not saying that mammograms are useless, but some people put all their faith into technology and think doctors are gods. Then again, I'm not quite where you are, Phoebe Jo, where I can be so sure that there is a God who's controlling everything, but I know there is more to this world than what we can see.

"A few days ago, Jaz accused me of living an imbalanced life. Too much on the physical plane, she said. It made me angry, but then I got to thinking about how I used to follow Ayurveda."

"What's that?" Phoebe Jo asked.

"Well, it's Hindu medicine, but more than that, it's being aware of your specific body type and needs, then taking care of it in a way that is healthy and balanced. Sometimes I think maybe I wouldn't have gotten sick if I'd stuck to it. I still think it's valid, but it's hard to live with an Eastern mind-set in the middle of Western culture. I guess that's one of the reasons why people like Jaz gather into these groups. But anytime you put a bunch of human beings together, human emotions will complicate things.

"I would like to get back into Ayurvedic cooking, but Phoebe

Jo," I shook my head, "you'd spend every minute of the day in the kitchen trying to work out who should eat what foods in what combinations, at what temperature and in which season, to keep everyone's doshas in balance. Then, of course, there's the matter of—"

"Oh, never mind, Miss Kate." Phoebe Jo held her head as if in pain. "Just stop licking the bowls."

The kitchen's back door opened with such force it crashed against the steel shelving behind it. Tony grunted as he backed in and deposited a case of wine on the floor, using it as a doorstop. He looked up. "Hey, Boss. Good to see ya. I'll be right back. Got some more stuff to unload."

Phoebe Jo and I continued our chocolate éclair assembly line, while Tony went back and forth, bringing in countless cases of wine and mysterious bulging grocery bags. Seeing Trader Bob's gorilla-in-a-pith helmet logo on the bags, I said, "Tony, you know that's my favorite place. How could you go there without me. Hope you at least brought me a surprise."

Tony grinned, reached into one of the bags and pulled out a small package.

My mouth started watering. "Double Gloucester and Stilton cheese! What a guy!" I reached for it, my taste buds anticipating the strong bite of the rich cheese, but froze in mid-action. Uh-oh. I gave Phoebe Jo a sheepish look. "I know. Rule Number Two: I'll make up for it, tomorrow."

Phoebe Jo shrugged her shoulders, an innocent expression on her face. "I'm not saying anything."

Tony studied the cheese in his hand. He frowned at me. "What? Did I bring the wrong stuff?"

"No, no," I answered. "Don't worry. By the way, thank you for prepping all these desserts."

"That was easy. Got it all out of the way real early. Then my cousin Carlo phoned. Got some news for you about Frankie Alberto."

158

I put the éclair I was about to fill back down on the tray and gave him my full attention.

Tony leaned up against the edge of one of the steel counters and raised his thumb. "One. This Frankie Boy's no Einstein. Carlo says there's stories about him always messing up and getting into trouble when he could've avoided it.

"Two." Tony raised his index finger. "Word has it that Frankie was thinking of quitting the job he had with Brad Holtmann."

"Why?" I asked.

Tony shrugged. "Nobody knows. *But*," he pointed to me, "he's been invited to the bachelor party and you'll be able to question him yourself."

22

JAZ'S ONLY REQUEST WAS THAT I pick out a restaurant where "we can hang."

By six-thirty we were settling into a booth at JJ's, known for expertly cooked steaks and a non-trendy menu. Great place to bring a vegetarian, right? Many of the area's chefs like to frequent this jazz club, located in a refurbished Colonial house in Old Montgomery, to wind down after working high-pressured shifts at their very trendy restaurants. JJ, a friend to all, roams from table to table sharing his bottle of wine and the latest gossip.

"Oh, Katie," Jaz said, slumping in her seat, "you don't know how good it feels to get away from all that energy at the spiritual center."

"What kind of energy?" I asked.

"You'd expect a group of people like The Circle to be able to handle a crisis in a mature and spiritual manner. But now I'm seeing what kind of people they really are. Everybody's bad-mouthing Charles, calling him a faker."

"Because he wasn't protected from violence by some energy field?"

Jaz nodded. "Yep."

"Well, you've all had the rug pulled out from under you. I

would think you must feel kind of duped. Or are some people still hanging on to their beliefs?"

"Oh, yeah. Bruno's going on and on about how this is all building up to The Final Battle."

"What does Mike say?"

"Well, Mike's trying to stabilize the situation. He's saying that even if Charles wasn't a true believer, it doesn't mean The Circle of Light's teachings are wrong." Jaz made a design on her napkin with her fork. "Mike says that Charles was led astray by his own big ego."

A stooped and bleary-eyed man trudged over to our table. It was The Man himself. JJ stroked his graying walrus moustache and smiled down at us, his bloodshot blue eyes looking even more tired than usual. "Saw your lovely face gracing the front page of *The Enquirer* again."

I said, "I hate that file photo. Want you to meet a friend of mine." I gestured across the table. "This is Jasmine Woods, one of my traveling companions from way back."

JJ made a very formal bow to Jaz. "A pleasure. And what can I bring you from my kitchen?"

I wanted a big, juicy steak. But this whole evening was supposed to be geared to Jaz's comfort and I didn't want to offend her with my carnivorous appetite. "How's the Paella Marinara tonight?"

JJ kissed his fingers. "Excellent choice. The shellfish is as fresh as it gets." He turned to Jaz. "And for you?"

Jaz stared at her menu. "Ummm. Let's see . . ." Her fingers slid across the page, underlining each item. "How 'bout . . . No. Okay." She snapped the menu shut. "I'll have the Pasta Primavera."

I ordered a glass of Chardonnay and Jaz opted for bottled water. JJ wrote it all down, took our menus and said, "Hope you'll come and visit my booth at Taste of Cincinnati this weekend, Kate."

"You're actually doing it this year?"

"Yeah, big surprise, uh? I was tired of seeing all this bizarre, so-called fusion food, and decided it was time for me to show what good cooking was all about. *Bah!*" JJ slashed the air with an upwards karate chop. "Don't get me started on that subject. I'd best get the kitchen going on your orders." He lumbered off.

I said, "So who's taken over the leadership?"

Jaz took in a deep breath, making the delicate gold ring piercing one side of her nose flare out. "Lowell's back as High One. I guess that's the logical thing to do until the elders can come up with someone else. No Circle decisions are made on the spur of the moment. Everything has to be meditated on for weeks. But Katie, Lowell just wanders around like some fool in a fog."

"Yeah, he came up to me just before I left this morning. Do you think it's all an act?"

"If it is, he's good at it. I've never seen him out of character."

"I got the impression that everyone was kind of embarrassed by him. So how did he become High One in the first place?"

Jaz was quiet for a moment. "Lowell used to make predictions, saying things that actually turned out to be truthful and quite profound. So, the elders were convinced he was receiving divine wisdom. But as time went on, he started muttering to himself and gradually turned into a silly but harmless old fool."

That would be a good disguise for a murderer. I wondered if any of The Circle members would consider the killer might be one of their own. "Is there any talk going around the spiritual center? You know, theories about who might've done this and why?"

"Theories?" Jaz grabbed a roll and started ripping the soft dough out of the center and rolling it between her fingers. "More like panic rumors. People are saying the killer's someone who hates The Circle of Light and what it stands for and wants to destroy it."

"You don't seem like a group that would incite hatred in other people."

"There've been some incidents like hate mail and graffiti on members' houses, but we just figured they were teenage vandals—or even if they were crazies the angels would protect us. Then there's the rumor about the killer being a volunteer with an axe to grind."

"Nobody's suspecting any of the elders?"

"Oh, no. That's too scary to think about. That would really destroy The Circle."

"Well, it has to be someone who knows the significance of the pendant. Sure looks like the killer was making a statement, shoving it into Charles' chest like that."

"Oh, yeah, that's the other thing I meant to tell you. The talk is Charles was hit on the back of the head with a tree branch. And that's what killed him."

That reinforced my observation.

"What am I going to do, Katie, if, let's say it's one of the volunteers or someone else who knows about my past relationship with Charles? They hear I'm the one who found him, so they tell the police and the finger gets pointed at me."

"Jaz. Tell the cops."

"But maybe I won't have to. Maybe the killer doesn't know about me and Charles and I won't get pulled into this situation any further than I already am. I don't know, Katie," she squeezed her eyes shut and shook her head violently, "I just wish it would all go away."

If Jaz was ever going to learn to confront issues, this was the time to start. But I knew I'd exhausted her capacity to discuss this topic any further, so I shifted the focus onto me. "I know what it feels like to be falsely accused of murder. Remember when I told you about finding the body of Brad Holtmann?"

Jaz nodded.

"Well, what I didn't tell you was that when I went to report it to the police, I was accused right there by some guy named Frankie Alberto who said he saw me bending over the body."

"That's totally ridiculous. You didn't even know the guy. Did you?"

"No, and yes, it is ridiculous. But what's frightening is that people have the power to turn your life upside down with their lies."

Jaz stared at the mound of rolled-up dough balls on the plate in front of her. Obviously, what I'd just said sent Jaz off on some kind of trek through her mind.

I broke the silence. "There's got to be a connection between those two deaths. Brad was wearing a Circle of Light pin, and Cincinnati is too small a place for that kind of coincidence."

Jaz snapped back to the here and now. "Oh, yeah." She slapped the side of her face. "That's another thing I wanted to tell you. I asked around about Brad Holtmann and nobody seemed to know the guy, but then Charles said he remembered Brad back in California."

Jaz sat forward and leaned across the table towards me and whispered, "Maybe Charles had something to do with Brad's murder? Do you think that's possible?"

That hadn't occurred to me. "I have no idea. You knew Charles intimately. Was he capable of that?"

Jaz looked down at her hands. "Oh, I . . . I don't know anymore . . . about anybody."

I laid my hand on top of hers. "This is only going to go away if the killer is found. Let's say whoever did it is attending the retreat. If there's something strange going on behind those white robes and smiling faces, you're in a much better position than the police to find out."

Jaz bit her lip. "You mean you want me to snoop around?"

"No, not exactly. Just keep your eyes and ears open. Watch and listen for anything unusual or suspicious."

Jaz looked to the side. "You know, maybe Charles knew something about Brad's killer and that's what got him killed. Maybe there's something in Charles' room that might point to the killer. I don't know. But I do know Charles, and he always kept things: receipts, records . . . he always made lists of the pros and cons of whatever before he made any major decisions." Jaz screwed up her face in disgust. "He was secretive, though. I learned that the hard way when he sold the business out from under me without my even knowing it."

A little devil whispered a suggestion into my ear. I relayed it to Jaz. "Can we get into Charles' room?"

"Yeah, sure. None of the rooms are locked. You're not supposed to be paranoid about things like that when you're attending a spiritual retreat. If anyone wants, they could have their valuables locked up in the office safe. Don't you think the police searched his room already?"

"So? Maybe they missed something important. They might not have known what they were looking at."

"Oh, there *is* one other thing I forgot to tell you, but I don't think it'll be a problem. We now have security guards."

"Security guards?"

"Yeah. The owners of the Golden Valley Spiritual Center are freaked about what's happened, so they've hired a private security company to patrol—"

The clanging and clattering of pots and pans rolling across a tile floor, followed by a string of loud profanities, caused everyone in the restaurant to simultaneously turn and stare at the entrance to the kitchen. JJ ran across the dining room and pushed through the swinging doors to check it out. A tense silence hung in the air. It seemed that every diner in the room was holding his or her breath. After a couple of minutes, the sound of muted conversation and eating gradually returned to its normal level.

Soon after, JJ emerged and headed for our table. He looked worried.

I asked, "What happened?"

"I have a new dishwasher. He's not too bright. It's gonna take a few weeks for the rules of the kitchen to sink in. And now I have a line cook with a broken wrist."

"Well, how did that happen?"

"You know how frantic it gets back there, Kate. My best line cook, who really knows his stuff, was doing his usual five things at once in front of the stove, rushed over to put something under the broiler and tripped over a big pile of dirty pots and pans. Stupid dishwasher. I've told him a couple of times already, 'Don't leave things on the floor!'"

JJ pulled a wrinkled red bandana out of his pocket and wiped his forehead with it. "Now I'm shorthanded, and it's not just tonight I'm worried about. It's the entire weekend. I was counting on him to man the booth at Taste of Cincinnati. Well, he sure can't work the grill with his arm in a cast."

I was half-expecting him to ask if I would go back there and cook our own dinners.

JJ pocketed his bandana. "Don't worry about your dinners, I'm going back into the kitchen to help keep things running. But chances are I won't be out here again tonight, so I want to ask you right now if you'd do me a huge favor."

"Sure," popped out of my mouth.

"Could you and Tony help me with the booth at Taste of Cincinnati? Think of it as a catering job you don't have to prep for. I'll pay your going rate."

As I slowly said, "Yes," I wondered to myself, *What's wrong with this picture?*

* * * * * * *

Boo-Kat raced me across the half-court as we both went for the basketball. I grabbed it just before he was able to attack it with his huge fangs and drooling tongue.

"That's not what they mean by dribbling the ball."

166

I was having a one woman mid-night madness basketball tournament. It's scheduled for those nights my brain is too hyperactive and I can't sleep.

After dropping Jaz off at the spiritual center, I tried to go to bed early. My body felt tired and I thought I would fall asleep quickly, but my mind wouldn't shut down until I filled in all the blanks. I was forgetting something important.

I can always think clearly in a dark, quiet room, so as soon as I turned off the light and laid my head on the pillow, it came to me. Damn. Taste of Cincinnati Weekend includes Memorial Day.

Trouble. Memorial Day is Mother's barbecue. All of a sudden, I couldn't look at my schedule as a list of individual events. It was one enormous avalanche thundering down the mountainside towards me.

In a few hours, on top of the usual catering jobs, I was going to help Jaz by searching through her murdered ex-significant other's bedroom, then try to personally question Frankie Alberto at an Italian stag party and get a straight answer as to why he accused me of killing Brad Holtmann. After getting by those boulders, I was faced with helping JJ with his debut appearance at Taste of Cincinnati, the tri-state's gastronomic event of the year.

Then the biggest boulder. Mother.

This barbecue of hers was important to her self-esteem and how she saw her position in Clairmont's social strata. I couldn't fail her, especially at a time when she felt ignored and rejected.

Then there was Jaz. I felt a responsibility to be there for her, too.

I had a sudden image of myself standing at the foot of the mountain, arms outstretched trying to catch all the boulders. Why did I think I had to hold them all up? I could just step aside and let them roll past me.

After flip-flopping around in bed for an hour, the muscles in my body were tied in knots. I decided it was tournament time, so

I got up and put on my sweats. Boo-Kat stared up at me from his bed. *Is this one of those nights?* he seemed to be asking.

"You don't have to come," I said.

Boo-Kat yawned, stretched, and trailed along behind as I headed down the stairs, through the foyer, and past the commercial kitchen. He scampered ahead as I pushed through the door into the gym.

I flicked on the overhead lights and shut my eyes against the sudden fluorescent glare. When I opened them, I saw Boo-Kat waiting for me beside a basketball, his stubby tail wagging in anticipation. For the next minute we played doggie soccer. The basics are: human chases after dog, who uses his nose to push the basketball across the floor and around the Soloflex machine. Boo-Kat loves it, but I lose interest at the fifty-eight second mark. Seeing that I wasn't going to continue the chase, Boo-Kat decided to attack the ball. I was close enough to give the basketball a surprise kick that sent it across the half-court, away from his drooling tongue.

As I said earlier, we raced after it and I gained possession. I slowly dribbled the ball to the foul line and began shooting baskets. The secret to getting the ball through the hoop consistently is learning how to access the Zone. Focus on the hoop, clear the mind of everything else, get into a rhythm. Bounce. Set. Shoot. "Yes." Bounce. Set. Shoot. "Yes." Gradually, I felt the knots in my back and neck muscles start to loosen from the rhythmic movements. I had entered the Zone—or as Lowell Lindsay called it, "the Bliss of No Thought."

It didn't last long. The boulders in my mind came thundering back, and the basketball started bouncing off the rim.

So, why didn't I just step aside and let that avalanche roll past me? Why was I standing at the bottom of the mountain, trying to catch and hold up all those boulders?

The honest answer to that question is: I have a need to be

needed. Guess that's my way of getting love and approval. I would rather get that love from one special person, instead of trying to fill my need by responding to every cry for help.

It's a vicious circle. I get myself all booked up and I'm so busy running around, thinking I'm taking care of everybody, that it's probably pushing away the people who might want to take care of me.

But for now, this was the only way I could operate.

I imagined Cindy Schmitz—or was it now Schmitz-Hoseyni?— guarding me as I drove to the basket for a lay-up. Cindy and I made the regional All-Star team in our senior year at Clairmont High. I was starting center and Cindy was at one of the two guard positions.

Guards. I wondered how The Circle of Light felt about the Golden Valley Spiritual Center hiring earth guards to take over for their failing spiritual protectors? I sometimes think there really are guardian angels trying to protect us from danger. I thought about my experience in Iran, only one of several situations my traveling companions and I were rescued from during our wanderings. Mother was right to be surprised we survived that trip.

And then there are my prophetic dreams. The most dramatic one occurred six years ago, saving my life. I don't know if it was a guardian angel whispering to me in the middle of the night, but I had a dream so startling, it made me sit bolt upright in bed.

In my dream, I was on the Greek island of Mykonos, lying on the hot, silvery sand, watching pelicans swoop over the turquoise water. Suddenly, a strange sensation made me look down.

My left breast ached as if a cold, hard stone was growing from somewhere deep in the center of the soft tissue. The aching pressure in my breast began radiating outwards and I watched, with horror, my nipple fall off.

23

Thursday, May 22nd

I REALLY FELT LOUSY and I didn't want to do this, but I followed Jaz up the steps into the spiritual center's dormitory building. Usually, my insomnia doesn't affect my energy level the next day, but I felt as though I was dragging all those boulders behind me everywhere I went.

"C'mon, c'mon, Katie," Jaz said, pulling on my sleeve, "we've gotta do this fast. I'm supposed to be working in the kitchen this morning, and the other volunteers are complaining about me leaving the grounds and not pulling my weight."

Jaz was in one of her bouncy states. It had to be nervous energy and I couldn't ask her to stop doing it, but it was really irritating the hell out of me.

As we walked down the hall towards Charles' room, I asked, "Where is everybody?"

"The elders are having another of their big meetings and the volunteers are cleaning up after breakfast and getting stuff ready for lunch."

We reached the door to Charles' room and stopped. Jaz nervously looked up and down the hall before pushing down on the door handle. The door swung open.

"Oh," Jaz said.

The two of us stared in surprise.

"Where's all his stuff?" Jaz asked, entering the bare room.

I followed and closed the door behind us. "I bet the police took everything."

"Oh. I didn't think about that."

Neither had I. Jaz's shoulders sagged with the disappointment that I felt too. "Let's search anyway."

I started opening drawers and Jaz looked under the bed

"Dust bunnies," she announced.

"Nothing in here, either," I said, shutting the last of the dresser drawers.

"Well . . . there are these things," Jaz said, picking up a small, brass dish and putting it back down. "But I don't think they're going to tell us anything."

I stepped across to the bed and looked at the items on the bedside table. Two half-burned candles and a brass incense burner.

"Would he have brought this with him?" I asked, picking up the incense burner and studying its complex filigree design. "Or does it belong to the spiritual center?"

"Naw. He would have brought that with him." Jaz turned to the closet door right by the bed. "Let's see what's in here."

My eyes caught movement outside the half-opened window. "Lowell."

Jaz's head whipped around. "Where?"

"Coming up the steps."

"Did he see you?"

"Doubt it. He's looking at the ground . . . I think he's talking to himself."

We both froze, waiting to see if Lowell was actually going to

171

enter the building. Sure enough, we heard the outside door open, and I strained to listen for his shuffling steps. As he neared the room, I could hear him muttering.

"Quick!" Jaz whispered frantically, and she pulled me into the closet with her.

I didn't think to duck and my head smacked against the clothing rod, sending wire hangers clattering to the floor, one of them catching in my braid.

"Shh," Jaz hissed in my ear as I tried to make myself shorter and pulled the closet door almost closed.

Through the crack I could see the bedroom door open slowly. Lowell shuffled in, mumbling something about rotten eggs. He stopped in the middle of the room, snuffled, and looked up at the ceiling. I could feel the heat of Jaz's body squeezed up against me. Her heart must have been pounding as hard as mine, but she was managing to stay very still.

Lowell gave a big sigh and scanned the room. I watched his gaze travel past the closet door and lock onto something. Lowell started walking towards us. I caught my breath, holding it as he came closer, and prayed he wasn't interested in checking out the closet. But then again I wondered, so what if he found us in here? What was *he* doing, snooping around in Charles' room? All of a sudden, spying on Lowell was more interesting than searching Charles' empty room.

Lowell's arm reached out. It was so close I could have poked my finger through the crack in the door and touched him.

"Ahh," Lowell said as he picked up something. A second later, I saw Charles' incense burner in his hand. Lowell turned the brass dish around, studying it from all sides. With a smile on his face, he held it up to his nose and sniffed. Lowell quickly stuffed it into a pocket in his robe and shuffled back out of the room without looking anywhere else.

Hearing the door close, Jaz whispered, "Can we get outta here now? I'm dying."

As we burst out of the closet, Jaz asked, "What did you see? He wasn't in here very long. What was he doing?"

I pointed to the top of the bedside table. "He stole the incense burner."

"Well, that's pure Lowell. Doesn't make any sense at all."

"Must've been what he came in for. As soon as he saw it, he grabbed it and left."

I looked around. "There's absolutely nothing else in this room." I took in a deep breath and blew it out, feeling totally frustrated. "Wait. Let's take a look inside the closet. We didn't really see what was in there."

Jaz opened the door and I looked in every corner, but it was empty.

"What should we do now?" Jaz asked.

"That incense burner must have some significance. You can't think of any reason Lowell would steal it? Didn't you say all the elders were at some meeting? And Lowell's The High One. What's he doing wandering around?"

Jaz shrugged. "Just another one of his endearing habits," she said with a smirk. "The elders are used to his wanderings. They just carry on without him."

I glanced out the window and watched Lowell stroll into the conference center. "Do you know if Charles ever left the grounds?"

"Oh, no." Jaz shook her head. "I can't imagine that. If he wasn't in his room or at a meeting, he was in the meditation hall. Charles was dedicated."

"I've never seen the meditation hall. Where is it?"

"Way over on the other side of the field behind us."

I really didn't think I'd see anything of interest there, but I was grasping at straws. "Let's go look."

* * * * * * * * *

AS I FOLLOWED Jaz down the dirt road that crossed the newly plowed field, I saw in the distance a man emerging from one of the trails. He was wearing a hat like a cop's and a white shirt with patches on the shoulders. It appeared he also had a gun holster slung around his middle. An earth guard.

We headed for the long, frame building with small, colored glass windows just below the roof line. It looked like a pioneer church—a sort of generic house of worship.

By this time, I was really in the mood to search and I could feel the curiosity gnawing at my stomach. After the disappointment of Charles' room, I'd have settled for a trash can with a few sheets of crumpled up paper in it. Or even just a book to leaf through.

Jaz and I climbed the two wooden steps and entered a vestibule crammed with metal folding chairs stacked against the walls. Immediately, we stepped into the main room, which could have held four hundred people. The air was thick with the smell of incense, and the sunlight coming through the colored glass windows bathed the room in a purple-amber glow. I could see why the chairs had been folded up and stored in the vestibule. The entire floor was covered with neat rows of flat brown cushions. At the front of the room, on a slightly raised dais, a wooden pulpit had been pushed to the side and one brown cushion was positioned in the center in front of a large, brass gong.

A center aisle had been left clear, and Jaz and I walked up to the front. The anticipation that had been building up in me was immediately extinguished. The room was stark.

I plunked myself down on the edge of the dais and stared out across the sea of cushions, chin in hand. There was a serene feeling to the room, but it did nothing for my irritated, sleep-deprived state of mind. My head began pounding as though I'd just slammed it against a brick wall. Now what? There was nothing to search.

I watched Jaz walk back down the aisle to the last row, where she intentionally counted three cushions in and sat down, cross-legged, on the fourth one. She closed her eyes and I watched her face transform from its anxious look to one of peace and calm. I envied her, but sat quietly and waited. Maybe an angel would tell her what to do next.

I've always been too impatient to meditate successfully. When I found myself counting the cushions just for something to do, I decided it was time to get up and move around.

Standing up, I stretched out my arms and turned around to look behind me. I assumed the cushion on the dais was where The High One sat and noticed how worn its cover was. Looking out at the rest of the cushions I discovered you could tell that some of The Circle of Light members had been at this for a long time, while others were novices. Some of the cushions had deep indentations and worn spots from hours of rubbing against devoted knees and butts. After watching Jaz go to a specific spot, I wondered if each person owned his or her cushion and brought it with them. Apparently, there was a seating plan of some kind.

I started pacing around the dais, walked over to the pulpit and leaned on it. Golden light streaming down from one of the windows reflected off the brass gong. I fought against an overwhelming impulse to grab the mallet hanging next to it and whack the shimmering disk as hard as I could.

Jaz must've been reading my mind. I heard her call out, "Guess you wanna go, huh?"

"Yeah, well . . . I do, but I hate giving up." I grasped at one last straw. "Is that your personal cushion you're sitting on?"

"Yep." She got up and walked towards me.

"Does everyone else have a place they're supposed to sit in?"

"Yeah." Jaz began pointing. "The High One's up there. Then the elders from the California circle get to sit up front because that's the biggest. And then you work your way back in order of importance. That's why I'm way down there," she said, indicating her spot with a jerk of her head.

"So Mike and Adam and Patricia and Bruno and all those guys are up here? Which one belongs to Charles?"

By this time, Jaz had reached the front and walked over to a well worn cushion in the front row. "This is it," she said.

Finally, something belonging to Charles that hadn't been taken away. "So he would've been sitting here the entire week?"

"Right."

Remembering what Jaz told me about Charles being secretive, I picked up the cushion and looked underneath. Nothing. Guess that was really grasping at straws. Seeing that the cushion cover was removable, I unzipped it and felt around inside.

Jaz clapped her hand over her mouth. "No. Wait a minute. Charles became The High One . . . at least for a few hours before he was murdered." She pointed to the dais. "He would've moved up there."

I replaced the cushion and moved over to The High One's spot. I checked underneath, unzipped the cover and slide my hand inside. Bingo. To my amazement, I pulled out several index cards.

"What's that?" Jaz stared at the cards, eyes wide.

"Looks like lists of some sort."

"I told you that's what he did."

The cards were filled with rows of initials and brief notations scrawled in some sort of shorthand beside them. I held the cards out to Jaz and asked, "Is this Charles' handwriting?"

"Yeah, that's him."

"What about these initials? Do they mean anything to you?"

She studied the first card for just a few seconds. "It's a list of all the elders."

"Oh? That's interesting. What's written beside each name?"

"I don't know." She shook her head. "This is some new system he's developed. I recognize some words but I'd have to

176

study it to see if I can make sense out of it."

Someone shouted, "Hey, you two. What're you doing in here?"

We both turned and looked down the long center aisle towards the entrance. Adam George, decked out in safron-orange, started walking up towards us. A set of gold wings glittered at his earlobe and I could hear the jingle of his heavy silver bracelets. I instinctively shoved the cards into my shoulder bag.

Jaz answered in a voice that was way too chirpy. "Oh, nothing. I was giving Katie a tour. She's never been in here before."

Adam frowned.

"Is there a problem?" Jaz asked.

Adam looked at me and back at her. "Have you seen Lowell anywhere?"

I piped up. "We saw him go into the conference center about fifteen minutes ago."

Adam twisted his mouth in disgust. "He never came back to the meeting. That guy's going to drive me crazy." He started to leave, but stopped and turned. "Jasmine, I think they need you in the kitchen. And Kate, I'd be more than happy to give you an official tour after lunch. Why don't you stay and eat with us?"

My mind quickly sorted through my Excuse File and came up with a truthful one. "Thanks, but I have to get back to my kitchen—can't leave my assistant doing all the work."

It seemed Adam wanted to play doorman.

I said, "Guess I better go, Jaz. We can finish our talk later." We walked down the center aisle, past Adam, and out of the meditation hall, letting him shut the door behind us.

From there, Adam went off in one direction in search of Lowell, and we headed to the parking lot. When I was sure we were out of earshot, I reached into my bag to pull out the cards. "Do you want to hold onto these and try to decipher them?"

Jaz placed her hand on mine, keeping me from taking the cards out. "No, no," she said, with a nervous shake of her head, "you hold on to them. I don't want anyone catching me with something like that."

"But you have to look at them. Why don't you come to my place tomorrow and we'll go over this stuff."

Someone called out from the kitchen window at the back of the conference center. "Jasmine!"

Jaz waved without looking. "Coming, coming. Katie, I've got to put in my appearances here. I'm gonna get into a lot of trouble with The Circle if I keep leaving the grounds."

"You want me to come back tomorrow morning? That's the first chance I'll get."

"Okay, great. If you can, Katie, take a look at those cards. Maybe you'll be able to figure them out." Jaz gave me a quick hug. "Thanks. Love you." She ran off across the parking lot towards the kitchen door.

AS I DROVE HOME, I could almost hear the cards in my shoulder bag shouting at me to hand them over to the police. "We're evidence," they yelled.

I wondered what kind of trouble I'd get into with Matt Skinner for not turning the cards in. Probably a lot. And of course I was going to hand them over. I just wanted Jaz and I to have a good look at them first.

On Route 126, I decided to bypass my turnoff to home and continued until I reached Loveland-Madeira Road. Going home this way I could stop at the Mailbox Place and make photocopies of the cards—then I'd turn them in. I didn't think there was any law against that. Besides, Matt Skinner would never know I had the copies. That raised a curious point: how is it that Jaz and I stumbled across what looks like important evidence while the police failed to find it? Of course, I didn't know what Skinner had found in Charles' room. Maybe the police didn't need any more evidence, or maybe they didn't know that the meditation cushions were personal possessions.

I made a left hand turn into the parking lot of the Loveland Towncenter Mall and drove past the free-standing red brick building with the giant gold crown on the rooftop. It was noon on a weekday and Crown Chili is a popular lunch place for the local workers, so the parking spots were filling up fast.

I parked close to the Mailbox Place and went in. One of the two copy machines was down and I had to wait for an elderly gentleman to slowly and carefully photocopy his tattered music scores. I pulled out the cards and gazed at them without any understanding of the information they contained.

The first set of initials on the top card was LL, and I assumed that meant Lowell Lindsay. What was the significance of the incense burner? The police had left it behind, but Lowell appeared to have gone into Charles' room specifically to get it. Lowell was such a simple soul. It was possible there wasn't anything too devious about his motive. He could've taken it just because he liked it.

"It's all yours, Miss," the elderly gentleman said, shoving the yellowing music score into a worn, leather briefcase.

I quickly copied both sides of the five mysterious index cards and went to pay the cute, young man at the counter. My stomach roared with such a sudden hunger, it startled the poor guy, who quickly recovered and said, "Sounds like it's an emergency. There's a Crown Chili parlor over there."

I said, "Thank you," fished around in my shoulder bag, and handed him a few coupons that startled him again.

"Free Crown Chili Coneys? How come?"

"For sending your customers over to my place."

EATING AT ONE of my family's fifty-plus chili parlors is something I rarely do, for two reasons. One, they are usually crowded. Two, I scare the staff whenever I show up. They know

179

what I look like and always think I'm on some impromptu inspection.

Sure enough, as soon as I walked in, the middle-aged woman cashier who was in the middle of saying, "Have a nice day," to the previous customer, saw me and froze in terror.

She swallowed hard and said in a very loud voice, "Hello, Ms. Cavanaugh." Her face was half-turned to the man ladling chili on top of spaghetti at the work station behind her. He—and it felt like everyone else in the restaurant—stared up at me.

I smiled and my stomach grumbled. I wanted to say, "Hand over a Coney. *Now!*" But instead I waved away their efforts to serve me first, and said, "I won't die. I can wait."

It must be handy being able to meditate, to push away reality for a few minutes and enter some blissful state whenever you wanted. I thought about the meditation hall and tried to picture hundreds of people sitting on their cushions. The room would be absolutely quiet, but were they sometimes sitting there thinking earthly thoughts? How could Charles still his mind when he was sitting on top of his secret notes about the other elders?

Yet another question popped into my head. Why was Charles', and not Lowell's, cushion still up on the dais? I guessed with all the problems the elders had to contend with caused by Charles' murder, switching the cushions around wasn't at the top of the list. Probably no-one thought of it. Of course, it was possible that when Lowell was reinstated as High One, he just decided to take Charles' cushion 'cause he liked it. Same as the incense burner. But I was wasting a lot of mental energy doing all this supposing.

I got a couple of Coneys, paid for them, and found an empty table by the front window. I set my tray down on the paper place mat with the official Crown Chili punch out crown. The first chili dog couldn't get into my mouth fast enough.

Once the rumbling in my belly died down, out came the photocopies and I placed them on the table far enough from me so they were out of range of splattering sauce. Checking all the initials, I saw that Jaz's weren't listed. That was one less connection between Jaz and Charles to worry about. I began nibbling on my second Coney.

A lot of the initials didn't mean anything to me, but I figured out the ones belonging to Adam George, Patricia Ebbes, Lowell Lindsay, Mike Dyer, and Bruno Marcello.

The information beside them looked like some kind of speed writing. Next to what I figured were Adam George's initials were the letters NO RCRT-OUT.

It didn't make any sense.

Running my finger down the list and stopping at PE for Patricia Ebbes, I read NO DEH-SPEV CORD.

A little knocking on the window beside my head made me look up. Grinning at me and doffing his Smokey Bear hat was Matt Skinner. I switched on my inherited Cavanaugh smile—an all-purpose, but meaningless flash of my pearly whites.

Skinner was definitely in a friendly mood. He waved at me as though he were happy to see me, came into the restaurant and joined the short line at the order counter. I knew I was going to hand over Charles' cards, but I didn't want to jump right into business. The photocopies went back into my shoulder bag.

The Crown Chili workers were on their toes that day and had his order up in a couple of minutes. I'm sure it had nothing to do with my presence. Anyway, the next thing I knew, Skinner was at my table, tray in hand. "Mind if I join you?"

I waved an open hand at the seat across from me.

Skinner hung his hat on a wall hook right under the *We are not responsible for lost items* sign and sat down.

I said, "I thought you ate here only on Sundays for a treat? Something about your cholesterol being too high?"

"Did I say that?" Skinner raised the first of two Coneys to his mouth. "Well, that was before Christmas. Diet and exercise weren't enough. Now the doc's got me on cholesterol lowering drugs—numbers dropped way down and I can eat what I want. Sort of." He bit into the cheese-and-chili-laden hot dog. I marveled at how neatly he could eat such a messy concoction, and gazed at the puddles of sauce on my own plate and tray.

Skinner wiped his mouth with a napkin and I admired his clean, neatly trimmed fingernails. He said, "And so Clairmont is getting to meet another of your unusual friends."

"Jaz? Oh, she's spending most of her time at Golden Valley."

"Yeah. I'm curious about something. I hear you've traveled to a lot of eastern countries, so how come you're not involved in one of these spiritual groups? Isn't that why you make that kind of trip?"

"Not necessarily. In my case, it was just plan old curiosity and a need for adventure." I looked down and inspected my mangled chef's fingernails. "Guess I'm more of an observer than a joiner."

I couldn't tell if Skinner was interested in me or if he was still on the job and this line of questioning was just another example of his disarming style of interrogation. I didn't know what kind of information he had on Jaz or—more importantly—on her relationship with Charles, so I dug my heels in. Didn't want to be swept away by his charms.

I started my own little interrogation. "What about you? The other day you mentioned something about Zen Masters. Sounds like you've some knowledge of spiritual disciplines yourself."

Skinner swallowed the last bit of chili dog and laughed. "You asking me about my college days? I read a lot of books."

An awkward silence followed. I was expecting him to reveal more, but it became apparent we were both overly cautious when it came to talking about ourselves.

Steering the conversation in a different direction, but one that was probably going to be just as touchy, I asked, "So, when you're gathering evidence, what are you looking for?"

Skinner's eyes brightened noticeably. "Oh, clothing, personal papers, books—very generally, I'm looking for anything that will tell me what happened to the victim."

"So in a murder investigation, do you always confiscate the victim's possessions?"

"Not always, but any time I think it's relevant."

Here was my chance to make sure there were others on the suspect list besides Jaz. "Why didn't you take Charles' incense burner?"

"Because I know that it was just that—an incense burner. Nothing mysterious about it. I'm not going to take items that I can confidently say have nothing to do with a person's murder." Skinner stopped suddenly and stared at me. "How do you know I left the incense burner? You doing your own investigation?"

"Jaz and I just happened to be around when we saw Lowell Lindsay go out of Charles' room, stuffing an incense burner into the pocket of his robe. Must have some importance to him."

Skinner's lips were clamped tight, and I could see a muscle on the side of his face twitch. "Okay. We'll talk to him."

I really wanted to hand over the cards, but it was bad timing. Then again, would there ever be a good time? Rechecking my priorities, I concluded it was more important to help my friend than try to work on my love life.

Mentally kissing off the fragile beginnings of our relationship, I dug out the cards and handed them over to Skinner.

"What's this?" Skinner wiped his fingers with his napkin and took the cards from me.

"Jaz and I found these hidden in Charles' meditation cushion. They're in his handwriting."

"Where was this cushion?"

"In the meditation hall with everybody else's."

"You looked through all of them?"

"No. Everyone has their own and they each have a spot to sit in."

"Oh, is that right? Why would you do that? Were you looking

183

for something specific?"

"No. But you'd already taken everything out of his room, so we went to see if you took his cushion, too." That wasn't exactly the truth, but it was close enough.

Skinner kept his eyes focused on the cards, but I could see his jaw tighten even more. I could almost hear him cursing in his head. Out loud he said, "You should have left them as you found them and just told us about it." He twisted his lips to one side. "Do you also happen to know what these notes say?"

"Jaz says it's a list of the elder's initials, but she didn't get a chance to study the shorthand notations beside them. You might want to show them to her. Maybe she can figure it out."

Skinner looked at me, keeping his face expressionless. "Yes. Well. Thank you for your expert advice, Ms. Cavanaugh. We'll check the handwriting on these." He got up and put on his hat. "Stay out of trouble."

24

I WAS STANDING AT THE STOVE, holding a yellow pepper over the gas flame with a pair of tongs. In a stainless steel hotel pan were orange, yellow, and red peppers, their skins already blistered and ready to be peeled. I couldn't let Tony do all the work himself, so I was helping him put together the sandwich trays for the Italian stag party that night.

My mind drifted back a few hours to lunch. Boy, Skinner sure is touchy. Quick to change moods. Warm and smiling one minute, with his I-think-you're-attractive manner, but show him I'm not some huge wallflower and *click!* those eyes become cold ice picks. Hell, if I hadn't found those cards, he sure wouldn't know of them or even suspect they existed. Burns my buns. My nose tickled with the smell of something burning.

"Hey, Boss," Tony yelled from the other side of the kitchen. "I think it's done."

I snapped back to attention and pulled the tongs away from the flame. The once perfectly-shaped, healthy pepper was charred and crispy—suitable only for the garbage dump. Just like my love life.

The phone rang.

I was closer than Tony, so I went over and picked it up, answering "'Round the World Catering," as I carried it with me back to the stove.

"Kate? This is Cindy."

"Cindy Hoseyni who hasn't had her honeymoon yet?"

"That's the one."

"I've been wondering about you. How're you doing?"

"I'm holding up, but everything else seems to be falling apart around me. Have the police been hassling you? They've been here a couple of times already and Ali is fit to be tied."

"Why? What are they asking? You really didn't know Brad that well. Did you?"

"I guess not, but we're getting to know him a lot better, now that he's dead. Seems Brad was doing drugs at the reception—"

I held my breath, expecting Cindy to say the police told her I caught him in Ali's bathroom.

"—at least that's what some informant told them. And that was confirmed by the autopsy."

I started breathing again. "You had no idea Brad was into drugs? You worked with him pretty closely on that flower show project."

"He seemed okay to me—I guess I don't have much experience with people on drugs. I figured Brad was a creative type and if he acted a little crazy now and then, that was part of his personality. Ha!" It was a nervous laugh, but I heard her customary snort tagged on the end.

"I've been wondering how you and Ali are getting along. The last time we spoke, you admitted you weren't ready for a romantic week in Paris."

"Well, Ali's been stomping around the house, furious with everybody but me. Seems his anger is directed at TC now. I heard them a couple of times, shouting at each other about drugs. I don't know what that's all about, and I know I can't ask. It's business between brothers and no women are allowed to butt in."

That marriage is doomed, I thought, picking up another pepper with the tongs and rolling it in the flames. "So, is everything going to be okay between you and Ali?"

"Seems so. It's going to take time to adjust to this marriage, but I know he loves me. We'll get to Paris some day. I just wanted to touch base with you and I wanted to tell you again, even with all the things that went wrong, you put together a wonderful wedding reception. Ali's family was very impressed. Thanks, Kate. I knew I could count on you."

"I'm glad to hear you say that. It wasn't exactly the smoothest running event of my career."

I told her to come to see me at JJ's Taste of Cincinnati booth if she happened to be there, and we said our goodbyes.

* * * * * * *

"CAN I FRESHEN that up for you?"

I pushed my glass of bottled water to the edge of the bar and let Dino fill it up again. He stuck a paper parasol into a maraschino cherry and plopped it into my "drink."

"Just trying to make it a little more festive," Dino said with a grin.

For an hour, I'd watched him work his bar, pulling draft beer from spigots into large pitchers, knowing exactly where to reach for a bottle and splashing just the right amount of liquor into glasses, then choosing some colored twist of peel or maybe an olive or cherry from his tray of garnishes. All of this was done with the fluid movement of someone who looked like he was born to tend bar.

Dino nodded towards the food-laden table where the testosterone-rich guests swaggered, strutted, and jostled each other to get to the goodies. "Those guys are all animals. They don't deserve the good food you put together." The all-guy partyers shouted bawdy jokes and personal jibes at each other,

187

but mostly at the groom-to-be, while piling their plates with huge helpings from every tray. They had to shout to be heard above the earsplitting decibel level of the Hits of the Eighties emanating from the jukebox in the corner.

I took a swig of water, popped the cherry in my mouth, and twirled the parasol. "Everybody deserves good food and, by the way, Tony did most of the work. Make sure you get some before they devour it."

Swiveling around on the bar stool, I took in the dark, smokey ambience of Bambino's Bar. I had no idea where we were. Tony drove the van, since we were traveling to the west side of Cincinnati and he knew the streets a lot better than I did.

It was fun watching Tony on his own turf, shooting pool and kibitzing with his buddies. Guess he felt like a fish out of water in Clairmont.

Speaking of fish, I was still waiting for the arrival of that small fry of a hood, Frankie Alberto. The whole purpose of my being at this bachelor's party was to have a chance to talk to him. Tony said his cousin Carlo, who "owes me a few favors", had promised to arrange for Frankie's appearance.

The front door opened and a clone of Dino walked in, lugging a few cases of beer. I instinctively turned to check that he was still behind the bar.

Dino laughed. "Everybody reacts the same way the first time they meet me and my brother Nino. They always think they've drunk too much. You're not seeing double."

Nino went behind the bar and dropped his load of beer. The sight of the two Bambino brothers standing side by side was a little disconcerting. The only way I could tell them apart in the dim lighting was by remembering that Dino wore a vest made out of some fabric with a silvery snake skin print.

I was so transfixed by the two that I almost missed Frankie Alberto's entrance and turned, just in time to see Carlo lead him past me. I wiggled my fingers in a little wave. Frankie's mouth

188

fell open when he saw me, and he jerked his head around a couple of times to check me out as Carlo pulled him towards a group at the pool table. Frankie shook hands with the groom-to-be.

They were too far away for me to hear their conversation, but it appeared Carlo next introduced Frankie to Tony, then led Frankie to the buffet table and invited him to help himself. All the while, Frankie kept sneaking sidelong looks at me. Carlo, playing the gracious host, guided Frankie to a booth on the quieter side of the room where Tony was now waiting.

A short conversation took place with Frankie doing all the listening and hardly any eating. I waited. A few minutes later, Tony waved. That was my cue. I picked up my "drink," minus the parasol, and sauntered over to the booth.

Frankie was essentially penned in. Carlo had moved across to his side of the table, forcing Frankie to squeeze up against the wall. I slide into the seat next to Tony.

"How's the food?" I said, staring diagonally across the table into Frankie's eyes. "Not hungry?"

"I—I—" Frankie's voice caught in his throat. He swallowed a couple of times and took a swig of beer to clear it. "I didn't know you were connected to these guys," he said, nodding at Carlo and Tony.

"You mean you wouldn't have accused me of murder if you did?"

Frankie raised his hands defensively. "Hey, lady. I didn't accuse you of knocking off that jerk."

"Jerk? Thought you said Brad Holtmann was a cool guy, lots of laughs?"

"He was. Then he became a jerk, but I wasn't going to tell the cops that's how I felt about him."

Why not? He was. I said out loud, "Let's cut all this preliminary chit-chat. We both know you didn't actually come into Brad's studio and see me standing over his body. My dog

189

would have been barking and yapping like crazy if you did. He loves people, strangers in particular, and tells them so whenever he can. In fact," I leaned forward, "we also both know you were in there before I got anywhere near the place."

Frankie looked down at the plate of food in front of him, his lips twisting back and forth as if chewing over his options. He lost another couple inches of his comfort zone as Carlo shifted a little in his seat and forced Frankie to squeeze tighter up against the wall.

Frankie's decision was made for him. "Okay, look. It's like this. I've had trouble with the cops before and I done my time—twice—and don't want to go back in for a third time. That Brad was into heavy stuff and when I found out what he was doing I decided to get the hell out. Last thing I wanted was my name connected with drug dealing."

So Brad the Stick man was not just a recreational drug user.

Frankie continued. "Worse thing is when a dealer starts overindulging in his own product and gets sloppy. I knew one of these days he'd mess up and I didn't want to be sitting there when the cops came barging in."

"You mean Brad was dealing out of his studio just down the block from the police station?" He couldn't have been that dumb.

"No, no. I never saw drugs in that place. But I never saw drugs in the old place, I just heard conversations and a lot of money flying around, but never knew who he was doing business with. I could see all the signs. He probably used drug money to fix up the new studio."

"Why didn't you just tell the police that?"

"Lady, you don't know how the world operates. Whoever was in on this with him would probably put a hole in the back of my head, too."

A snapshot of Brad's oozing head wound flashed in my mind. "So you got close enough to see he was shot in the back of the head. You still haven't answered why you were there. If you didn't want to be connected with him anymore, what were you doing there at six o'clock on a Sunday morning?"

"Well," Frankie shrugged and began drumming his fingers on the table, "I wasn't expecting anyone to be there and so I figured it was the best time to get into the computer and delete my employee file. That's the only reason I stuck around the last couple of weeks helping Brad move into the place—I wanted to have access to the computer. If I'd quit, I had to give Brad back my studio keys."

"What's the big deal about being one of his employees?"

"Like I said, lady, he was getting sloppy and I've seen him use people to protect himself. He could've messed up my life big time and he knew I already had a prison record. Wouldn't put it past him to plant evidence against me if the cops started sniffing around. I just wanted out."

He couldn't be that dense. "Just deleting your name from the employee files wasn't going to keep people from knowing you had worked for him. You must've been filing taxes, and there are government records all over the place that you can't delete."

Frankie was that dense. In his eyes I saw a twenty-five watt bulb switch on. Tony gave my leg a playful kick, Carlo smirked and looked up at the ceiling.

Frankie quickly covered himself with his macho I'm-still-in-control attitude. "Well. That was no big deal. It was only supposed to take five minutes. I wasn't expecting to find anybody there—living or dead."

"So, when you saw the body, what happened? You panicked?" I still had a vivid picture of him running away from the storefront.

"No. There was no panic. I just move fast when I have to."

Yeah, and make some pretty stupid snap decisions on the run. "What made you go to the police?"

"When I reached the end of the block, I turned the corner and saw you and your dog walking across the street towards the

191

studio. I figured you'd seen me run outta there. Okay, I say to myself, I can't say I never worked for the guy, and I knew you'd go to the cops and describe me to them. And I knew they had a file on me, so I decided to be the loyal jerk coming in to work."

"Why'd you lie about seeing me standing over the body?"

"Just to get the attention off of me. Your word against mine, lady." Frankie turned to Carlo and Tony. "Look, guys, I've told her everything that happened. What more do you want?"

Tony asked, "Anything else, Kate?"

There were a few things. "Frankie, who is Big Gabe?"

His face scrunched. "Big Gabe?" He laughed. "Where'd you get that name from? Some Godfather movie?"

"Never heard that name mentioned around the studio?"

Frankie shook his head.

"Okay, what about seeing an emerald green car? A four door sedan? Did any of Brad's friends or clients drive one?"

Frankie shook his head again.

I wasn't too surprised that he didn't have any answers for me—I wasn't sure I could trust anything he told me anyway. But I had one last question. "Did Brad talk about angels? Or The Circle of Light?"

"Ha! Ha! Ha! Angels? You mean that stupid pin he wore all the time? I never did know what that was all about. He never talked about it or mentioned anything."

"Well, what kinds of things would you hear Brad talking about? You said you knew he was dealing because you heard conversations. Who was he talking to?"

"He'd be on the phone talking about shipments and money and things. None of it had to do with the studio, just general talk. But you can tell. You know, the tone of voice and everything a big secret like he's talking in code. Oh, yeah. I remember a couple of times him saying—yeah, just last week—he told someone, 'The flying carpet has landed.' "

25

Friday, May 23rd

I WOKE UP THE NEXT DAY after an all-night marathon dreaming of objects with wings: angels, horses, dark scary things chasing after me, even winged pigs like the ones adorning the entrance to Bicentennial Commons down by the Ohio River. But the scariest image was of a flying carpet with a dark skinned, white-tuxedoed man sitting cross-legged on it. I could only assume it was Ali Hoseyni.

What else could I think? The connection was made and it seemed to fit. A major portion of Ali's business was importing carpets. Maybe that wasn't all he was importing. He lived in the wealthiest part of Clairmont, and I wondered if you could make that much money selling carpets and furniture. There weren't a lot of people in the Cincinnati area who could afford his prices.

But Ali was always ranting about the decadent American culture, complaining that his employees were always coming to work stoned out of their minds. Maybe all that talk was just a cover-up. As I witnessed at his wedding reception, Ali was very adept at switching from anger to amiable civility when the situation called for it. I wondered if anyone, Cindy included, knew the real Ali. Sometimes when people try to convince you they're something other than what they really are, they overdo the act.

Maybe, in this case, Ali's anger wasn't because of Brad's drunkenness at the wedding reception. Could be Ali knew Brad was sampling too much of the "merchandise" and, as Frankie Alberto told me, saw he was "getting sloppy."

In any situation, sloppiness would enrage Ali Hoseyni.

Now I wished I didn't believe so much in my dreams and their messages. I didn't like what this one seemed to be telling me.

Tossing and turning this latest message around in my brain, I sat at the breakfast table and gazed out the bay window at the steady downpour. Boo-Kat was on guard at his usual spot in front of the center window, staring at some imagined varmint hiding in the flower bed. No meditative walk for us this morning.

Phoebe Jo's leftover corn pones with syrup poured over the top brightened the morning a little. I abandoned the dream trail and was starting to go down the road laid out by Charles Sutcliff's cryptic cards when the phone rang.

"Kate? You up? It's JJ."

"Of course I'm up. I answered the phone, didn't I?"

"It's raining."

"Yeah."

"They say it might rain all weekend. I wished I'd never agreed to do this dumb Taste thing."

I swallowed a mouthful of coffee. "JJ, you know it almost always rains on the Taste, but people come anyway. Besides, weather forecasters are usually wrong."

"I just wanted to make sure you're still going to stand in for my cook."

I didn't realize JJ was such a worrywart. "Don't worry, of course I'm going to do it . . . even if it rains. Tony will fill in for me on Monday. Unfortunately, I've got another job to do that day." Mother's I-Hate-Pink-Flamingos Memorial Day Barbecue.

"I really appreciate it, Kate. It'll be easy—just ribs and sweet potato fries. I'll be there handling the dessert and three or four of my wait staff will take care of the customers."

"Sounds good. What time do you want me there tomorrow morning?"

"Eleven-thirty?"

"Okay, no problem." We said our goodbyes and I added, "Don't worry, it'll be fun." Seeing hundreds of thousands of happy people wandering around, sampling all kinds of food, was my idea of a positive spiritual experience. I figured it would be a break from the darkness of drugs, doomsday cults, and murder.

Sometimes I figure wrong.

26

ONE THING I'VE ALWAYS hated about living here in Clairmont is the rain. There is no such thing as a gentle shower. No Gene Kelly-ish dancin' and singin' and twirlin' your umbrella in this neck of the woods. The storms are of biblical proportions and you better be ready to start dodging lightning bolts and tornados.

I pulled on a hooded jacket, ran out into the heavy downpour, and jumped into my Jeep. Photocopies of Charles' notes were safely stuffed in my pocket and I was anxious for Jaz to take a look at them. After coming home from the bachelor party, I had tried to decipher Charles' notations but couldn't make any sense of them.

Cursing the rain, I splashed through the muddy ruts in my laneway and pulled out onto the highway.

It must've been raining heavily all night. The Little Miami River was raging well above flood stage, and tree branches and big chunks of garbage were shooting past, just a foot below the bridge, in a wild rush to get downstream to the mighty Ohio. I hoped by the time I came back later the road wasn't flooded over. If it was, I was in trouble—I hadn't started building my ark yet.

My brain felt like mush. Snippets of my conversation with Frankie Alberto were getting all mixed up with flashes from the flying carpet dream and I was having extreme difficulty focusing away from that train of thought. I needed to switch tracks and concentrate on the murder of Charles Sutcliff. Maybe the clues to the identity of his killer where sitting right there on the photocopied lists in my pocket.

Even though, at first glance, the two murders appeared to be very separate events, each in its own different world, I knew somewhere and somehow they were going to connect. And I was sure it would be Brad's Circle of Light trinket that finally pinned them together.

The windshield wipers were useless. It was a good thing I knew the roads as well as I did. Every muscle in my upper body was tensed as I tried to peer through the curtain of water I was driving through.

"Yuck!" The road leading up to the Golden Valley Spiritual Center was in worse shape than the laneway on my farm. The right wheel of my Jeep plunged into a huge pothole, sending a small tidal wave of muddy water five feet straight up into the air. The jolt rattled my teeth, and I hoped my axle wasn't damaged. I hate this weather.

I bumped and slipped my way up the road that would soon be no more than a mud slide, and started looking for a parking spot close to the conference hall.

I went down one row of parked cars and, on my way up the second row, noticed someone opening up the trunk of a car and looking inside.

I slammed on the brakes and stared in disbelief.

It was like a spotlight had cut through the torrential downpour and isolated the car with a bright glow.

An emerald green glow.

It was the same car I'd seen outside of Brad Holtmann's studio that Saturday morning before he was killed.

But who was that, jacket pulled over their head, rummaging around in the trunk? It was a Circle of Light member—I could see long legs in white pants.

The person must have heard my Jeep idling, because whoever it was turned towards me and waved. I scrunched my eyes, trying to see through the rain. Whose face was under the dripping wet jacket?

The person retrieved something, slammed down the trunk of the car, turned and came a few steps towards me. My stomach tightened into a little knot. I knew I hadn't breathed in a while, so I took a few shallow breaths and stared hard at the approaching figure. Now I could see it was a man.

He waved again, friendly and smiling.

He lifted the coat away from his face, and I lip-read, "Hi, Kate."

It was Adam George.

I was stunned, but I still managed to slap on my Cavanaugh smile and wave back at him.

Adam pulled his coat back over his head and ran into the conference center.

I just sat there in my Jeep not knowing what to do, my mushy brain jumping back and forth between the Brad and Charles tracks. There was a possibility the car wasn't Adam's. I tried to replay the argument I overheard in Brad's studio and match up one of the voices to Adam. But all I could remember was they sounded angry.

A streak of lightning shot across the sky, followed by an enormous clap of thunder. What the hell was I doing out here?

I know they say sitting in your car is the safest place to be in a thunder storm, but I wasn't going to solve any murders doing so. Up ahead was a parking spot—not as close to the conference center as I wanted it to be—but this was not the time to engage in my usual habit of exploring parking lots until I found the perfect spot.

I pulled in, cursed the rain once more, and tore across the stretch of gravel and gray muck to the kitchen door of the conference center. Not bothering with any courteous knock, I pushed through the screen door, startling the volunteers who were busy prepping for what I assumed to be some incredibly healthy meal.

"Hi, Katie. What an entrance," Jaz called out from the other end of the kitchen. She was chopping something green and leafy.

I pulled off my hood and stood in the entrance for a few seconds, waiting for all the water to drip off my jacket. Didn't want to create a hazardous situation by leaving puddles along the tile floor as I walked through the kitchen.

Jaz laid her knife down. "I can take my break now. Do you want me to come over there or shall we shout at each other?"

"I'm coming," I said, taking off my jacket and rolling it up. I was happy to see the bruise on her face was healing—just a few tinges of yellow around the eye. There didn't appear to be any new ones.

Jaz grabbed my arm and steered me out of the kitchen, across the main hall where Circle of Light members were gathering, and into one of the small side rooms. It really wasn't a room—more like an alcove with a pulled out accordion door separating it from the main hall. It wasn't sound proofed and I could clearly hear conversations coming from the other side.

I asked, "How are you doing?"

"Oh, Katie." Jaz sighed noisily, held her head in both hands, and stuck her tongue out. "I don't know how you can stand working in a kitchen all day long. I'm so sick of chopping, I wanna go home."

As usual, Jaz seemed unable to give a direct answer. I tried again. "How's Mike? You two doing okay?"

"Yeah." Jaz gave a little shrug of her shoulders, as if to say "no problem." She continued. "He's so preoccupied with all that's happened, it's been easy to stay out of each other's hair.

We're still sharing the same bed, but we're not sleeping together, if you know what I mean."

I knew very well what she meant. But I still wouldn't curl up next to a snake, no matter how preoccupied it was.

Shifting the topic of conversation from one slime bucket to another, I asked, "Does Adam George drive a green car?"

Jaz frowned. "Huh? . . . yeah . . . an ugly Saint Patrick's green. Why?"

I wanted to keep my suspicions to myself until I had more concrete evidence, so I white-lied, "Just wanted to know who waved at me out there in that deluge."

"Did you get a chance to look at those cards?"

"Yeah," I said, unrolling my jacket, "but first I photocopied them. The cops have the actual cards."

Jaz's mouth dropped. "What? How did that happen?"

I quickly related my lunchtime conversation with Matt Skinner and said, "We want the person who murdered Charles to be caught, right? It doesn't matter who solves the case."

Jaz nodded and reached out. "Let me see those copies. They won't know what they're looking at."

I handed over the slightly damp and crumpled pages. "I figured out some of the elders' initials, but the entries beside them are unintelligible to me.

Jaz studied the papers, frowning slightly. After a few seconds, she said, "Oh. I get the drift of this. I've typed up stuff for The Circle before, using these abbreviations for job titles."

She pointed to Adam George's initials. "See? This notation NO RCRT means 'no recruit' and OUT means just that, I guess."

"He was going to kick him out?"

"Looks like it."

I looked down the list and pointed. "There's Patricia Ebbes' initials next to NO DEH-SPEV CORD. What was his plan for her?"

"Ha! That's a good one. We all make jokes about how Patricia isn't reaping the benefits of dynamic energy healing. Obviously, Charles agreed and figured she'd be more of an asset to The Circle if she were behind the scenes."

"So what's SPEV CORD?"

"Special events coordinator. She'd be sitting in an office, talking on the phone most of the time, arranging things like this retreat."

"So Charles was planning to clean house and shift people around?"

"Looks like . . . yeah. Charles was always preaching about how we were veering off our spiritual path and turning The Circle of Light into some commercial venture. These elders have been in their present positions right from the start."

"I'd guess removing them from their little empires and putting them in charge of something they weren't familiar with would make them all dependent on Charles for leadership."

"Yeah, that sounds like his kind of planning."

"Why wouldn't they all just get up and leave?"

Jaz was quiet for a moment. "We've been inside The Circle for so many years, I don't think any of us knows how to function outside."

"If Charles had lived to see his plans go through, I bet there'd be some very unhappy people."

"Well, he was already upsetting a lot of the elders with his strict ideas about getting back to the fundamentals."

I thought of the political statement the killer had made by jamming the golden wing medallion into Charles' chest. "I think there's a case to be made that someone on this list was very upset about him being reelected as High One."

Charles was obviously keeping this list secret, so I wondered who found out about it? Or was there an outside chance his murder had nothing to do with any of this? I didn't have enough brain power to go off in tangents, searching for new possibilities.

It was enough of a challenge just focusing on what I had in hand.

I asked, "Who were the biggest headaches on this list?"

"Adam George," Jaz said without hesitation, "Head Recruiter also known as The Big Stud. He and Charles were always getting into loud arguments over his jerky, tasteless recruiting methods."

An image of an arrogant, good-looking Frenchman decked out in heavy, silver bracelets on both arms and ropes of silver hanging around his neck came to mind. "Remember that guy on the beach in India? He would charm his targets into thinking he was interested in them romantically. He'd always pick the youngest and most innocent types. They were so overwhelmed he'd chosen them, they'd join the cult just to be near him."

"Exactly," Jaz said, nodding her head vigorously, "that's exactly what Adam was doing as Head Recruiter. And Charles was furious that he didn't have the power to remove him."

"So . . . Adam's motive for murder is wanting to hold on to his position of power? I don't know . . . " That didn't explain why he was arguing with Brad Holtmann. If it was him.

Then again, as Head Recruiter Adam probably would've known Brad in California. If so, why did Adam lie when I asked if he had ever heard of him? Could this be what I was looking for to connect the two murders?

I asked, "Who else created problems for Charles?"

"I guess you couldn't really call Patricia Ebbes a problem. She was more like an embarrassment to Charles, hanging around like some kinda pathetic, middle-aged groupie trying every way she could to climb into his bed. But he'd always turn her away and sometimes not very gently. Whenever she saw him talking to another woman, she'd barge in on the conversation hoping to grab his attention. Charles would get pissed off, and that seemed to make Pattycake try even harder the next time."

"She certainly appears to be an angry woman. Her eyes were shooting daggers at me for shaking hands with Charles at your Open House."

I recalled squatty Patricia's violent drum-banging dance. It was meant to be cathartic, but I think anger was her fuel and she kept going back to Charles for a refill. Maybe she finally got fed up with the service she was getting at the pump.

I asked, "Do you think Patricia would get angry enough to kill?"

Jaz was peeking around the edge of the accordion door, sounds from the main hall had attracted her attention. She turned back to me. "What did you say?"

I repeated the question.

"You think it was a crime of passion? A woman scorned?"

"At this point anything's possible. I'm just going down the list. How about Lowell Lindsay? There's just a question mark beside his initials."

"Hahaha. You funny girl. That man picks up bugs and moves them off the path so he won't step on them."

"Why did he go snooping around Charles' room and take his incense burner?"

Jaz shrugged. "Lowell does all sorts of things nobody understands. He's just a senile old man."

Who just so happens to have regained his position of power as The High One. I admitted it was supposed to be temporary until someone else was elected, but Lowell was back on the throne—or cushion.

I looked at Jaz's yellow-green rimmed eye. "I . . . I have to ask you this, Jaz. Just curious."

She stared back at me expectantly and started twirling one of her frizzy curls around her finger. "Okay. Shoot."

"What did Mike think of Charles? How did they get along?"

"Oh." Jaz waved my question away. "There was nothing much there. I never heard Mike complain about him, but I know Charles didn't like Mike. They ignored each other most of the time . . . probably because of me . . . I mean . . . well . . . Charles probably didn't like the way Mike treated me."

I was taken aback. I hadn't anticipated we'd be talking about that issue. I was thinking, maybe the usual politics and friction between two leaders, and had momentarily forgotten they both were part of Jaz's love life. But the most surprising thing was Jaz taking the first step to admitting she was physically abused by Mike the Snake. I wanted her to take another step forward into freedom from that dark pit of a relationship, but kept myself from reaching out to pull her. Knowing Jaz, if I forced the issue, she'd deny there even was a pit. I had to wait and just be there for her to come at her own pace.

The racket from the main hall had crescendoed to the point where it was intruding on our conversation. Obviously, the room had filled with more elders since we walked through, and it echoed with their excited chatter. Everyone had a lot to talk about. They were no longer on a quiet, meditative retreat.

The sound of a gong brought the hubbub to a sudden close.

Jaz's attention was drawn to the silence. "Oh, I better go," she whispered loudly, "they're going to have a meeting."

I grabbed her before she was able to pull the accordion door open. "No, stay with me. I want to hear this and I might need you to explain some things I won't understand."

Jaz bounced nervously. "I—I don't know . . . I'm supposed to be working in the kitchen . . . what if they find us here?"

I shrugged. "So? What's the worst that could happen? They tell us to leave. Don't let them control you."

Jaz stared at me and then at her feet for more than a few seconds. She pressed her lips together tight with determination, let go of the door, and stepped back.

I heard a low, monotonous drone start up. I raised my eyebrows and looked at Jaz.

"Circle meetings start with a chant," she whispered. "It's a prayer for wisdom."

I thought, that's a good beginning and hoped someone would grant me the same. I sure as hell didn't know what I was getting myself into.

The chanting went on for a minute or two until, I guess, Lowell Lindsay got a fresh message from some angel, because it was his voice I heard break into the chant.

"I've heard some talk amongst you that we have come to the end of our path. Do we no longer believe we are on an endless journey? And will our spirit guides no longer lead us through the chaos? Angelic voices still shatter the darkness, their anger will be for us the Way to Joy."

I scratched my head. Lowell had a way of making his words sound sensible, but for the life of me I couldn't tell you what they meant. Jaz was listening with rapt attention.

Lowell continued. "It is my duty now to call for an election of the new High One to lead us through the next two years. But before I do, we have yet to hear from a final elder, Bruno Marcello."

For some reason, I hear better when I can also see what's going on, so I moved over to the edge of the accordion door, slowly pulled it open a crack, and watched the gigantic Bruno walk to the front of the gathering.

"Yes! We are still on an endless journey," Bruno said in a loud and almost shouting voice, "but we are witnessing only the end of our earthly time. Some of us see where the spirits are guiding us and others do not. Charles did not, and that is why we are having to deal with this so-called chaos."

Jaz touched me on my arm. "He's saying Charles was not a true believer and that's why the angels did not protect him from death."

Bruno started pacing back and forth, twirling his string of worry beads. "This is only the beginning. Destructive forces are building and not all of us will survive. Only the true believers will be left after the final confrontation between the Hosts."

I looked at Jaz and mouthed, "Hosts?"

"Armies of angels," Jaz replied.

Bruno shouted, "And is that not our goal—to survive the final battle and evolve into the angelic beings we were destined to become. We will not be helpless victims of violence and mass destruction. Those of us who are truly on the path are from seeds that germinated and crawled up out of the muck, walked for a while on our two legs, and now await the final reincarnation of our spirits. Have we not been longing for this time? It is here and now."

This take on evolution—survival of the spiritually fittest—was a new one on me. Maybe Bruno thought he was getting angelic messages telling him to help the process of natural selection along by getting rid of Charles . . . maybe Brad, too?

I wasn't going to have anything else to go on in that direction, because Bruno brought his sermon to an end and sat down. Mike Dyer took his place.

Immediately after Mike's greeting, I turned to look at Jaz. She avoided my eyes and continued to stare at the floor and chew on a fingernail. Either Bruno's talk made her as uneasy as it did me or the sound of Mike's voice caused her anxiety.

Mike announced, "It's time for the election of the High One. Do we have any nominations from the floor?"

This was greeted by deafening silence—seemed nobody wanted the responsibility. Maybe they were afraid to put their spiritual fitness to the test. The job, after all, could be a killer.

Finally someone I didn't recognize, a woman sitting in the front row, shouted, "Bruno Marcello."

Several male voices immediately seconded it.

Bruno jumped up out of his chair and shook his head violently. "No, no. I am not worthy."

Mike asked, "Do you wish to withdraw your name?"

"Yes." He sat down amidst the chatter of a few disappointed supporters.

Jaz wiggled in under my arm so she could look through the crack and witness the proceedings for herself.

Adam George stood up and said, "I nominate Lowell Lindsay."

Patricia Ebbes, slumped beside him, got to her feet—I think—and in a high, squeaky voice said, "I second that."

Lowell Lindsay stared up at the ceiling, a serene smile on his face.

"We need some more names," Mike said, surveying the room.

There was another period of stubborn silence.

Finally, Mike walked to where Lowell stood. "All those in favor of Lowell Lindsay continuing as High One for the next two years, please signify 'yes' by standing."

Chair legs scraped across the floor as almost everyone in the room got to their feet.

Jaz looked up at me with an incredulous expression and whispered, "That doesn't make sense."

I stepped away from our peep hole. "Tell me why."

"For the past year, people have been complaining about Lowell being such a dimwit. They were looking to Charles for real leadership." Jaz stared at the accordion door as if she could see right through it. "And now with things in such a mess . . ." She turned back to me. "I don't think they know what they're doing."

Sounds of the meeting breaking up was our cue. I said, "Let's get out of here," and slowly pulled the door open. I looked out into the room. Nobody was facing our direction. People were standing around in groups, engaged in very focused discussions. They were probably making plans for the next two years—unless of course, the world came to an end first and all the little seeds sprouted wings and flew away. That would solve everything.

Jaz and I slipped out of our hiding place and walked along the edge of the crowd, towards the exit.

"Greetings, friends." Lowell Lindsay shuffled up to us.

Jaz and I stopped and said, "Hi," in unison.

Lowell reached for my hand and held it, his touch soft and warm. He craned his neck to look up at me and I noticed how thin and sunburned the skin on his forehead was. The man should wear a hat when he goes on his wanders.

Lowell asked, "Do you smell something?"

I sniffed the air. Jaz sniffed the air.

"No," I answered.

Lowell looked over my shoulder and up at the ceiling. "If there is stench in the air, somewhere there is a rotten egg."

27

IF IT WEREN'T FOR the fact the Health Department would shut me down, I'd just close the door on the mess Tony and I made that afternoon in the kitchen. By five o'clock we had platters of olive tapenade on crostini, a savory cheesecake with marinated artichoke hearts and sun-dried tomatoes, tiny biscuits with sliced turkey and mango chutney, vegetable chips with a garlicky sour cream dip, crab and potato balls, and mini tostadas ready for the Clairmont Business Association's monthly cocktail party. At least we didn't have to deliver. They sent someone to pick the stuff up.

It always amazes me how much energy it takes and what a huge mess you can make preparing hors d'oeuvres—little works of art that people pop into their mouths without thinking twice about them. I would rather prepare some impressive full course meal that would be in itself the topic of conversation, after the guests first pulled out their cameras and captured the moment for posterity.

What other kind of artist has to deal with the realization that her patrons will stuff her little masterpieces down their throats—usually without even looking at them first—only to flush it all down the toilet the next day?

Business is business, though, and hors d'oeuvres pay the bills.

I finally closed the door on a clean kitchen, grabbed the *Enquirer* off the table in the foyer, and tramped wearily up the stairs to my room. Unfolding the newspaper I read the headline *Murder Stirs Up Cincy's Rich and Powerful* and plopped down on the bed to read the full report.

As expected, the events at the Golden Valley Spiritual Center had given new fuel to the argument over the controversial use of such valuable real estate. One especially irate citizen, a CEO of a Fortune 500 corporation, was quoted as saying, "They're not the type of people we want here in Clairmont. Who knows what kind of weird voodoo they're practicing out there?"

Another equally irate and important resident added, "We told City Hall it would come to this and we don't even get any tax money out of them to clean up the mess."

The report ended with a quote from Clairmont Ranger Matt Skinner, who was in charge of the investigation. "It has only been two days since Mr. Sutcliff's body was found, and the Department is making the case its highest priority. We are getting full cooperation from the group presently staying at Golden Valley and are following all possible leads."

Yea, Matt. I tossed the paper aside and wondered how he was going about deciphering Charles' list. Maybe Matt was meeting with Lowell and sniffing around the grounds for rotten eggs.

I stripped off my kitchen clothes, which were decorated with samples of the afternoon's works of food art, unwrapped a bar of Chandrika soap, and stepped into the shower. The hot water felt good. I lathered up my body with the unusually scented, herbal soap, and wondered what kind of stench the not-so-loopy Lowell had been sniffing in the air earlier that morning.

I had just started to ask him what he meant, when Patricia Ebbes rushed up to us, shot me a look that said, "stay away," and hauled him off. I guess age or looks didn't matter to

Pattycake—could be she was simply attracted to power.

By that time, I was quite happy to leave. The rain had let up and at least I knew the world wasn't coming to an end by way of some great Biblical flood. On the other hand, there was Bruno's comic book version of the final days to look forward to. Remembering I'd picked up a booklet outlining some of The Circle's beliefs at the Open House, I decided it was time to do a little homework.

I turned off the shower, kicked Boo-Kat off the mat, and stepped out to towel myself off.

"Thanks, Boo. You're a big help," I said, as he licked the water off my ankles.

I threw on a silk kimono, combed through my hair, and went to get the booklet out of my shoulder bag. Rolling around in the bottom of my purse was the little glass bottle of "Fiery" Ayurvedic oil I had also purchased at the Open House. I reread the label. "Application of this oil provides inspiration, courage, and determination—most important for self-realization and growth."

Rubbing in the oil on my neck and forehead, I breathed in the warm, musky scent which stirred up something more primitive than inspiration and courage. This stuff was prepping me for a night of passion under a tropical moon and was wasted on my just going downstairs to eat dinner with the Boones.

I grabbed the booklet and curled up on the loveseat by my bedroom window. Bypassing the introductory pages describing how The Circle got started, I flipped through until I found the section describing the various classes and duties of angels.

There were beautifully rendered drawings of androgynous beings with steroid-pumped wings and flowing robes. Beside each drawing was a paragraph describing specific physical characteristics and the responsibilities of each class of angel. There were even long lists of names for the angels and I wondered, How do they know all this? Who made up all this stuff?

All of them looked fierce, except for the first one, The Healer. I read "The Healer's voice is easily recognized—always speaking to us in a warmer, higher-pitched voice than the other angels. Once summoned, Healer angels guide you to a more balanced path where the believer's energies are lined up in accordance with the vibrations of the harmonic center."

Following this was a chant written out phonetically that was supposed to be used in times of physical or mental imbalance to call forth such Healer angels.

Hmm, I wish I'd known this when I was diagnosed with breast cancer. It might've saved me the misery of twelve months of poisonous chemotherapy and having my boob whacked off. Then again, no time limits had been listed as to how long it took for a Healer to answer. For all I knew I could've died while on hold because there weren't enough of them to go around.

The section on Protectors showed a dramatic picture of one of these big-armed beings whisking some lucky believer out of the path of a runaway truck. The call for help chant looked long and complicated. By the time, you got it all out, the truck would've run over you and the angel would probably arrive just in time to pick up the pieces.

"Miss Kate?" Phoebe Jo's voice squawked out of my telephone's intercom across the room.

Putting the booklet down, I went over to the bedside table and picked up the receiver. "Yeah?"

"I got a nice vegetable stew and your favorite baked beans ready. We're sittin' down. You ready to join us?"

My stomach growled with hunger even at the thought of filling it with a lowfat, high-fiber, vegetarian meal. "Okay, thanks. Be right there."

I quickly skimmed over the parts about Messenger and Warrior angels, recognizing Bruno's favorite topic of conversation, and briefly admired the drawing of the giant being brandishing a sword and shield, ready for the final battle. The angels' teeth were clenched so tightly, it made my own jaw hurt just looking at them.

Thinking the Boones would probably get a kick out of seeing what New Agers had done with their angels, I brought the booklet downstairs with me after changing into a pair of baggy, drawstring pants and my favorite purple T-shirt.

"Those beans and veggies sure smell good," I said, taking my place beside Julie Ann at the kitchen table.

I waited in silence, while Robert led his family in a brief prayer, after which he hoisted the pot of beans and passed them over to me.

"You start, Kate," Robert said, "I know you're starving."

He frowned and nodded at the booklet I'd placed on the floor by my chair. "Expecting the dinner conversation to get boring?"

"No, it never does. Just want to show you this after we've eaten. It's all about angels."

Phoebe Jo asked, "What kind of angels? You mean Jaz's kind?"

I filled them in on what I'd read and heard that afternoon. They listened respectfully until I reached the part about chanting to bring the angels to your side and The Circle of Light's belief it was their destiny to evolve into angelic beings themselves.

"What's the problem?" I asked, noticing the identical look of incredulity on each face.

Julie Ann reached out. "Can I see that?"

I handed her the booklet.

"Well," Phoebe Jo said, "the Bible does talk about angels. Lots of times. It's different from what these Circle people believe in."

"It's a free country," Robert said. "Everyone's entitled to believe what they want."

I said, "So, do your angels have names and different jobs?"

Phoebe Jo started counting on her fingers. "We have an archangel and angels, then there are the cherubim and seraphim, but they stay in Heaven around God's throne. The angels are the ones who come down to earth to guide and protect us, but the word angel just means 'messenger'. The Bible doesn't name them all—well, we have Michael and Gabriel."

Robert piped up, "And of course there's Lucifer the fallen angel."

Phoebe Jo passed me a basket of hot rolls. "Michael is the angel above all angels, but Gabriel is the angel mentioned most often in scripture. He was the Lord's messenger and his name in Hebrew means 'the mighty one.'"

My heart started to flutter. I looked at Julie Ann who had her nose buried in the booklet. "Turn to the page that has the list of angel names."

Julie Ann flipped back a few pages. "Yeah? Now what?"

"Is Gabriel listed there?"

"Let's see . . ." Julie Ann pushed her glasses back up onto the bridge of her nose and ran her finger down the list. "Uriah, Rapha El, Lucius, Gabri El. Wait a minute, they spelled it differently but it sounds the same as Gabriel."

I wanted to snatch the booklet out of Julie Ann's hands, but I counted to three—ten was too long—and asked, "What kind of angel do they have him listed as?"

"Kind of angel? Umm . . . Oh, yeah, here we are. 'Protector.'"

Bingo. Another piece of the puzzle fit, linking the murder of Brad with The Circle of Light.

Big Gabe can't protect you now.

28

Saturday, May 24th   11:00 AM

THERE'S SOMETHING VERY empowering about strolling down a stretch of pavement that's been closed off to the usual stream of automobile traffic. Sort of gives you a sense of reclaiming the land from some evil enemy.

Central Parkway between Elm and Main streets was bustling with people staking out their territory, and this major artery of downtown Cincinnati had taken on the appearance of a frontier town. Booths and tents and trailers lined both sides of the street—there must've been a hundred or more setups.

I was glad I decided to wear shorts. The sun was blazing hot and the air was getting stickier by the minute. JJ was probably having fits. Every station reported the possibility of severe pop-up thunderstorms for every afternoon of this Memorial Day Weekend. I was also wearing my trekking sandals and JJ's T-shirt with the slogan "We're Cookin'—Great Food and All That Jazz!" printed on the back. With my braid hanging out the back opening of a bright orange baseball cap, I was as ready as I could be for a long, sweaty grill gig.

The crowds wouldn't start arriving until noon, so it was easy to get a parking spot right behind one of the kiddie venues—a playground where hassled parents could unleash their whining brats. This deposited me right in the center of Taste of Cincinnati. I had intentionally come early so I could tour the whole site and take note of who was there and—more importantly—what kind of food they were serving. On my breaks, I planned to revisit the restaurants offering the most interesting dishes.

Right across from where I began my tour was the Hassenbacher Brewery tent. Obviously one of the big guys on the block, the Hassenbachers had taken over a large area of pavement for their beer garden—groupings of small tables and chairs, shaded by a huge red and white striped canopy. Thomas and Carl Hassenbacher were standing in front, arguing with a giant beer can with legs. I wondered what poor soul had been condemned to an afternoon of hell inside that mobile steam bath.

Walking east towards Main street, I breathed in a world of smells as I made my way down the line of little booths. They were cooking up everything from Thai spring rolls to Pulled Pork barbecue to Indian pakoras. I was glad to see there were more Indian restaurants this year. Mom and pop shops for the most part, it looked like they had drafted their entire family to work the booths. Most of them were dressed in saris and tunic and pant outfits, which reminded me of The Circle of Light costume.

Some unhappy restaurateurs were standing, arms crossed, in front of their setups, waiting for the inspectors to come and do their health and safety checks. I knew one of these perturbed owners—Manny, whose restaurant, The Hairy Rhino, was a college student hangout well known for its signature dish, Fried Banana Cream Won Tons with Mexican Chocolate Sauce. There's something for everybody at Taste.

Manny nodded at me and waved his arms in exasperation. "People are going to be here soon and I can't even heat up the

216

fryer yet. I don't know," he said, shaking his head, "this event is getting bigger and more complicated every year."

I waved back. "Don't worry, people'll wait for your goodies. I'll be back for my won ton later this afternoon."

I knew this was a big headache for all these restaurant owners, trying to duplicate their kitchens in a little tent on the side of the road. But to me, it was a perfect way to spend a summer afternoon. Walking around, sampling every kind of food imaginable reminded me of walking around Bombay where every few feet some little guy with a pushcart was cooking up complicated snacks and the air was always filled with such a mix of contrasting smells that your olfactory nerve center could go into overload. I *love* food.

Walking towards Main, I passed a TV news sound truck. Channel Nine was on the job, and I recognized one of the female anchors, a glamorous blond who I was glad to see looked a little less perfect outside of my TV screen. She was short, too.

Microphone feedback suddenly screeched from one end of the Parkway, followed by "Testing. One, two, three," and an ear-splitting twang of an electric guitar.

One of the Channel Nine sound men poked his head out the back of the truck and shouted, "Time to put on your earplugs. B-105 is here."

A surge of teenage adrenalin—or you might call it groupie fever, which was still alive and well inside of me—made me step up my pace and head for the stage. I can be just as easily seduced by the sound of six strings strummed together as I am by the smell of food.

The stage, shaded by a canopy, had been set up in one of the parking lots. A huge banner emblazoned with "Good Times! Great Country! B-105" stretched across the front of the platform. An audience of early-comers, sitting on lawn chairs they'd brought from home, watched the stage crew as they bustled around taping down cables, setting up mikes, and positioning speakers.

Taking their places on stage were a drummer and the guitar player. Both looked like good ol' boys with their big silver belt buckles and worn-out cowboy boots. The drummer started up a beat and a curvy young woman with big hair, wearing sprayed-on jeans and a scoop-necked T-shirt two sizes too small, stepped up to the front microphone and started belting out one of my favorite Martina McBride songs. I started to sing along, but a few bars into it, the sound system complained with another screech when the guitarist joined in.

While they busied themselves adjusting their equipment, I studied the billboard, taking note of the lineup of bands scheduled for the weekend. I'd try to make it back in the evening to catch the Dixie Chicks.

Glancing at my watch, I saw I still had fifteen minutes before having to report to JJ, enough time to quickly check out the rest of the booths. I walked on.

Next to the WAVE stage, another of my favorite radio stations, was the Hassenbacher beer-drinking "garden."

The giant Hassenbacher beer can was sitting with its back to me at a table under the red and white striped canopy, looking very crumpled and dejected. I walked up and rapped twice on the foam rubber costume.

"Hello in there," I said, feeling very sorry for whoever was being subjected to this cruel and unusual punishment.

The can tried, but failed, to turn around in its seat.

I walked around to look through the cutout in the face of the costume and saw a pink, pushed up nose and a pair of sad eyes.

I was about to ask which one of the Hassenbacher brothers it was, when a muffled voice said, "Oh. Hi, Kate. It's me. Henry."

"Did your big bad brothers do this to you?"

"Yeah." Henry shook his head. "Me and my brilliant ideas."

"So, you gotta spend all day in the can?" I chuckled at my own stupid joke.

Henry said, "Sure. Go ahead and laugh. This is going to be the worst weekend of my life."

"Good to see you, Kate." I turned at the sound of Thomas Hassenbacher's voice and found myself staring at another pink and freckled face. Thomas was already sweating through his Hassenbacher Gold T-shirt. "I heard you were going to be helping JJ."

I said, "Yeah. I've never worked down here before. This is going to be fun."

Thomas wiped a handkerchief across his brow. "Well, maybe."

Henry's voice cried out of the can, "Aren't you worried about your little brother?"

"Stop whining." Thomas smacked the top of the rubber suit. "This was your big idea to test the reaction to our new mascot. Just take the damn thing off until we've got a crowd here."

Funny how you can tell what adults were like as little kids. People never change—they just get more extreme with age. As an only child, I always longed for brothers and sisters, thinking it would be fun to have constant companions—loyal, trusting friends connected to you by blood. But I've yet to meet any brothers and sisters who didn't want to spill some of that blood while jockeying for higher positions in the family pack. Still, after the knives have been put away, some adult siblings actually have tolerable relationships. That's one of the holes in me I don't think will ever be filled.

Henry began squirming out of his foam rubber shell. I noticed the small army of college-aged workers unloading beer kegs, rearranging tables and chairs, and hanging Hassenbacher Brewery flags all around the tent. One blond, broad-shouldered hunk was nailing up a wooden menu board.

I read down the list of items. "Soft pretzels I understand, Thomas. But strudel and cream horns? With your beer?"

"We're trying to be a family-oriented venue. We want Mom

and Pop to enjoy their brew, so we have cream horns and apple strudel to keep the kiddies quiet. And here we are, right next to the WAVE stage. Great location, huh, Kate? My Dad, God love him, wanted us to have accordion music."

"Yeah, seems like he's kinda stuck in that Oktoberfest mode." But cream horns and apple strudel didn't sound like kiddie fare and sure wasn't proclaiming, *We're hip! We're cutting edge!* Those poor Hassenbacher boys weren't even aware they were following in their father's polka-dancing footsteps. Taking over the family business can be dangerous. You get stuck in a way of life and image someone else invented and, in the meantime, the rest of the world passes you by. So far, I've avoided that situation by having my own business. But someday I'm going to have to confront that very thing when I inherit Mother's controlling stock in Crown Chili. Oh please, Mother, don't die.

Henry, drenched in sweat, joined us. "It's going to be great at night when the WAVE puts on their jazz concerts. People can sit here, drink our beer, listen to some cool music—"

Thomas barely let him finish his sentence before butting in. "I think we'll get a classier clientele than those snotty-nosed microbrewers with their rock 'n roll crowds, down there." He indicated with a nod of his head the WEBN Rock stage which was anchoring Taste at the Elm street end.

"Winged Pig Ale." Thomas snorted. "More like pig piss."

I DON'T KNOW how many frozen strawberry-mango coolers I poured down my throat that afternoon, but with the sun setting, relief was in sight. At least from the heat. Standing at a smokey grill cooking up ribs over and over again for an intimate party of a few hundred thousand is like being sentenced to Hell's Kitchen. I found myself using the squeeze bottle full of JJ's special sauce to squirt *I hate ribs* across the three slabs of meat in front of me before slathering it with a basting brush big enough to paint a house.

Every once in a while I'd look over at JJ, who was busy dishing out his double chocolate, raspberry brownies, and barking out orders to his young, boisterous wait staff. Now and then, he'd stop and nervously look up at the sky. But he wasted all that worry energy. The clouds never opened up, and the hot afternoon stretched on in front of us like the great Gobi Desert.

One good thing about setting up your kitchen in the middle of a street, you can watch all the people. You're not hidden away in the back of a restaurant, where all you can see is a stove and the harried wait staff. This way, you can see all the action in "the front of the house" and the customers can watch you. On my short breaks, I'd tour around Taste, seeing a lot of chefs and cooks I knew. They all seemed to enjoy being on display and showing off their repertoire of fancy knife flips and spatula twirls. Kind of like watching a combination episode of Julia Child and the old Ed Sullivan show.

People came to JJ's booth in a steady stream, and it was interesting to see how the crowd changed throughout the day. The early afternoon was filled with the AARP crowd and young families trying to maneuver big strollers around them, while constantly shouting "No!" to their kids. By eight-thirty, the street lights were turned on and the bands got louder. Party time.

The WAVE was right next door—our booth was on the opposite side of the stage from the Hassenbacher's tent—and one of Cincinnati's favorite jazz bands was warming up the already overheated crowd that was gathering. Those people who were still trying to make their way down the culinary midway were having to squeeze through an ever-narrowing corridor. Central Parkway was filled to capacity. I wondered if I was going to make it down to the more popular B-105 stage.

"Hey, Kate."

I turned from the slabs of ribs on which I'd been writing *Die, Pig!* "Skip! You brought me a beer? What a sweetie."

Skip Enburg, wearing a straw hat and a Life's Short Eat Hard

T-shirt—one of Taste of Cincinnati's official souvenir items—handed me a jumbo-sized plastic cup filled almost to the top with a frothy brew. "You're looking kind of limp. Figured you could use this. By the way, you have some JJ sauce on your nose."

"Drat, you've discovered one of my beauty secrets." I took care of the tangy facial cream with the last clean corner of my apron, and gulped the beer. "Oh, boy. That sure tastes good." I took another swig. "This isn't Hassenbacher."

Skip's face crinkled up in mock disgust. "Of course not. I brought you some Winged Pig Ale."

Hmm, Pig Piss. "You carried this all the way down through that crowd? For me? That must've been a tricky balancing act."

"Well . . . a few spills landed in my mouth."

My inner timer went off. I turned back to the grill, flipped the ribs over and painted them with more of JJ's famous sauce.

"Getting any good ideas for your column down here," I called over my shoulder.

"Nah," Skip replied, "that's why I've come to hang out with you. If only you'd talk about what goes on at those fancy Clairmont parties you cater, I could fill my column seven days a week instead of only three."

"So that's why you're plying me with alcoholic refreshments. Trying to loosen a girl's tongue?"

Skip gave me his mischievous leprechaun grin. "Sometimes it works. But never with you. You're the most tight-lipped woman I've ever met."

I bowed my head slightly. "Taken as a compliment."

"Well, if you won't talk about your parties, how about this new side-line career of yours?"

"Huh? What're you talking about?"

Skip pulled his hat down, shading his eyes and in his best Bogart said, "Kate Cavanaugh, Private Eye. Oh!" With an index finger, he pushed his hat to the back of his head, and smiled.

"Sorry. I'm short-changing you. The papers have crowned you 'The Amazon Chili Heiress Detective' for solving that murder last December. And now I see you're at it again."

I slapped down a new batch of ribs, causing flames to shoot up through the grill. I felt a flame of anger shoot through me, too, as I thought back to a few months earlier when Matt Skinner and the rest of the Clairmont Rangers had been willing to roast an innocent friend of mine over the flimsiest of evidence. "Yeah. Well, the cops don't always go chasing down the right rabbit hole, do they."

Skip jumped back a foot. "Whoa! Guess I'm standing a little too close to the fire."

I took a swig of beer to cool myself down.

He sidled back up again and in a low conspiratorial whisper said, "Maybe we can do some business."

"What kind of . . . 'business'?"

"A barter. I'll tell you what I know about the murder in Loveland and you can give me what you know about the victim, Brad Holtmann. He's becoming quite a story now with the value of his artwork going through the roof." Skip shook his head slowly. "It's a shame. He was becoming an important local artist, but he had to die to be truly appreciated."

I'd seen Brad's work without knowing whose it was. He was half-decent as a commercial artist, but he sure wasn't the second coming of Picasso. "I don't know anything about Brad Holtmann."

Skip rolled that around in his mind while rubbing his thumb and forefinger along his lower lip. "Hmm. Alright. Then I'll make a little investment in our relationship. I'll tell you something about this case nobody's supposed to know. Down the road, maybe you'll slip me some information."

I'd worry about "down the road" later—at that moment, I was too excited at the prospect of learning something new about the case.

Skip took my silence as a "yes". He continued. "According to my reliable source in the Loveland Police Department, there was a very unusual pin found on the floor by Brad's body."

My clients' secrets were safe. "Tell me something I don't already know. It's a Circle of Light pin—I saw Brad wearing it the day before. It must've popped off his jacket when he was killed and my big foot kicked it across the floor when I discovered his body."

Skip laughed and waved his hand. "Oh, no. You don't know everything, Kate Cavanaugh. Our murdered friend was still wearing his Circle of Light pin."

My stomach flip-flopped. "You mean there was another . . .?"

"Yeah. The pin you saw was a second pin. Solid gold. The one Holtmann was wearing was a cheap gold electroplate."

29

IN MY MIND I saw Adam George decked out in his fancy jewelry. Every time I saw him over the past week, he'd be wearing a different combination of bracelets, pins, and earrings. Put that together with the fact he appeared to own the same emerald green car I had seen outside Brad's studio and the picture on my jigsaw puzzle was beginning to look a hell of a lot like him. But the biggest piece was still missing. Why would he kill Brad?

I was aware of Skip watching me closely as I worked with the new information he'd just given me. I was never good at playing poker or lying—I'm always slapping on my Cavanaugh smile a split second too late, after I've let my true feelings flash across my face.

Skip, looking very pleased with himself, wagged his finger at me. "Aha. I see I've told you something you didn't know. Remember, you owe me."

I spent the next half hour trying to figure out how to pay off my debt without breaking my lips-are-sealed honor code. By this time, cooking JJ's ribs was pretty mechanical—my hands worked like an automaton and I could trust my inner timer. I was also thinking about calling Matt Skinner. I had real information about Adam George, his car, and "Big Gabe" connecting the Loveland murder with Clairmont's by way of the Circle of Light. It was my duty to report it. So it was appropriate for me to pick up the phone and call him, right?

So why did I feel weird about doing that?

This time I hadn't gone snooping. The information had just landed in my lap. Sort of. Ranger Skinner couldn't accuse me of tramping through a crime scene, sticking my big nose into places it shouldn't be. Anyway, who cared if he didn't like me helping him do his job? I'd been falsely accused of Brad's murder, and Jaz was probably high up on his suspect list for Charles'.

If Skinner had personal problems accepting the solid leads I was about to hand over to him, the hell with him. I'd just go over his head and talk to the mayor—she's one of my best clients. So there.

I whipped my cell phone out the pocket of my shorts and was about to punch in the number to speed-dial the Clairmont Ranger Headquarters, when I heard, "Kate. Over here."

I looked across to the front of the booth, where Cindy, Ali, and TC were picking up their orders of ribs and sweet potato fries. All three of them waved at me, big smiles on their faces. They looked like a happy, carefree trio. In my mind, I heard Brad Holtmann announcing "the flying carpet has landed." At the same time, a dream-clip of a white tuxedoed Ali sitting cross-legged on top of one of his magic Persian carpets rolled across the screen in my mind's private viewing room.

I waved back, my Cavanaugh smile firmly in place.

With all the new leads pointing at Adam George, I had completely forgotten about my suspicion of Ali's possible involvement in Brad's death.

I realized there was something odd about seeing the Hoseyni clan all smiles and jovial. It occurred to me I'd never seen them *not* arguing. The last I'd heard from Cindy was that Ali, feeling hassled by the police with all their questions about Brad, was directing his anger at TC. According to her, they were shouting at each other about drugs.

And then there was the fact that Ali and TC were the last people to officially see Brad before his death. But the police already knew that.

There were too many suspects and my brain was beginning to hurt.

"How's it going back there?" Cindy shouted across from the front of the booth.

"Real busy," I replied. "You having a good time?

Ali smiled and said, "Very much. We're going to listen to some jazz."

TC added, "And drink some beer."

Ali made a sour face at his brother and looked back at me. "Little brother says he can't listen to jazz without having a drink."

Next door, an announcer's voice boomed from the stage and the Happy Hoseynis waved again, and trundled off with their little plastic plates full of JJ's delights.

I took a big breath and punched in the Rangers' number. On the second ring, a half-bored male voice answered, "Clairmont Ranger Station. How can I help you?"

"I'd like to speak to Officer Skinner, please." As soon as I asked, I realized it was almost nine o'clock on a Saturday evening and he might not be there. On second thought, I figured the guy's always working and expected, any second, to hear his voice at the other end. Instead, much to my surprise, I caught sight of him walking towards our booth, wearing a short-sleeved shirt in some kind of purple and green batik print, and a pair of khaki shorts showing off his long, hairy legs. In my ear I heard, "He's not on duty this evening."

"Never mind." I clicked off.

Skinner was not alone. Hanging onto his arm was a petite and very attractive woman. Attractive in a downtown artsy kind of way. Short, jet black hair, wraparound sunglasses (in the middle of the night, no less), and a black knit dress (hardly longer than a T-shirt) hugging her body, making sure the world knew how perfect and tiny her female frame was. I guess she spent her days sleeping and only came out at night, because her face had a vampire-white complexion, against which her fire engine red lips pouted in a frozen "kiss me" expression. I didn't like her.

And I didn't like the confusion Matt Skinner stirred up inside of me. Whatever I was feeling—defensive, jealous, catty—it was an ugly part of me I didn't want to acknowledge, so I pushed my emotions away and focused on what I needed to tell him.

I waved, trying to catch Skinner's eye. He was busy counting out his change, oblivious to me—which told me how some evidence could pass by his nose unseen. After all, how can you miss a six-foot-three blond. I know, that was unfair. A cheap shot. Anyway, his little trophy girl finally noticed after I shouted, "Hey, Skinner." She gave him a nudge and pointed in my direction. Skinner did a slight double-take when he finally looked up and saw me. I motioned for him to come over.

Skinner said, "Always helping out your friends, aren't you, Kate. Or is this a new job?" He was using his friendly tone of voice.

I said, "Yeah, JJ needed help. I have to talk to you."

His eyebrows shot up. "Oh?"

"I've got some new leads."

He gave me a weary look and was opening his mouth to say something, but I jumped ahead. "Now before you get pissed off at me, I was not 'playing detective.' I have information that was dropped into my lap."

When he just stood there and stared at me with an I'm-going-to-be-patient look on his face, I took that as my cue to continue. His date-in-black stared back at me, too. At least I think she did, but I couldn't see her eyes through the dark lenses. I hate that.

First, I told him who I thought "Big Gabe" was and how it connected the argument I heard Saturday morning, while walking past Brad's studio, with The Circle of Light. In the meantime, Skinner started munching on his serving of ribs. As I explained my understanding of The Circle's beliefs and told him about the protector angel Gabriel, I could see this was testing Skinner's patience. He didn't look very impressed, but that was okay. I presented the rest of my case, saying, "I happen to know the Loveland murder is connected with your investigation because of the second Circle of Light pin found at the scene."

Skinner scowled at me, dropped the bone he'd stripped clean of meat and picked up another one. "How did you know that?"

"Like I said, information just landed in my lap."

"Well, that is all very interesting, but . . . "

"Wait. I have more. I think that pin belongs to Adam George."

"Yeah? How so?" The scowl was still on his face.

"Maybe you haven't noticed, but he's into jewelry, big time."

Skinner laughed. "They *all* wear jewelry."

"Yeah, they all wear those cheaper pins and earrings, but the one found beside Brad's body is solid gold. That's Adam's style."

"Pretty flimsy, Kate." The caveman tore off a chunk of meat and chewed it.

"Hang on. I'm not finished. When I was in front of Brad's studio and overheard the argument and the stuff about 'Big Gabe,' I also noticed an emerald green car parked outside. I think it's Adam George's car. I saw it in the Golden Valley parking lot yesterday. Adam was getting something out of its trunk."

Skinner's eyes betrayed his sudden interest in my information, but he quickly snapped back to his bored look. "And have you told this to the Loveland police?"

"No."

"I suggest you do."

Skinner's date was squirming alongside him, dropping not-so-subtle hints that she was bored and it was time to move on. He looked from her to me and licked his sauce-covered fingers. "Good ribs . . . See you around . . . "

They turned and walked away. Skinner's petite, pouting companion looked up into his face and said something. They shared a laugh. I was so angry at being brushed aside and not taken seriously, I could've broiled the rest of the ribs on my forehead. Picturing Skinner's face peering up from the slab of meat on the grill in front of me, I squirted barbecue sauce right into his eyes and slapped him hard across his cheek with my paint brush—several times. What was I expecting Skinner to do? Throw his arms around me in a bear hug and call me his "beautiful Amazon Detective?" Oh, grow up, girl.

"Kate?"

I looked up. Skinner had come around to the back of the booth. "Yeah, what?" I asked.

He pointed to me. "You have sauce on your nose. Just wanted to say thank you for the information." He smiled, the corners of his eyes crinkling. "Stay out of trouble," he said, and strode off before I had a chance to say anything. I don't understand men. I like them, but their wiring is all screwed up.

A few minutes later, I suddenly realized the jazz concert at the WAVE stage had come to an abrupt halt. There was a lot of shouting. "Let them through. Let them through."

I heard the little hiccups of a siren and then saw the flashing lights of a medical emergency van trying to make its way slowly through the crowd and past our booth. People were shouting "Get outta the way." Everyone stared at the van like dumb sheep, eventually getting the point and moving out of its path.

JJ said, "I'll go see what all the commotion's about," and disappeared into the crowd.

Five minutes later, JJ was back. "It's over in front of the WAVE stage. It's one of your friends, Kate. I think he had a heart attack."

"That tall good-looking guy who was just here?" I knew part of Skinner's medical history included a close brush with that very thing. Did JJ's ribs finally do him in?

"No. It's the carpet guy," JJ said, nudging me away from the grill. "I'll take over if you want to go see what's happening."

I handed him the tongs, and went bobbing and weaving through the crowd towards the stage. The first person I recognized was Skinner, standing by the open rear door of the medical emergency van and talking to three uniformed Cincinnati police officers. Two paramedics were pushing a gurney towards the vehicle. It was then I noticed Cindy, eyes wide with shock and both hands clamped over her mouth, standing next to TC and across from Skinner. It was Ali who was being loaded into the van.

"Cindy," I shouted, and pushed my way through the herd. "What happened?"

Cindy turned in my direction, moving her hands away from her mouth. "Kate? Oh, God, I don't know what happened."

I reached her side. "JJ said something about a heart attack?"

Cindy waved her hands, helpless. "Ali's never had any problems before. One minute, he's laughing and having a good time, and the next he was on the ground, clutching his chest. It looked like a heart attack."

"No warning? He didn't complain earlier about feeling bad?"

Cindy shook her head.

"Was he eating anything? Maybe it's an allergic reaction."

"No, Ali can eat everything. He was having a piece of strudel while TC was drinking a beer." Cindy froze and stared at me for a few seconds, her eyes widened with a realization. "The strudel! He took a big bite and immediately spit it out, complaining it tasted awful."

Cindy grabbed one of the medics and told him.

Skinner overheard and asked, "Where's the rest of it?"

TC answered, "I don't know, he dropped it back where we were sitting by the stage."

The second medic called out to Cindy, as he was closing the back door to the van. "We have to get him to the hospital fast. You want to ride along?"

Cindy quickly climbed in and said, "TC, follow us in the car. Call you later, Kate." The van started up, blared its siren, and moved through the stupid crowd.

Skinner's date was hanging back a bit, looking inappropriately bored. He ignored her and asked TC, "Where's the rest of the strudel and where did he buy it?"

"Ali just dropped it on the ground." TC pointed at one of the umbrellaed tables right in front of the WAVE stage. "Over there I guess."

One of the Cincinnati police officers, who'd been listening, came up beside us. "So where did he buy it?"

"Hassenbacher's." TC jerked his head toward the beer garden tent. I looked in that direction and saw Thomas Hassenbacher, who'd probably been attracted by the spectacle of someone else's misfortune. The horrified expression on Thomas' face indicated he'd heard the entire conversation and now realized it was also going to be *his* misfortune. He charged up to us.

"There's nothing wrong with my strudel," Thomas shouted.

The Cincinnati officer raised his hand and in a patient tone said, "'Fraid you're going to be shut down until we know that for sure."

"No. You can't do that. Nobody else got sick. We've sold hundreds of pieces today."

"It's just a routine—"

"No, you don't understand. This is a conspiracy." Thomas' pink face was turning a bright red, and he shook a fist towards the WEBN rock and roll stage. "Those damn microbrewers down there are trying to kill our business. Word gets out that Hassenbacher Breweries is accused of serving tainted food, we might as well shut down for good. There won't be any customers—and I'm talking our entire business. Done. Kaput.

Who'll trust a company—"

I said, "Thomas, don't you think you're overreacting a little? No one's made any accusations."

Thomas kept huffing and puffing and cursing under his breath, while Cincinnati's finest went about doing their duty. TC led one of the cops back to the area, where Ali collapsed, to search for the partially-eaten pernicious pastry. Skinner tagged along. Guess I was right—he's always on the job. I looked at his date. She had taken off her wraparound sunglasses and was chewing on one of its plastic arms. Her annoyance with Skinner was obvious and I almost felt sorry for her.

I went back to JJ's booth. It was nine-thirty, and by that time people had stuffed themselves silly. JJ seemed to be able to handle the dwindling orders and gave me an hour to go enjoy myself. I went down to listen to the Dixie Chicks and drink some more Winged Pig Ale—no matter what Thomas was accusing the microbrewers of doing, I still thought it tasted better.

It was midnight by the time I finally dragged myself home. I was all Tasted out clear through to the bone, with another full day of the same waiting for me twelve hours down the road. I had a good time, but my body was complaining at the thought of serving another ten-hour stretch in front of that smoking grill.

I was greeted by a sleepy Boo-Kat and my answering machine's flashing red light. Beside the phone was a stack of messages in Phoebe Jo's handwriting, so I guessed the call on the machine must've come in after the Boones had gone to bed.

I pushed the message button.

"Katie? It's Jaz. Guess you're busy at that food festival thing. I'm doing okay, but I wanted to tell you what I've been thinking. I hope we get a chance to talk soon. The retreat's going to be wrapped up on Tuesday morning and we all gotta be out of here by that afternoon. I . . . I feel like things are changing. Actually, I'm going a little nuts.

"All of a sudden, I feel like I can see through the people in The

233

Circle. None of them is on a spiritual path. They're all in it for something else."

Jaz sighed. I thought, Way to go. Smart girl.

She continued. "And my relationship with Mike . . . well, I guess that's dead. At least when we fought, I figured it was his way of showing he cared about me. Now in the last few days there's been nothing. With all that's going on, you'd think he'd talk to me. At least ask me how I was doing. He just goes to elders' meetings or disappears for long stretches. Meditation walks, my ass. The bastard's probably spending time with his girl friend. The only time I see him is when he crawls into bed. Can't even say 'good night.'"

There was a catch in her voice. Jaz paused.

Good. I was hoping it would get to this point. Maybe Jaz was finally going to consider herself worthy of something better than the same old destructive relationships she was always getting into.

She cleared her throat. "Well, anyway, I'm going to meditate on what my next step should be. I don't know where to go or what to do."

Another pause. She forced optimism into her voice. "Maybe I just need to be a little more patient with Mike."

"Jaz! No," I shouted at the machine. I wanted to grab her before she jumped back into that dark pit.

"Oh, Katie, I don't . . . I'll meditate on it. 'Bye."

A groan escaped from my worn-out body. Jaz. Skinner. Relationships. Screw 'em. I went up to bed.

30

I LAY IN BED AS LONG AS I could, but it was already three hours later than my usual rising time. Boo-Kat was trying to coax me out of bed by fidgeting, scratching, and chewing on his feet. He knows I can't stand listening to that for long. His devious plan worked—I got up, but in stages, which taunted *him*. Boo-Kat sat, tail wagging in tense anticipation, while I slowly pulled off the sheets and in super-slow motion swung my legs down onto the floor and straightened up my stiff and aching body. I shuffled into my bathroom, took a quick shower, and threw on my shorts and a clean T-shirt.

Boo-Kat bounded down the stairs ahead of me and went straight to the kitchen cupboard where his supply of lamb and rice doggie treats were stocked. Instead, I opened the back door and gently kicked him outside. He was on a diet. And I was in a bitchy mood.

I was glad the Boones had gone to an early church service and I had the kitchen to myself. Didn't like subjecting them to my moods. I started up a fresh pot of coffee and, while it burbled through the filter, I began leafing through my pile of phone messages. Most of them were business related and would have to wait until Tuesday. A few were from acquaintances I knew wouldn't be up at that time on a Sunday morning (and I didn't want to speak to them anyway), and there were messages from a couple of reporters still on their mission to get an "in depth interview" with the Chili Heiress Detective. I hadn't been keeping up with the newspaper coverage, but apparently Brad Holtmann was now getting the publicity he would have died for when he was alive.

Sighing, I read the two messages from Mother, written in Phoebe Jo's precise school teacher script. "Mrs. Cavanaugh is very upset," said the first note. "She thinks you're ignoring her and is worried about her barbecue on Monday."

The second message, taken down eight hours later said, "Your mother is frantic. I tried to calm her down and told her how busy you were, but that everything was under control and not to worry. She said that you were a negligent daughter and she doesn't know what she's done to deserve this kind of treatment."

I crumbled up the two messages into one little ball and tossed it into the sink. Two points.

I prioritized my calls and made the first one on my list to the Loveland police, as I promised Skinner I would. The officer on duty didn't sound all that impressed, but thanked me just the same for the information and stated they'd be in contact if they needed to clarify anything.

Well, at least that was one less obligation to drag around that day.

Next, I called Cindy on her cell phone. She was still at the hospital and had spent the night sitting by Ali's bed. I was shocked when she told me he was in a coma. And even more shocked when she told me it was due to a hypersensitive reaction to cocaine.

I said, "Cocaine? Ali? That's impossible."

"That's what I told the doctors. But they found it on his tongue and in the lining of his mouth along with a lot of sugar. Obviously, it had to be from that pastry he bit into."

I remembered Thomas Hassenbacher's accusation and wondered if this was the work of a malicious microbrewer. That sounded too crazy to be real, but I told Cindy about Thomas' conspiracy theory.

Cindy said, "Yeah. TC told me about that last night."

I said, "Guess Ali was just in the wrong place at the wrong time."

"Well, no. TC was in the wrong place at the wrong time. He's the one who bought the beers and pastry, while Ali and I picked out a table to sit at. But I don't think whoever did this had a specific victim in mind—it could've been anybody. Whatever the case, the doctors said that, normally, the amount of cocaine found in Ali's system would not be enough to put someone into a coma. If anyone else had eaten that pastry, they probably would've just felt bad for a few hours. So they figured Ali must have been hypersensitive to cocaine or he was already suffering from high blood pressure which would have had the same affect."

"Did he have high blood pressure?"

"I don't know. Nobody would've known. He never went in for physicals."

I ended our conversation with some optimistic and reassuring statements, and promised to call her the next morning. I poured myself a cup of coffee and stood at the bay window for a few minutes, watching my dog trample all over the day lilies. This latest incident had my thoughts spinning around in total confusion. I had so much information, but I didn't know how to put it together and make sense of it. In my mind's private screening room I saw that Persian rug flying around Brad's body lying on his studio floor, down West Loveland Avenue past Frankie Alberto pointing at me, through the Taste of Cincinnati crowds on Central Parkway, and stopping to hover over the Golden Valley Spiritual Center.

Which made me think about Jaz. I really needed to talk to her, but it was impossible to get her on the phone. The least I could do was leave her a message.

I went back to sit at the kitchen table, picked up the phone and punched in the number for Golden Valley. Ten rings later, someone finally answered in a chirpy, singsong voice, and I was almost convinced that life was just grand at the spiritual center. I left a message for Jaz, saying, "I won't be free of my obligations until Tuesday morning, but I want you to come stay at the farm for as long as you need. If I'm not here, I've instructed Phoebe Jo to help you get settled." Better not forget to leave a message for Phoebe Jo.

Last on my list was Mother. I admit I did not want to talk to her. My fear was that a conversation with her had the potential for cranking me up several notches from feeling slightly bitchy to wanting to go out on a rampage and chew off the head of anyone who looks at me funny because I'm so tall.

But I had to admit Mother was right, I was neglecting her. And so, with my teeth gritted and tail between my legs, I called. Thankfully, she only had a few minutes to talk, but managed to get in a dig by saying, "You know I always go to church at this time. Why are you calling now?"

I had forgotten. Truly. I counted to ten as she launched into her you-should-come-to-church-with-me sermon. That gave me a great opening to show that I was trying to be the dutiful daughter. I said, "I'm sorry. I'm far too busy preparing for your barbecue tomorrow." A little lie told in the heat of battle.

Mother couldn't think of a good come-back. She just said, "Oh . . . well . . . thank you, Kathleen. I'll see you in the morning. Don't be late."

Dig, dig, dig. My teeth hurt, but innocent bystanders' heads were safe. For the moment. But I had to eat something. The day was not starting out well: I slept in and made all those phone calls with only coffee sloshing around in my stomach. My whole routine was off, so the day was destined to be a weird one all the way through. Foraging around in the refrigerator, I found a fried chicken leg and the chunk of Double Gloucester and Stilton cheese that Tony had brought me. I nuked one of Phoebe Jo's homemade bran muffins and sat down to a fine feast.

I sensed I was being watched. Sure enough, a pair of big, brown eyes begged at me through the kitchen's screen door. Boo-Kat was sitting on the step, whimpering quietly. His routine was messed up too. I let him in and gave the poor little bugger his morning's diet ration of doggie biscuit. He left a trail of drool as he carried it across the kitchen floor to his spot, and devoured it.

"DAMMIT. The produce was supposed to be delivered yesterday." I let go with a few choice curse words that bounced off the steel walls and shelving of my walk-in refrigerator. I'd have to call Trolley Brothers, my emergency backup, and pray they'd have enough salad greens and fresh corn and berries. If not, Mother's menu was going to be an all-meat medley.

"Is that you in there, Miss Kate?" The door opened and Phoebe Jo stuck her head in. She was still wearing one of her many flower print Sunday dresses.

I shouted, "Why didn't the produce guy show up yesterday?"

Phoebe Jo backed away. "They had some kind of problem with their trucks. I told them it was okay as long as they delivered this morning after eleven."

"Well, they better," I said, kicking a big, plastic bucket full of potatoes. "Otherwise I'm not using them again. What if they don't come today? Then what? I should never have switched suppliers just to save a few bucks. And I've got this stupid Taste of Cincinnati to do today. I won't have Tony to help me 'cause he has to do it tomorrow. Me and my big mouth—when am I going to learn to say no?"

"Shh, shh." Phoebe Jo made a motion with her delicate fingers as if patting the air in front of her. "Stop and take a breath, Miss Kate. Julie Ann and I will help. Robert can go to Trolley's and get what we need if the deliveryman doesn't show up. It's not good to get yourself all riled up like that. We're not going to just sit by and watch you try to handle this all by yourself."

I had the image of myself appearing on the old Ed Sullivan Show, juggling bowling balls, knives, and eggs. It's a very difficult act to perform under the best conditions, but almost impossible when the next act, the Unknown Murderer, tosses in a couple of bodies from offstage.

By eleven o'clock, I had written out a list of instructions for the Boones, simple things they could do for me in the kitchen. But only if they really wanted to. It was already steamier than the day before at the same time. Even a T-shirt was going to be too hot to wear, standing in front of JJ's grill, so I went upstairs to change into a tank top.

Taking a final check in front of the mirror, I lifted up my arm to see if the arm hole was cut high enough so people wouldn't be startled by the sight of my prosthesis. Okay, that was good enough. But then, if I leaned over, which I did, you could look right down my front. It wasn't an ugly sight—just odd seeing the gaping hole between the plastic boob and my flat, bony chest. I grumbled. I got enough weird looks as it was because of my height—I didn't need any more. Yanking off the revealing piece of clothing, I went to my closet to find something else to wear. The next tank top I tried on fit tight against my chest, but I was going to have to keep my arm down if I didn't want anybody viewing the harsh reality of my Amazon body.

"Oh, for crying out loud. I can't stand this." I ripped the top off and threw it across my bedroom. I wish I had the nerve to go without a prosthesis, but I have a hard time handling the stares of people even when I look perfectly proportioned.

I could feel myself getting into one of my poor-me-why-can't-I-be-normal fits, and I was running late. This was not going to be a good day. I threw on a plain white, short-sleeved T-shirt, grabbed my orange baseball cap and stomped out of the bedroom.

JJ GREETED ME WITH, "I'm thinking of changing the menu."

"Huh?" I said, tieing on my apron. "Isn't it a little late for that?"

JJ rubbed the sagging pouches of flesh under his bloodshot blue eyes. "I counted yesterday and half of the restaurants here are serving ribs. I thought they were all going to do their froufrou rattlesnake and portobella with raspberry vinegar whatsits."

I cringed at the imagined combination and said, "But your ribs are still the best. Let's just cook 'em and think of the next two days as War of the Ribs."

"Yeah, well . . ." JJ looked up into the sky. "It's gonna rain, too. I'm never doing this again."

That's good.

I went into my automaton chef act: pick up ribs, slap 'em on the grill, squirt, brush, flip. Some time around one o'clock, I saw the giant beer can slowly listing from side to side as it shuffled past our booth. I imagined Henry Hassenbacher frothing inside from the heat and half-expected to see a gusher of foam explode out the top of the costume.

I yelled out at JJ, "What's happening with the Hassenbachers'? I guess they're open?"

JJ was scouting the sky, on the lookout for dreaded severe thunderstorm clouds. "Yeah, they can sell their watered-down brew, but they can't sell any food."

The threat of rain wasn't keeping anyone away. The crowd was larger than Saturday's. And hungrier. By nine o'clock that evening, I was ready to quit. Thankfully, business was dropping off, just like it did the night before, and JJ told me, "We can handle the rest of the night by ourselves. Go have yourself a good time, Kate. You deserve it."

I walked around, checking out which bands were playing where. But I wasn't having a good time. WEBN's rock n' roll stage was the launching pad for some screeching guitar and booming bass assault music that definitely was detrimental to my ear drums. B-105's country music act was a tall handsome cowboy with a black Stetson. The young girls in their sprayed-on jeans crowded the edge of the stage, but he was a little too twangy and nasally for my taste. I was tired and the crowd was too much. It was hard to walk around without having to elbow my way through, and everybody seemed to be carrying some sticky-gooey food or drink sloshing around in a plastic cup just millimeters away from spilling on me. The WAVE's jazz was so cool and laid back I was afraid I'd fall asleep.

Nothing was going to satisfy me. Except my big, comfy bed. And with Mother's barbecue starting to loom over me, I decided it was best to go home and get some sleep.

Just as I was approaching my Jeep in the parking lot, I caught sight of TC Hoseyni leaning down and talking to someone in a car stopped in the street about fifty feet away. Though it was dark, they were under the orange glow of a street lamp. No mistake. It was the emerald green car.

Why was TC talking to Adam George? How did they know each other? I desperately wanted to hear what they were talking about but didn't want to be seen. Crossing over to the other side of the parking lot, which wasn't as well lit, I started creeping along beside a brick wall so I'd come up behind them. But by the time I got within hearing range, the conversation had ended and Adam's car pulled away. TC headed towards the Taste crowd on Central Parkway.

I wanted to ask him how he knew Adam George, but not on a dark, empty side street at ten o'clock at night. TC was a big guy and now, with this little meeting, could possibly be connected to Brad's murder. I decided to follow him back into the Taste and talk to him in a safer environment, with people around us. I waited for him to go on ahead and put a little distance between us. Then I started to trail behind.

Adam George, Brad Holtmann, and drugs were already linked in my mind. Ali hated drugs. He also disapproved of TC buying into the American culture and hanging out with Brad at the furniture store, when Brad was one of the employees. Did TC buy into the drug culture, too?

On the phone, just a few days earlier, Cindy had said the two brothers were arguing violently about drugs. Yet, they show up at Taste of Cincinnati like one big happy family—that is, until Ali finds himself at the wrong place at the wrong time, playing Russian Roulette with a piece of cocaine-dusted pastry bought by his brother. What a unhappy coincidence. The flying carpet had a new flight crew—TC, Adam, and Brad.

TC suddenly stopped walking and turned back towards me.

I froze and held my breath.

He took a step or two in my direction.

I figured my spy game was up.

He raised his hand, tossed something red into a city trash bin, turned on his heel and headed towards the crowd.

Of course I had to see what he had thrown away. But if I kept this distance between us, by the time I reached the trash bin, TC would have disappeared into the crowd and I'd risk losing him. So, instead, I took the even bigger risk of his seeing me and ran to the trash bin.

There was only one piece of red garbage sitting on top of the pile. I grabbed it. Yuck. It had something sticky on it. What a dumb waste of time. I peeled the Popsicle wrapper off my fingers.

TC was just approaching the fringe of the crowd and I was going to lose him if I didn't get going. I picked up my pace.

Sometimes there are advantages to being tall. My giraffe legs enabled me to catch up and I could look out over the heads of the munching festivalgoers. TC was only about thirty feet away, sauntering down the middle of Central Parkway, giving nothing more than casual glances at the booths he was passing by.

Okay, so there I was, tailing this guy. Now that I had him in my sights, I moved on to the next problem. What would I say when I caught up to him? Better start the conversation in a non-threatening way. I could ask, "How's your brother doing?" Then look for an opening to make an innocent-sounding statement like, "I was just getting something from my Jeep and saw you talking to someone in a car I recognized." That was good. It allowed me to prod for the information I really wanted—how did TC know Adam George?

I felt ready to approach him and began weaving through the crowd, closing the distance between us. My heart pumped faster as though I was in the middle of a championship basketball game, dribbling down the court and getting ready to make my move to the basket. I knew I could hit this shot.

TC stopped to read the menu at one of the booths.

I cut around a teenaged couple kissing in the middle of the court, er, street. I was fifteen feet away from making contact. Suddenly, my arm was held back, stopping me in my tracks. I expected to hear the referee's whistle calling for a foul. Instead, "Where you going Kate?"

It was Skip Enburg.

I answered, "Oh, hi. I can't stop. 'Bye." I tried to move away.

"Wait a minute." Skip kept hold of my arm. "You went right by me and you've got a funny look in your eyes. What's up?"

"Nothing. Just saw someone I know." I wrenched my arm out of his grasp, spun around, and slammed into three teenage-punk-rocker-head-shaved-nostril-pierced males, launching beer, wieners, and expletives into the steamy atmosphere.

The expletives were mine.

The kid with the silver stud through his lower lip yelled, "Hey, lady, what's with you?"

"Yeah, watch where you're going," said his buddy with the bull-ringed nose.

The biggest of them, sporting a spider web tattoo on his bald head, shoved at the other two. "Shaddup, you jerks. It was an accident." He whipped out a grimy-looking bandana and dabbed at the Taste samplings clinging to my shirt sleeve. "Sorry about the mess, lady."

Skip, mortified, was wiping sauerkraut off my other sleeve. "I'm . . . so . . . sorry, Kate. How can I ever make it up to you?"

The three guys took off. I looked around, scanning the crowd for TC. "I don't know. He's gone."

"Who's gone?"

"TC Hoseyni. I don't think you know him. It's okay, I'll see him again some time."

Skip gently tapped his forehead. "That's who it was. Ali's brother. About half an hour ago, I saw a man who looked vaguely familiar walking with someone down towards that parking lot." He pointed in the direction I had come from. "I met TC at a couple of parties. You know me, I meet lots of people. Never forget a face, but names . . . that's another matter all together."

"Did you know who he was with?"

"No."

"What'd he look like?"

"Well, I was kind of far away. Didn't get a real good look. I'd say he was average height, short, dark hair, and he was dressed in a white, exotic outfit. I thought maybe he was one of the guys from the Indian restaurants, or that religious organization meeting over at the Golden Valley Spiritual Center."

"Short, dark hair? You sure it wasn't a long ponytail?"

"Nope. Just a regular haircut. Why? What's the matter? You've got that funny look in your eyes again."

31

Monday, Memorial Day, May 26th, 9:00 AM

I WAS SO SURE Skip had seen Adam George, it threw me for a loop when he described someone else. I stayed up all night, thinking about the possibilities. There were lots of Circle believers fitting that description. Maybe all this anguish was for nothing, and TC just happened to be talking to someone from an Indian restaurant who drove an emerald green car. *Sure.*

But now it was time for Mother's Revenge of the Unflocked Memorial Day barbecue. I had a ton of work ahead of me.

Good thing it was Tony's turn to help JJ—I'd had my fill of ribs. There weren't going to be any of those damn sticky things on Mother's menu.

While I was placing the blueberries and raspberries in the middle of the half-frozen ice star that would eventually float in the bowl of patriotic punch, I remembered I hadn't checked my phone messages from the day before. The only one of importance was from Jaz.

"Thanks, Katie, for offering me a place to stay. But I've got to work this out on my own. I promised myself, I'm not going to run and hide from my problems anymore. Really. I'm doing okay. Tuesday, everybody goes home and I'll come see you then . . . maybe stay a few days. We'll have some fun. 'Bye."

That was bullshit. I wanted to believe it, but she was waffling. Why couldn't she just get up and walk away. That's what I would have done. A long time ago.

I mixed up the dough for the shortcakes, put them in the oven, and wiped the sweat off my forehead with the corner of my apron. Ridiculous. It was still only May and the air conditioning wasn't keeping my kitchen comfortable. I switched on the radio to catch the latest weather report, hoping there was some relief in sight. They were repeating the same litany they'd broadcast all weekend. "Hot, hazy, and humid, with a possibility of severe thunderstorms late this afternoon and through the evening."

I let fly a string of my favorite four-letter words. Now I knew how JJ felt. I was wondering how Mother was dealing with it. I could imagine the prayers she must have been shooting up to God in her desperate attempt to control everything. Well, nothing to do but carry on. I put together a few different salad dressings and sliced up oranges and red onions for a salad that also included avocado. That would have to be finished up at Mother's place.

Phoebe Jo had already made the spicy butter for the grilled shrimp and an herb butter for the corn on the cob. I sliced up a variety of veggies which would be grilled and used as toppings on the Blue Cheese Burgers. Remembering Mother's "see you in the morning" and noticing the clock said almost noon, I rang her up and assured her that we'd be there in an hour and not to fret, everything was ready.

Robert helped me load all the food into the 'Round the World Catering van. I got behind the wheel.

Robert asked, "You sure you don't want me to come along and set up that grill?"

"No thanks, I can handle it. You just have yourself a restful day."

I drove to the Cavanaugh castle followed by Phoebe Jo and Julie Ann, who were coming along in their car to help me set up.

Mother's groundskeepers had been busy. I laughed. Huge red, white, and blue balloons bobbed in the air, attached to her mailbox. Little American flags were stuck into the ground at two-foot intervals down both sides of the long, winding driveway. Hanging from a flagpole on the front of the imposing stone house was an Uncle Sam windsock. Mother was getting downright carried away. I should've made that sheet cake after all. I did manage to get a red, white, and blue theme into the menu with the punch and its floating white ice star, and the shortcakes with red and blue berries and whipped cream. If you were inclined to add ketchup and white onions, even the Blue Cheese Burgers qualified.

We drove around the back, parked next to the kitchen door, and transferred the food into the refrigerators. One of Mother's housekeeping staff had already set up the eight-foot-long grill, filled it with charcoal, and lit it. Phoebe Jo and Julie Ann helped me set up the tables on the huge multi-leveled deck. We covered half of them with blue tablecloths with white stars; the other half got red tablecloths with white stars.

Mother graciously invited Phoebe Jo and Julie Ann to stay, but they just as graciously declined and went back to Trail's End.

Mother was unusually quiet and easy to get along with all afternoon, asking me if I had everything I needed in her kitchen, offering to make me iced tea, and checking her watch, the sky, and her lipstick every half hour. I reminded myself of how important this was to her and kept the lips of my own sometimes-smart mouth sealed.

By four-thirty the guests began to arrive. Betty Zender and Mabel Crank were amongst the earliest, probably because they always liked to stake out the smoking zone.

Betty loaded up her cigarette holder and asked, "Kate, dear, have you experienced Taste of Cincinnati yet this year?"

"Yes." I quickly juggled a few figures mentally. "About forty thousand servings worth."

"Oh, Kate. You're so cryptic. What on earth does that mean?"

I explained about helping JJ.

"Oh, well then, you were there when that big to-do went on at the Hassenbacher's beer garden. By now, everybody in Clairmont knows that Mr. Hoseyni is in the hospital because of eating something he bought from the Hassenbachers."

Betty directed Mabel and I, with a wiggle of her bony finger, to come closer. "I heard something very interesting about that from a very dependable source."

She resorted to a whisper. "It was coke."

Mabel said, "Aw, he got sick from drinking pop?"

Betty made a sour face at her.

"What?"

"Cocaine, dear." Betty took a drag of her cigarette and blew a smoke ring for emphasis. "Rumor has it that Henry Hassenbacher was in one of those rehab places for drug dependency."

"Well," Mabel said, lighting up another cigarillo with the still glowing butt of her previous one, "I wouldn't put *anything* past those boys. Hey, Katie, remember at your friend's wedding last week I was calling the Hassenbachers my 'angels?'"

I nodded.

"Hell, they're no angels. More like wolves in sheep's clothing, devils in disguise. They didn't want to help me—they were planning to take over my hockey team."

I was horrified at what Mabel was implying. "Are you accusing the Hassenbachers of intentionally spiking their own pastry? That sounds kind of dumb on their part."

Mabel went into a coughing fit and, between splutters, said, "Naw, I'm just mouthing off 'cause I'm mad at them."

Betty cleared her throat. "I'm going to get myself something to drink. Kate, dear, we shouldn't be listening to this. Mabel is always 'just mouthing off' and spreading idle gossip and dangerous rumors."

And of course, Betty *never* did such things in her monthly gossip column.

ASIDE FROM A couple of offensive conversations, the barbecue was going well. I figured about sixty people showed up. By eight o'clock everyone had been fed, which was good because one of Mother's staff came up to me and said, "We just heard the Channel Nine weather reporter issue a severe storm and flood warning for the tri-state area."

The air was still and heavy and all the little American flags hung like limp rags. I suggested to Mother we move the party indoors. At her instructions, all the guests carried their drinks into the large gathering room. It always reminded me of a hunting lodge, with its stone fireplace, leather sofas, and oversized prints of fox hunting scenes. Mabel and Betty pitched in and helped me bring the food inside.

We were in the kitchen, stacking dirty dishes on the counter, when Mother joined us and finally chose to "casually" launch into the topic that was uppermost in her mind.

"Betty," Mother said in a voice perkier than was normal for her, "has anyone discovered who's responsible for starting that tacky pink flamingo business?"

"I suspect Skip Enburg knows, but he's keeping mum about it."

Mother picked up a plastic straw and began winding and twisting it around her finger. "Yes, I've been reading Skip's column. It was quite interesting yesterday. Apparently, some poor souls are out buying pink plastic flamingos and sticking them in their front lawns. They're flocking themselves so everyone will think they're on the A-list. Clairmont does not have an A-list." She shook her head. "Some people are so insecure they'll stoop to anything."

I was glad Mother started unwinding the straw. She'd twisted it so tightly, the tip of her forefinger was turning purple. It was difficult watching her try to hide her bruised ego, and I hoped I was the only one seeing her struggle. I felt embarrassed for her.

"I agree," Betty said. "Even the most powerful people are little kids underneath. But I guess that's natural. Everybody needs to feel they belong to some group."

Mabel waved a fistful of dirty forks in the air. "Yeah, it's always been like that. I went to my sorority's annual get-together last month. When I was in college, that was the sorority to belong to. You were nothing if you didn't have one of those pins."

"At that age everything is drastically important," Betty said, rolling her eyes up to the ceiling. "I'm sure you don't wear it now. A mature adult should have outgrown the need to tell the world she belongs to some select group."

"Oh . . . I don't know about that. Everybody still has their pin and wears it when we have these get-togethers. It would be very strange if any of the gals didn't. *I* wouldn't show up without it. Sisters come from all across the country for those meetings and anyone not wearing her pin would stick out like a sore thumb."

All this talk about belonging to a group and wearing pins made me think of Jaz, her need for The Circle of Light and her difficulties in breaking away from them and leaving Mike. I almost gasped out loud. The sore thumb. I suddenly remembered an observation I made at the Open House.

Mike Dyer was the only believer not wearing a Circle of Light earring, pendant, or pin. That could have been his pin I saw on the floor of Brad's studio. Skip said it was solid gold, not a cheap electroplate like Brad was wearing. I remembered Jaz accusing Mike of disappearing and flying into the arms of some

251

girl friend. She said, "I gave him a special gift and I'm sure he just turned around and gave it to her. That's what we were fighting about when you heard us."

Well, in my books a solid gold pin is pretty special. But in this case Mike might not have been spending time in a tryst with a secret lover.

But what about the emerald green car I saw outside of Brad's studio? After seeing Adam George get something out of its trunk in the Golden Valley parking lot, I assumed it was his, and Jaz confirmed it.

So then who was TC talking to in the emerald green car when I saw it again at Taste of Cincinnati? Skip saw TC, just a few minutes earlier, talking with a short-haired man dressed in Circle-style clothing. That knocked out Adam, with his long ponytail. It could have been Mike.

And who killed Charles Sutcliff? And why?

I couldn't answer those questions logically, but my gut told me to get the hell over to Golden Valley and drag Jaz away from there.

"Kathleen? Are you in there?"

I looked down into Mother's puzzled face.

"I was asking you a question, but you seemed mesmerized by something over by the back door."

"Sorry. I'm here, but I have to leave for an hour or so."

"Oh, for heaven's sake! In the middle of my party? What could be that important?" Mother had those little puckers that appeared in the corners of her mouth whenever she was really ticked off.

"Don't worry, you'll be fine for an hour or two." I grabbed my purse and headed for the back door. "I'll be back in time to clean up."

"Kathleen!" Mother's puckers grew larger, but I waved and sprinted to my Jeep.

32

THICK, HOT AIR PUSHED IN through the opened windows as I drove the seven miles to the spiritual center. Still no sign of rain, but it sure felt like the atmosphere was soaking up moisture like a heavy blanket that would either suffocate us or break open in one of Mother Nature's torrential displays, with thunder and lightning as her way of celebrating Memorial Day. I wanted to be safe at home when that show started.

Pulling into the parking lot, I noticed the conference center was dark and the only lights were coming from the dormitory building. I went straight to Jaz's room, hoping that Mike wasn't there.

I banged on the door. "Jaz. It's Kate."

The door flew open.

Jaz stood there, dressed in a white caftan. Her frizzy hair was pinned up on top of her head in a wild-looking topknot. "Katie? What're you doing here? What's the matter? Come in. Come in."

I stepped into her room and looked around for the snake. "Where's Mike?"

"He went out for a walk with Bruno," Jaz answered, shutting the door. "Bruno said he had something to discuss with him."

"You've got to come stay with me at the farm. It's not safe here."

Her eyes grew wide. "Why?"

As I blurted out my whole line of thinking, Jaz's expression turned serious. She nodded her head several times, and I could see in her eyes she was putting the pieces together and getting a much clearer picture of what was going on than I had.

By the time I concluded with, "I think Mike is Brad's killer," the color had drained out of Jaz's face, which made the faded purple and green bruise around her eye show up even more. She stared at me, frozen. I thought she was waiting for me to tell her what to do next. Instead, her eyes snapped into an expression of rage I had never seen in her.

"That bastard! That sonofabitch!" Jaz shouted. Her fists hammered the air in front of her as if trying to pound some invisible image into the ground. "So that's why Mike got so pissed off with me when I pointed out his pin was missing. You guessed right, Katie, I did have a solid gold Circle pin made up special for him. That arrogant scumbag refused to admit he'd lost it but wouldn't say what he did with it. I figured he gave it to some other woman he'd been sneaking away to see. What else was I to think? The asshole bashed me when I brought it up again last Tuesday night. That's how I got this." Jaz pointed to the still ugly bruise around her eye.

I asked, "Did Mike do a couple of his disappearing acts around five, six o'clock last Saturday morning and then again Sunday morning?"

Jaz took a few seconds to search her memory. "He left this room around that time, but didn't tell me where he was going, and I don't ask him questions like that because he only gets mad at me."

I said, "That's when he probably met with Brad in his studio in Loveland and killed him. But why?"

Jaz shrugged. "I don't know, Katie. It doesn't take much. The guy's got a short fuse . . . when he thinks he can get away with it."

Adding Frankie Alberto's suspicions about Brad's drug connections into this mix, I asked, "Was Mike involved in drugs?"

"No. He never touched the stuff."

"Maybe Mike was dealing. Had he ever come to Cincinnati before this?"

"It's possible. He used to tell me what he was doing, but as he got more involved in his duties as an elder, he kind of put me away in a closet. Just pulled me out when he wanted something."

"Oh, Jaz." I reached out and gave her a hug. "Let's get out of here."

She nodded and began to stuff clothing, books, and toiletries into a knapsack. At one point she stopped and stared at the floor. It was obvious Jaz's mind was elsewhere, but I still had some questions to ask. "You told me Adam owns that emerald green car. Does Mike ever borrow it?"

"Sure. He hates how I painted the van. Says it's too silly-looking and too big to drive around for quick trips."

"More likely it's too recognizable—like driving around with a giant neon sign flashing 'Look at me. Here I am.' It'd be pretty dumb to park that outside the place where you were putting together drug deals."

I don't think Jaz heard my last comment. She was standing, arms folded, staring absently into her half-filled knapsack. A second or two later, her head jerked up. She'd made some decision.

"Katie, I want to go to the police and identify that solid gold pin as belonging to Mike. Let him try to explain his way out of that! But first, I want to find that SOB and tell him I'm leaving him."

"Are you crazy?" I grabbed her by the arms and stared, flabbergasted, into her eyes. Maybe there was a possibility I could shoot a bolt of common sense into that old hippie.

"Yeah, I'm crazy and I have to do this. I've never done anything more important for myself in all my life."

"Mike's had you under his thumb for a long time. You think he's just going to let you walk away? He's a dangerous man, Jaz."

"Mike's a coward. He won't do anything in front of witnesses. He's out with Bruno and there's probably a lot of people out there walking around." She pulled an arm free from my grasp and waved at the window. "It's still light out there."

I looked out. "Not for long."

"Yeah. So I gotta do it right now."

I kept hold of her other arm. "Just come to the farm with me."

"Katie, if I don't face Mike right now . . . if I just sneak away . . . I'll be transferring my dependency from him right onto you. I've got to do this if I'm ever going to have any self-respect."

Okay. "Well, at least take your flashlight." I let her go and followed her out of the room and into the woods.

33

HUGE BLACK CLOUDS SAILED across the darkening sky like a fleet of battleships heading out on a mission. Tree tops were beginning to swirl a little in the breeze that had just picked up. The last thing I wanted was to get caught in a thunderstorm out in the woods. We'd already gone up and down several of the meditation paths. As Jaz had said, there were other people out there, but they were being smart, heading back to their rooms. No sign of Mike or Bruno.

"Fifteen more minutes, Jaz, and then I don't care what you say, we're going home."

"Oh . . . okay. Let's try one more path, Katie—the one behind the conference center."

We trudged along the dirt tractor road that ran between the conference center and the old barn we'd explored a week earlier. Just as I was thinking this was a waste of time, Jaz said, "Over there," and pointed.

Standing by the barn was a little huddle of Circle people. As we got closer, I could see it was Mike, Bruno, Adam, and Patricia, and three other large men I hadn't been introduced to but recognized as the followers who had supported the nomination of Bruno for High One. Bruno appeared to be acting kind of chummy with Mike, standing next to him, an arm around his shoulder. But the expressions on everyone's face as they turned to stare at us didn't say "chummy" at all.

Obviously—to me—Jaz and I had stumbled onto some private elders meeting and we weren't welcomed. But she had only one thing in mind.

Jaz strode up to the group. "I've got something to tell you, Mike."

As I focused on Mike's startled face, I noticed a string of beads around his neck that looked familiar. Suddenly, Patricia stepped in front of Jaz and said to both of us, "Go away. This is none of your business."

At that moment I remembered where I'd seen those beads—they were Bruno's worry beads. And Bruno wasn't holding Mike in some friendly embrace—he was gripping his beads as though they were a choke collar around the neck of a vicious dog. Or, in this case, a snake.

This was certainly not your ordinary business meeting. I grabbed Jaz's arm and said, "Write him a letter."

Jaz wrenched her arm free. "No. It's gotta be now."

I heard a voice, singing softly, behind me. The words were more rambling than coherent, and the melody was the kind a child would make up on the spot. The group of elders all shifted to look around me and see who else was arriving.

"Oh, that's all we need," said Adam.

I turned and saw Lowell, head down, shuffling towards me. He must've been singing to his angels because he obviously wasn't aware of what was happening here on Earth.

Lowell greeted me first, most likely because I was the one he almost crashed into. He looked up at me and said, "Ah. Lovely." He took my hand and said, "I'm glad you're joining us. You are most welcome."

I shook my head emphatically. "No I'm not."

Lowell then realized others were there. "Oh, how fortunate to meet you all here. I've been having so much trouble. My mind is shrouded in fog and I cannot hear any clear messages, but the fact that you are all here at this time is most likely a divine circumstance. I think the angels want to talk to all of us, together."

He turned to Jaz. "Ever since Charles' death, I've been troubled. There is always a right path and I've been trying to find my way through the chaos and the interfering voices to a solution. Our beloved Circle, this community of love and brightness, is rotting from the inside, and we must remove the infection without destroying the body of believers. The love of money is such an insidious thing, it—"

I saw Bruno and Adam both try to silence Lowell with nervous hand gestures. Patricia said, "Lowell! Shut up!"

Lowell blinked. It seemed liked he momentarily lost his train of thought. Focusing back on Jaz, he said. "You know Charles valued The Circle over everything else, and he came to me last week with a problem he was struggling with. He had found the rotten egg."

Lowell pointed to Mike. "This man you have chosen to be by your side did not hold precious The Circle and used it for selfish gain. I did not see this during my two years as High One. This man had the important responsibility of distributing our healing oils, enlightening books, and holy music to the Circles around the country, but he polluted that with the destructive drugs he was more interested in spreading. When Charles met his violent end, I knew who had done it, and I told these elders."

Jaz glared at Mike, who was grabbing at his choke collar and trying, unsuccessfully, to loosen Bruno's grip.

I wondered about the theological implications of the High One being abandoned by his angelic secret service agents, but instead asked Lowell, "Why didn't you call the police?"

Adam opened his mouth for the first time. "And let The Circle of Light be destroyed by the media?"

Lowell's head bobbed up and down slowly. "Yes, that is what would happen. Unbelievers would only know what is in the headlines and judge us according to the worst of the half-truths they heard. The Circle must be protected."

I didn't really care how they solved their problem. I just wanted to get the hell out of there.

Before I had a chance to drag Jaz away, she blurted out to Lowell, "What about Brad Holtmann?"

Lowell gave her a blank stare.

Bruno said, "Brad Holtmann?"

Patricia answered, "Yeah, that's the local guy they found shot to death last week. Someone said he was a Circle member."

Adam looked at me. "Oh, yeah. You asked me about him." He turned to Mike. "You said you didn't know him, either . . . or did you?"

Mike suddenly tried to yank himself free, but Bruno tightened his grip, giving the leather thong a quick twist. Mike's face turned red. He started gagging and coughing as the large amber beads dug deeper into his neck. Bruno swung him face-down towards the ground and pulled up hard on the choke.

Lowell stared back at Jaz, his face almost as white as his robe.

Jaz said, "Didn't Charles suspect any connection between Mike and this Brad guy?"

The old man stared down at the ground. "No. Charles said nothing of that to me." He looked up and sighed. "Now that he is dead, it is up to me as High One to take care of the matter."

Bruno lifted Mike up by his collar. "It has to be settled before we leave tomorrow."

A heated discussion erupted amongst the elders, each having their own idea of how to deal with Mike. But I wasn't interested.

Taking Jaz by her hand, I turned to run. Unfortunately, I hadn't anticipated our escape path being blocked by Bruno's henchmen at his command, "Stop them!"

I struggled, but even though I was taller and knew from my basketball-playing days how to swing my elbows—smashing at the noses of the two who went after me—I couldn't slug my way free.

Jaz was easily captured by the third one, who asked Bruno, "What should we do with these two?"

Just then I heard the ominous sound of thunder rumbling towards us.

Before Bruno could answer, Mike spat at him and shouted, "You're all losers. Even your wonderful Charles. Without this Circle crap you're nothing. You've got no importance."

The look on Mike's face as he scanned the circle of elders made me think he was going to spit on all of them. "You're no better than me. You all manipulated Lowell for the past two years, grabbing whatever power you could get and building your own little personal empires."

Mike laughed. "And you all think you're so holy. All this spiritual talk about meditating and being guided by messenger angels. What a load of crap. Every one of you went ahead and did what you damn well pleased anyway, whether you heard voices or not."

Jaz leaned forward, straining against the hold her captor had on her arms, and shouted, "Charles was different!"

"Oh, yeah. He believed. But there were no angels around when I killed him," Mike said with a smirk. "The guy really thought nothing would happen to him. He takes me out on one of his meditative walks and actually gives me an ultimatum: 'Stop with the drugs or I'll turn you in to the police.' He says this to me at eleven-thirty at night in the middle of the woods."

Mike looked at me as though I would understand. "I couldn't let him ruin this sweet operation I had put together."

Lowell raised his arms as though trying to embrace the entire group. "You possess the wisdom that could cure the sickness of the world, if you stay to the path. We must be severed from our attachments and ambitions to manipulate. There are those who are out to entrap you. They carry a poison that could destroy the—"

"Lowell, stuff it," Adam shouted.

Patricia added, "This isn't the time for your holy ranting," and flicked on a large flashlight. I hadn't realized it before, but we had been standing in the dark.

Okay. Now that they had us, what were they going to do? Mike was the one killing people who got in his way, but these others? The two guys who were twisting my arms up behind my back until they burned with pain seemed to enjoy my wincing. Jaz and I exchanged looks—mine was worried, hers was totally freaked out.

Bruno jerked Mike's head around so he could look him straight in the eye. "I don't care what you say. And I can't speak for the rest of you," he said turning to the others, "but I certainly know I'm receiving messages from guiding angels. What they said came through loud and clear. We are to destroy anyone who would try to harm The Circle."

Jaz whispered to me, "We're dead."

I smashed my heel down on the foot of one of my captors and struggled to escape. The other one said, "Hey Bruno, this tall one is a real handful."

"Okay," Bruno answered, "throw them in that old barn."

Patricia led the way with her light, followed by Adam, who gave one of the double doors a heave. It creaked loudly as it opened. I wondered how they were going to secure us in such a rickety old building.

Jaz and I were pushed and pulled across the straw-covered floor. I breathed in the musty smell of old wood, earth, and rusting metal that reminded me of my grandfather's garage and felt a sudden deep sadness. Maybe Jaz was right. This was it. No, my mind immediately kicked that thought out. We'd get out of here somehow.

There was a rustling of wings in the rafters above our heads. For one crazy second I wanted to think guardian angels were up there, ready to pluck us away from these mad people. I had a sudden rush of spiritual adrenaline and a deep understanding of how deathbed conversions could actually happen. But I wasn't dying yet and, despite my usual cynicism, I felt disappointed when whatever was up there settled down.

Bruno, still holding Mike by the worry bead choke collar, headed to a back corner of the barn, past several rusting hoes and shovels hanging from nails on the wall. I saw a pitchfork. If only my hands were free.

Bruno motioned for the unholy procession to halt. He took Patricia's hand, the one holding the flashlight. "Here." He pointed the light at the floor, where the straw had been pushed aside. Unlike the rest of the barn, this corner had a wood floor. A trapdoor had been cut into it.

Bruno said, "I was exploring the place a week ago and discovered this old vegetable cellar. Throw them in there."

Adam grunted as he pulled up on the heavy wooden door, revealing a dark hole. I saw a dilapidated stairway when Patricia aimed her light into the pit. At least we weren't going to be tossed in.

I'd reached the desperate bargaining phase of the evening. "Look, Bruno, we won't say anything. Just let us go."

The only response was a snicker from one of the elders standing in the dark and a strong push on my back. I almost tumbled down the stairs, regaining my balance by grabbing onto the trapdoor ledge, and taking the last few steps in a jump. I turned and caught Jaz, who'd been shoved the same way.

The door was slammed shut, and I had to duck so I wouldn't be hit on the head. The cellar was pitch black and a little flutter of panic started up in my stomach. I couldn't stand up straight—the ceiling must have been less than six feet high.

I could hear something being rolled over my head and set on top of the door. Bruno's voice came through loud and clear. "That'll keep them out of the way for now."

Then the enlightened ones were gone.

The darkness was a heavy black curtain wound tightly around my body and I wanted to beat at it with my arms to free myself. That little flutter in my stomach was threatening to turn into a full-blown panic attack. I was hunched down and suffocating.

"For God's sake, Jaz, turn on your flashlight! I'm claustrophobic!"

"Oh, yeah! Sorry, Katie. I forgot I had it."

It seemed to take forever, but eventually one corner of our prison was just barely illuminated by a thin shaft of light. The light helped me think clearer. I sat down on the bottom step and put my head between my legs and forced myself to breath deeply, counting slowly to ten. I figured I must have counted to ten three or four times before I started breathing normally again and raised my head.

"You okay, now, Katie?"

"Yeah. Fine."

Out. We had to get out. It couldn't be that difficult. I stood up and, placing the palms of my hands against the door, tried to bench press my way out. No way. The door didn't budge an inch.

"Jaz, put that light down and help me."

She set it on top of some boxes, aiming it as best she could at the door, and climbed up one step so that we were approximately the same height.

"On three," I said, "one, two . . . ugh!" We pushed with all our might. Nothing happened. Whatever was pinning the door down was too heavy.

Jaz said, "If they've put that big old sleigh on top of us, we'll never get out."

"No, I don't think that's it. Sounded like a wheel rolling

across. It's probably that wheelbarrow full of bricks."

There was a loud rumble of thunder.

"Katie, I'm scared," Jaz said, sitting down on the step. "I'm sorry I got us into this mess."

"We'll get out. Let's just poke around and see what we've got here." I grabbed the flashlight and sat on the step below her.

I made a slow circle around us with the light, exploring every corner. It didn't take much time—the room couldn't have been more than ten feet square and there was nothing in it except for some bare shelving and a stack of empty wooden crates. Very old. Very dirty. I heard some little squeaks under the stairs, trained the light down underneath, and followed a tiny brown mouse scurrying across the dirt floor.

I said, "Cute."

"Okay, Katie. You're the smart one. What do we do now?"

I was so angry I wanted to punch my fist through that door. I imagined the wood splintering and immediately remembered the barn's floor giving way under my foot the day Jaz and I were exploring. I must have been standing over the cellar because the rest of the barn had a dirt floor.

Handing the flashlight to Jaz, I said, "Hold the light up and follow me around. Somewhere, there's a weak spot in this ceiling. I'll try to find it."

This was not going to be easy. I couldn't stand up straight and had to scrunch my head down into my shoulders and Chuck-Berry-Duck-Walk over to the furthest corner. Staying in a crouched position, I started pushing up on the ceiling with my hands, hoping to feel a loose or rotting board. I made the mistake of looking up. Dirt fell into my eyes.

"Shit! This is what I get for going along with your flaky ideas, Jaz."

"I said I was sorry! You don't have to chew my head off!"

"Well, I should have known better. Every time you decide to do something, it turns into a major disaster."

"Oh, I guess you still haven't forgiven me for that time in Iran."

"Yeah, right! Playing chicken against an Iranian truck driver on a mountain road just as it was getting dark is pretty flaky in my books. We almost got killed. Now here we are more than twenty years later and it looks like we will get killed this time."

I took a squatty sidestep and shoved hard at the planks above my head. This time I kept my face down. Everything felt solid. I continued this process up and down the length of our little dungeon.

Jaz said, "Wanting to tell Mike I'm leaving and why I think he's an asshole is *not* flaky."

"Why didn't you tell him that a long time ago? You should have marched out the door the first time he socked you in the face. You always picked the jerks."

"Oh, yeah. I see your love life is perfect. You haven't changed since those days yourself. You were incapable of having a relationship then, and you're still alone."

Damn. This was getting downright catty. But Jaz was right. No! Wait a minute! "Having a relationship with someone means opening yourself up and I did that with you when I tried to talk about my going through cancer. But you didn't want to hear it. So don't you come on telling me I'm the one who's incapable."

"You're sore at me about that? Well I happen to think I'm right. You wouldn't have got sick if you'd been living a more spiritually balanced life."

"Jaz, these people you've been hanging around with are not spiritual. At best they're phonies—some of them are criminals. And stupid ones. Their thinking is so faulty, all it takes is a strong personality like Bruno to lead them down some weird road. Next, they'll all be drinking Kool-Aid laced with arsenic hoping to shed their skins and beam up to join aliens riding on the tail of a comet."

"Yeah . . . I see that."

266

I continued moving along with my methodical squat-step-push-on-the-ceiling routine, but Jaz wasn't keeping up. "Hey, shine that light over here, I can't see where I'm going."

"Sorry." Jaz re-aimed the flashlight. "You know, Katie, this is just like when we were stuck in the van after the accident. I was *so* pregnant and you stayed with me while Colin and Cherry went back and forth to town trying to get someone to help. By the time they were able to get a truck to tow us—how long was that? A week? Anyway, by that time we'd kind of worked things out and come to a truce. You were so pissed off at me. But I thought by the end of that week we were friends again."

"Yeah, we were. We still are. And when we get out of here, we'll celebrate and go get us a couple of men."

The sound of footsteps overhead put a halt to our conversation.

Jaz whispered, "Oh, God, Katie, they're coming back to kill us."

"Keep quiet."

I grabbed the flashlight out of Jaz's hand, clicked it off, and pulled her to one side of the staircase, figuring the darkness might actually give us the advantage when they came down to get us. I hoped the flashlight would make a good club—it was the only weapon available.

Up above, Bruno said, "You two guys, roll this off the door."

I heard a couple of grunts and the sound of something being wheeled away. The trapdoor was opened and the strong beam of their much larger flashlight temporarily blinded me. I stepped back, ready to attack with my club.

34

I WAITED, EXPECTING SOMEONE to come down the stairs. It might've only been a second, but it was a long second before anything happened.

A live snake was thrown into our pit.

It was Mike.

Bruno shouted down, "You'll all just rot down there. Protector angels don't save unbelievers."

The trapdoor was slammed shut and the weight was rolled back over it. I expected to hear footsteps leaving but, instead, I heard Lowell say, "We must seek the favor of the protector angels for ourselves. The divine way is not always so clear. Sometimes we must search for a long time to find the truth."

Bruno answered, "Well, you go sit on your cushion and meditate, Lowell. In the meantime, this is what I was told to do."

Once I was certain our captors had left the barn, I turned on the flashlight and pointed it into Mike's face. It was gratifying to see the snake wearing a necklace of purple bruises where the holy choke collar had been.

Mike got to his feet, and I noticed he was able to stand to his full height with an inch or two to spare between the top of his head and the ceiling. He climbed the stairs and shoved against the door, but couldn't budge it. "There's—" He coughed and rubbed at his bruised neck, ". . . there's a wheelbarrow full of bricks on top of this. It's heavier than it looked."

Out of the darkness, Jaz shouted, "This is all your bloody fault. Why'd you kill that artist guy in Loveland?"

"Shut up. None of your business." Mike gave what seemed like an automatic response.

Jaz didn't shut up. "Did you get angry at him and lose it the way you do with me all the time?"

Mike laughed and shrugged his shoulders. "What the hell. We ain't getting out of here alive." He sat down on the middle step.

Jaz kept her distance and leaned against the stack of wooden crates.

I squatted on my haunches like a Hindu waiting for a Bombay bus, kept the flashlight trained on Mike's face, and watched his beautiful lips move as he talked. "Brad had a sweet deal with me and that furniture importer. But no, the selfish bastard had to ruin everything and get greedy. Well, I told him the angels wouldn't protect him."

"You mean 'Big Gabe', right?" I said.

Mike looked in my direction and squinted against the spotlight in his face. "Who told you that?"

I kept quiet.

Jaz asked, "Where'd you get the gun?"

Mike's lips parted into a snake-like smile, "A tool of the trade. It's been stashed under the front seat of the van all this time."

"You never told me the truth about anything, did you?"

Mike answered Jaz with a smirk.

I said, "The furniture importer—is that Ali Hoseyni?"

"Nay. The brother. TC. He had a great connection in the middle east. Smuggled pure cocaine in the hollowed-out legs of large antique furniture pieces he'd import. Brad was the connection between us."

"I know Brad used to work for TC. I guess you two met in California when he joined The Circle there."

"You're pretty quick at putting things together, aren't you." Mike didn't wait for an answer. "Brad designed the jewelry and the cover artwork for The Circle merchandise. When he got the drugs from TC, I'd come here and help him repackage them so the drugs got shipped around the country through the merchandising network of The Circle. But he got greedy and wanted half of everything."

"So after you had your argument with Brad on Saturday morning, you decided it was time to get rid of him?"

Mike looked at me with disgust. "You're everywhere, aren't you."

"You didn't answer my question. What did you do? Call Brad after your argument and set up a meeting for Sunday morning, giving him the impression you were ready to negotiate and he was going to get what he wanted?"

"Yeah. He showed up pretty wasted. It must've been a good party he went to the night before. But he surprised me and put up a struggle before I managed to push him off me and put him away."

Since we were having such a chatty, friendly conversation, I decided to go fishing for some more answers. "So, the incident at Taste of Cincinnati—when Ali almost died from eating a Hassenbacher strudel—that was no microbrewer's sabotage."

"Yeah. So much for brotherly love. These Arabs. Ali found out about the drugs—a shipment was supposed to come in while he was on his honeymoon. But the happy couple didn't go, so Ali was still in Cincinnati and decided to check in the furniture himself. He started asking TC questions when he saw that the furniture wasn't what he'd ordered."

Mike rubbed his neck. "TC sure screwed that up, trying to get rid of Ali by dusting a piece of pastry with cocaine."

"So that was you talking to TC at Taste of Cincinnati. You've been driving around town in Adam's car."

Mike nodded. "I sure wasn't going to try getting around in that monstrosity of Jaz's. TC suggested we meet last night at that food festival to discuss how to replace Brad. Figured we'd be part of the crowd. Nobody would question what we were doing there." The snake looked straight at me. "Except you."

But TC knew I was working at JJ's booth. Did he forget? Maybe he's just stupid. That was easy to believe—I hadn't seen any smart thinking over the past week.

Suddenly, the conversation wasn't as engrossing. Mike was staring back at me with a relaxed expression. He'd stopped squinting, even though I was still aiming the beam of light straight into his face. Damn batteries were going. I shook the flashlight. I sensed the heavy dark curtain around me, closing in again, threatening to pin my arms to my sides and start pushing on my chest.

I had to get out. "Maybe the three of us can get that door open."

Mike lifted an eyebrow and cocked his head to one side as though wondering what my ulterior plan was. This wasn't one.

I straightened up as much as I could, set the flashlight on top of the crates, and placed my hands against the door. "C'mon, Jaz."

It was pretty cramped with all three of us trying to position our hands on the unhinged side of the trapdoor. Jaz was on the middle step and Mike and I stood on the bottom one. We crouched, knees bent, so that when we straightened up our legs would give us more power in our push.

I said, "Ready? On three. One, two—"

We pushed and strained. The trapdoor lifted a little. I heard what must have been a brick toppling out of the wheelbarrow and falling onto the door.

Mike said, "Again," as though this was his idea.

My back went up. It was hardly the time for pettiness, but my ego couldn't stand the thought of the bastard taking credit for getting us out of there. I heard myself say, "I wasn't thinking of quitting."

Jaz said, "He doesn't like women telling him what to do."

"I don't care what he likes or doesn't like—just push!"

Panic was starting to build up in me again. Not only was our prison growing darker as the flashlight faded, but the air was getting stuffier and hotter. The heat from our efforts seemed to intensify the smell of the sandalwood oil Jaz wore. Mixed in with that was an evil, sweaty smell emanating from Mike's body, which I was certain would poison the little air left in our dungeon.

There was a sudden loud clap of thunder. The kind that makes your eardrums ring.

"C'mon," I said, "One, two—"

We pushed. The door lifted a crack and a couple more bricks rolled off and clattered onto the wooden floor above us.

An idea popped into my head. "Maybe we can keep bouncing the bricks out of the wheelbarrow."

We pushed and let go. Pushed and let go. Every time we did, a brick or two fell out, but it was still too heavy. We were all panting.

Another push and let go.

I heard the sound of cracking wood. "The wood's rotten. Keep bouncing this thing."

Again and again. Each time we did, the center of the door felt like it was buckling a little more. The wheelbarrow stopped bouncing—its legs must have sunk into the door's splintering top.

The cracking grew louder and turned into a continuous crunching. My fingers felt the old wood coming apart.

I shouted, "Get out of the way!" grabbed the flashlight, and moved to the furthest corner of the cellar.

The wheelbarrow, bricks and all, came crashing through the door and past the faint spotlight I was aiming at the top of the stairs. Dust clouds filled the cellar, tickled my nostrils, and billowed up towards the opening. My eyes were stinging, but I saw Jaz pick her way through the piles of bricks, push the wheelbarrow off the stairs, and scramble up our escape route.

Mike the snake stepped out from his dark corner and picked up a couple of bricks. "Too bad," he said with mock sorrow.

I trained my flashlight on his face.

He stepped in front of the stairs, blocking my way, and smacked the bricks together. "Too bad the whole pile fell on your head while we were trying to escape."

"Why do you have to kill me?"

"If I disappear, those stupid Circle people won't go to the police. But that's the first thing you'd do, and I can't let that happen."

This guy is brainless, I thought. I kept the flashlight trained on his eyes and picked up a brick to defend myself. "What about Jaz?"

"I'll handle that dumb bitch the way I always do."

"Up here, asshole!" Jaz shouted.

Mike turned to look up through the opening. The blade of a shovel swooped down, smashing him in the forehead. He reeled in my direction. I swung my arm, catching him full in the face with my brick.

The snake went down.

My hand hurt from the force of the blow, but I held the brick at the ready to swing again if necessary. The rapidly dimming light showed it wasn't—Mike, blood dripping from the huge gash on the side of his face, was out for the count.

"Katie?" Jaz stood on the top step, holding her shovel like a baseball bat. "You okay?"

"You bet," I answered, dropping the brick as I climbed the stairs. "Let's get the hell outta here."

Just as we reached the barn doors, a burst of lightning blazed overhead so brightly, it seemed as if the sun had momentarily appeared in the moonless sky, making my failing flashlight irrelevant.

Another ear-splitting crash of thunder followed. Strong gusts of wind were bending the tops of nearby trees.

I swallowed my hesitancy to expose myself to the storm that was obviously just minutes away, and said, "Jaz, run as fast as you can to the parking lot."

We were no more than fifty feet down the trail, when the clouds unzipped and a curtain of water fell from the sky. Our feet pounded the clay road, which was quickly turning into mud. I raised my arms to shield my eyes as I ran against the wind and rain that buffeted my face. Turning to check on Jaz, I saw she was having trouble keeping up with my long-legged strides.

Jaz yelled, "Keep going. I'll get there."

Just the same, I slowed down to keep her in sight. I didn't want us to get separated. This was not the time to be alone.

My dreams came back to me—the one where I was running through a dark forest, chased by the sound of beating wings, and the other when I awoke in a van and was attacked by wings on strings.

I knew my dreams were prophetic, but sometimes I couldn't make the connection until I was right in the middle of the situation. Were there angels trying to warn me of danger? Why couldn't they speak plainly and just tell me to stay away from certain situations? Maybe they were. I promised myself to start listening more carefully.

"LO-WELL!"

Who was that?

"LO-WELL!" Another voice. Even through the pounding rain, I could tell it was Bruno and Adam. I saw the beam of their flashlight. We were running right towards them.

I stopped, grabbed Jaz as she caught up to me and clamped a

hand over her mouth.

"Quiet!" I whispered and pulled her over to the side of road, almost tripping over a large tree branch downed by the gusting wind. Good weapon. I picked it up. We stood in the darkness and listened. The Circle elders were closer than I thought.

Plain as day, I could hear Patricia say, "Bruno, this is awful. Why'd you tell him to go meditate? He could be anywhere."

"I told him to go sit on his cushion."

Adam said, "You know he'll just wander, even in this rain. The guy's senile."

Before I could alter our route, the whole gang emerged out of the darkness right in front of us. We stood there, staring at each other.

Suddenly, another pair of lights cut through the heavy downpour. Headlights.

Bruno pointed his flashlight at the van that came to a halt on the muddy road.

The front passenger's window rolled down and Lowell's head peered out.

The driver's door flung open and out stepped Mr. Short Round, my Anonymous Angel security guard, his gun drawn and ready. "Okay. What's going on here?"

CONCLUSION

Two weeks later . . . June 9th

I SAT ON THE BACK STOOP, outside my kitchen door, a mug of coffee in one hand, the *Cincinnati Enquirer* in the other. The steamy month of May was behind us. Temperatures had come down, the air was dry and I just sat, enjoying the feeling of contentment. Boo-Kat nosed around in the overflowing flower beds. I felt like we were the only two beings for miles around. Out in front of the house, though, Jaz was in the midst of tearing apart her van in preparation for her trek back home to California. Chattering excitedly the whole time, she climbed in and out of the van, littering the driveway with bags of clothing, Indian drums, flutes, bells and various odd-looking percussion instruments. There were boxes of food, a collection of multicolored baskets, purple blankets and fringed pillows. I told her I couldn't stand watching the chaos and to just come and tell me when she was packed and ready to go.

For the past couple of weeks, the local media had been having a field day reporting on the I-told-you-so debate over the strange people coming in to Clairmont to attend the questionable gatherings at the Golden Valley Spiritual Center.

Unnamed sources leaked to reporters information about the Loveland Police Department finding a partial print matching Mike's thumb print on the gold Circle of Light pin I'd found beside Brad's body. Traces of skin and blood on the edge of the pin matched Brad's torn fingernail, which indicated a struggle of some kind.

A strand of hair along with threads from Mike's white tunic top were found on the winged medallion he plunged into Charles'

276

chest. No fingerprints. The police theory: threads and hair were left on the medallion when Mike used his tunic to wipe his prints off. DNA tests were ordered to confirm the hair was Mike's.

The TV stations were so hot on this story they even went so far as to run a human interest piece on Lowell the High One, who mentioned in passing that he stole Charles' incense holder as a memento of him.

It didn't end with that. There was still the matter of Adam, Patricia, Bruno and his three henchmen kidnapping Jaz and me. Lowell urged us to press charges, saying he'd received a message that "if the truth came out, The Circle would survive." And so we did. Fingers were pointed in all directions. Wackos from out of state called in to radio talk shows and defended the concept of crimes committed in the name of religious beliefs. The ACLU was asked to comment. TC was brought up on drug trafficking charges and he, in turn, implicated Mike. On and on it went.

I sighed. Folding the newspaper, I put it down on the step beside me and sipped my coffee.

Having offered Trails End Farm to Jaz as a place to stay for a while and regroup, I now wondered if it was a good idea. She kind of surprised me when she accepted the offer so enthusiastically and said she'd turn around and come right back once her life in California had been "closed down and packed up . . . Just give me a couple of weeks."

I supposed I could look on it as the sibling relationship I never had. It certainly promised to have its ups and downs, like all the other relationships I'd witnessed the last couple of weeks. Take TC and Ali—now there was a very complicated one. When Ali had come out of his coma and was told about his brother's alleged attempt on his life, he refused to press charges, stating, "We are family. This is between us." Despite this act of forgiveness, the Hamilton County Prosecuting Attorney charged TC with attempted murder.

277

Then there was Ali's relationship with Cindy. It looked like they were finally ready for their honeymoon in Paris. Cindy told me Ali's near-death experience was just what their marriage needed.

In a different way, a close encounter with death was good for Jaz and Mike's sordid relationship, too. Coming face to face with the possibility your life is ending has a way of bringing everything into sharp focus. All of a sudden you know what's true, what's really important. Jaz admitted to me that her use of Mike's head for batting practice with that rusty old shovel was the most spiritually uplifting moment she'd ever experienced.

I thought about their relationship and wondered, for the hundredth time, if I'd handled things properly. The abuse that Jaz allowed in all her relationships was still a touchy subject. There were issues I knew she would never discuss with me, just as I would probably never talk about the struggles I had with loneliness—which was nobody's fault but my own. I can't play the games and jump through all sorts of hoops in order to conform and be accepted, like Mother does.

I wondered if relationships were worth all the trouble, anyway. I'd always spent a lot of time by myself, even as a kid, and enjoyed it. Even needed it. But when all was said and done, when Jaz and I were safe at home, sitting in my kitchen drinking wine and marveling at how we'd escaped, I wished we *had* gone out and picked up a couple of men to party with.

Face it, Kathleen Frances Cavanaugh—you're an oddball. Always have been, always will be.

I emptied my coffee mug in one gulp, got up from the step, and walked around to the front of the house to check on Jaz's progress. Rounding the corner of the house, I saw that the driveway was cleared of all her worldly possessions. Jaz waved and called out to me, "I was just coming to get you. It's boogie time."

The lump in my throat surprised me. I didn't know why I

278

thought it would be easier to say goodbye to Jaz than it was watching Cherry take off on her motorbike last December. Both of these visits were emotional roller coaster rides, something I could get addicted to despite my need to control my surroundings. I found that once the ride got rolling I started having a good time and didn't want to come down. Tomorrow it was back to the same old routine.

Jaz came towards me, dressed in her hippie skirt and gauzy Indian top. We gave each other big hugs. For the third time that morning I said, "I'm worried about you making that long drive all by yourself."

"I'll call you every couple of days. Okay, Mom?" Jaz pulled on my braid.

"Okay."

She jumped into the driver seat, put on her sunglasses and stuck her head out the window. "Thanks again, Katie, it's been wild. See ya soon."

I waved, hoping the angels painted on the van's back corners pushed her safely across the country. Halfway down the gravel lane, Jaz stuck her hand out the window. I laughed. She was waving the rubber chicken and beeping her horn—probably steering with her knees.

Just then, Mother's pristine white Mercedes came roaring around the bend, her chirpy little horn blasting away.

My laugh turned into a gasp.

The two swerved around each other at the last moment, narrowly avoiding a crash. The Mercedes kept right on coming towards me as though nothing had happened.

Mother stuck her hand out her window and waved a pink plastic flamingo. "Kathleen! I've been flocked!"

THE RECIPES

✳ ✳ ✳ ✳ ✳

KUFTEH TABRIZI
Meatballs Tabriz style

1 lb. ground beef
1 egg , beaten
1 onion, chopped
1/2 c. yellow split peas, cooked
Pinch of saffron threads
1 tsp. Persian allspice (advieh)*
Salt and pepper
1/2 c. chopped walnuts
8 whole, pitted prunes
8 whole, dried apricots

2 onions, thinly sliced
2 cloves garlic, minced
1-10 oz. can beef broth
1 c. tomato juice
1 Tbsp. tomato paste
1 Tbsp. lemon juice
Pinch of saffron

Cook split peas in 2-1/2 cups of water for about twenty minutes, until soft. Sauté one chopped onion in butter or olive oil. Combine in a bowl the cooked, drained split peas, sautéed onions, beaten egg, ground beef, pinch of saffron, Persian allspice, salt and pepper (to taste). Knead mixture until thoroughly combined and pastelike. Shape into large patties (about 3" in diameter).

Holding a patty in your hand, place in the center one prune, one dried apricot, and a spoonful of chopped walnuts. Mold the meat around filling and shape into a meatball. (Recipe makes approximately 7-8 large meatballs.)

In large, shallow saucepan sauté minced garlic and two sliced onions in butter or olive oil until browned. Add 10 ozs. beef broth, 10 ozs. water, tomato juice, tomato paste, lemon juice and saffron threads. Place meatballs in saucepan in single layer and simmer, covered, over low heat for 40-60 minutes. Turn and baste a few times during cooking. Serve sliced in broth, with flatbread and Iranian pickled vegetables on the side.

*Persian allspice (also called advieh–a mixture of cloves, cinnamon, rosebud, ginger, cardamom and other spices) can be purchased at Iranian or Middle Eastern grocery stores.

(If you want to be absolutely authentic, each meatball should also contain one, whole hard-cooked egg!)

CRUSTY PERSIAN RICE

2 c. white basmati rice
Peel of 1 orange, julienned
2 carrots, julienned
1/4 c. pistachios, shelled, unsalted
1/4 c. almonds, slivered
1/2 c. golden raisins
3/4 tsp. Persian allspice (advieh)*
1/2 tsp. saffron threads, crumbled in 2 Tbsp. hot water
5 Tbsp. butter
2 tsp. sugar
2 Tbsp. oil
2 Tbsp. plain yogurt

Put rice in a bowl and cover with water. Drain. Repeat
procedure 5 times, or until water looks clear. Return rice to
bowl, cover with cold water and let stand at least 6 hours,
room temperature. (Can let stand overnight.)

Boil strips of orange peel and julienned carrots in 1 cup of
water for 5 minutes. Drain, pat dry. Sauté in 1 Tbsp. butter
and 2 tsp. sugar for one minute. Stir in 3/4 tsp. Persian
allspice, the pistachios, almonds and raisins and continue
sautéing another minute.

In a non-stick pot, bring 4-5 cups of water and 2 tsp. salt to a
boil. Add soaked, drained rice. Water should cover rice by 2
inches or more. Boil rice for 6-10 minutes until rice is soft to
bite. Drain and rinse in lukewarm water.

(cont'd. over)

In small bowl, mix 2-3 spatulas of cooked rice with 2 Tbsp. yogurt and half of the saffron water. Melt 1 Tbsp. butter and 2 Tbsp. oil.in same pot used for cooking rice. Spread rice/yogurt mixture on bottom of pot, pressing down with spoon–this will form the crust. Cover with alternating layers of remaining rice and carrot/raisin/nut mixture, mounding it in a pyramid shape. With the handle of a wooden spoon, make three holes in the mound of rice to allow steam to escape. Drizzle remaining saffron water and 3 Tbsp. melted butter over top.

Cook, uncovered, over low heat for 6 minutes. Meanwhile, wrap lid in small towel, securing ends of towel under or around handle of lid. Cover pot with towel-wrapped lid and continue cooking over very low heat for 40-50 minutes more, until rice on the bottom of the pot is golden and crusty. Remove pot from heat, let stand 10 minutes.

To serve: Spoon rice onto a serving platter. Detach crust from bottom of pot, break into large pieces and arrange around the rice.

*Persian allspice (advieh) can be purchased at Iranian or Middle Eastern grocery stores.

MANGO LASSI

1 c. plain yogurt
1/2 c. water
1 mango, chopped
3 Tbsp. sugar (or to taste)
Pinch of ground cardamom
8 ice cubes

Process all ingredients in blender, until smooth.
Serves 2.

CHAI
(Spiced Tea)

1 c. water
1/3 c. milk
2 green cardamom pods, split open
2 whole cloves
Half of a 3" stick cinnamon
1 heaping tsp. loose black tea

Boil first five ingredients together in a small pot for 5
minutes. Add one heaping teaspoon of loose black tea. Steep,
covered, for 5 minutes. Strain into cup. Add sugar to taste.
Serves 1.

RAITA

1/2 tsp. whole cumin seeds
1/2 tsp. whole black mustard seeds
1 tsp. canola oil
2 c. plain yogurt
1 c. chopped, peeled cucumber
1-2 Tbsp. chopped fresh mint
salt and pepper

Heat canola oil in a small pan. Add cumin and mustard seeds and cook until they sizzle and pop, less than one minute.

Combine yogurt, chopped cucumber and mint in a bowl. Stir in the seasoned oil and seeds. Add salt and pepper to taste.

Serve immediately as a cooling accompaniment to balance hot, spicy dishes. May be held in refrigerator for a couple of hours. Stir again before serving.

NOTE: There are countless variations to this recipe. Instead of the cucumber and mint, here are some suggestions:

Tomato, scallions, jalapeno pepper, cilantro

Mango, red onion, cilantro

Pineapple, almonds, raisins and cardamom (in place of cumin and mustard seeds)

Cooked potato, toasted walnuts and cilantro or mint

THE AMAZON CHILI HEIRESS
DETECTIVE IS AT IT AGAIN!!

CARVE

A WITNESS TO SHREDS

A Journals of Kate Cavanaugh Mystery

Available Fall 1999

If you are interested in receiving
Kate Cavanaugh's free newsletter

Thoughts at 3 A.M.
UPDATES FROM KATE
AND NEWS OF FUTURE BOOKS & EVENTS

Please send your name and address to:

**CC Publishing
PO Box 542
Loveland, Ohio 45140**

CATHIE JOHN is the wife/husband writing team of **CATHIE and JOHN CELESTRI**.

Cathie left her native Canada at the age of twenty and embarked on a trip, which turned into a two year odyssey, traveling overland through Europe and parts of Asia to India and Nepal. She has always had a passion for food—she's either cooking it, fantasizing about it, or wishing she had room for that third cannoli. Cathie has worked as a chef in the catering and restaurant industry, and in advertising and marketing research. She is a breast cancer survivor.

John has been a Directing Animator in charge of developing characters for twenty years. Through his pencil he has acted in over fifty feature-length films and half-hour TV specials, his roles ranging from the dramatic to the slapstick. He also makes a half-way decent lasagna dinner.

They live in Loveland, Ohio with their Welsh Terrier.